Armchair Travel Guides

# Scotland

Copyright © 2021 Moseley Road Inc.

All rights reserved. No part of this publication may be reproduced, distributed, or transmitted in any form or by any means, including photocopying, recording, or other electronic or mechanical methods, without the prior written permission of the publisher, except in the case of brief quotations embodied in critical reviews and certain other noncommercial uses permitted by copyright law.

Produced by
**MOSELEY ROAD INC.**
www.moseleyroad.com

**President:** Sean Moore
**Art and editorial director:** Lisa Purcell
**Production director:** Adam Moore
**Project editor:** Finn Moore

Printed in China

ISBN 978-1-62669-216-9

10 9 8 7 6 5 4 3 2 1

## Armchair Travel Guides

# Scotland

**mri**

MOSELEY ROAD, INC.

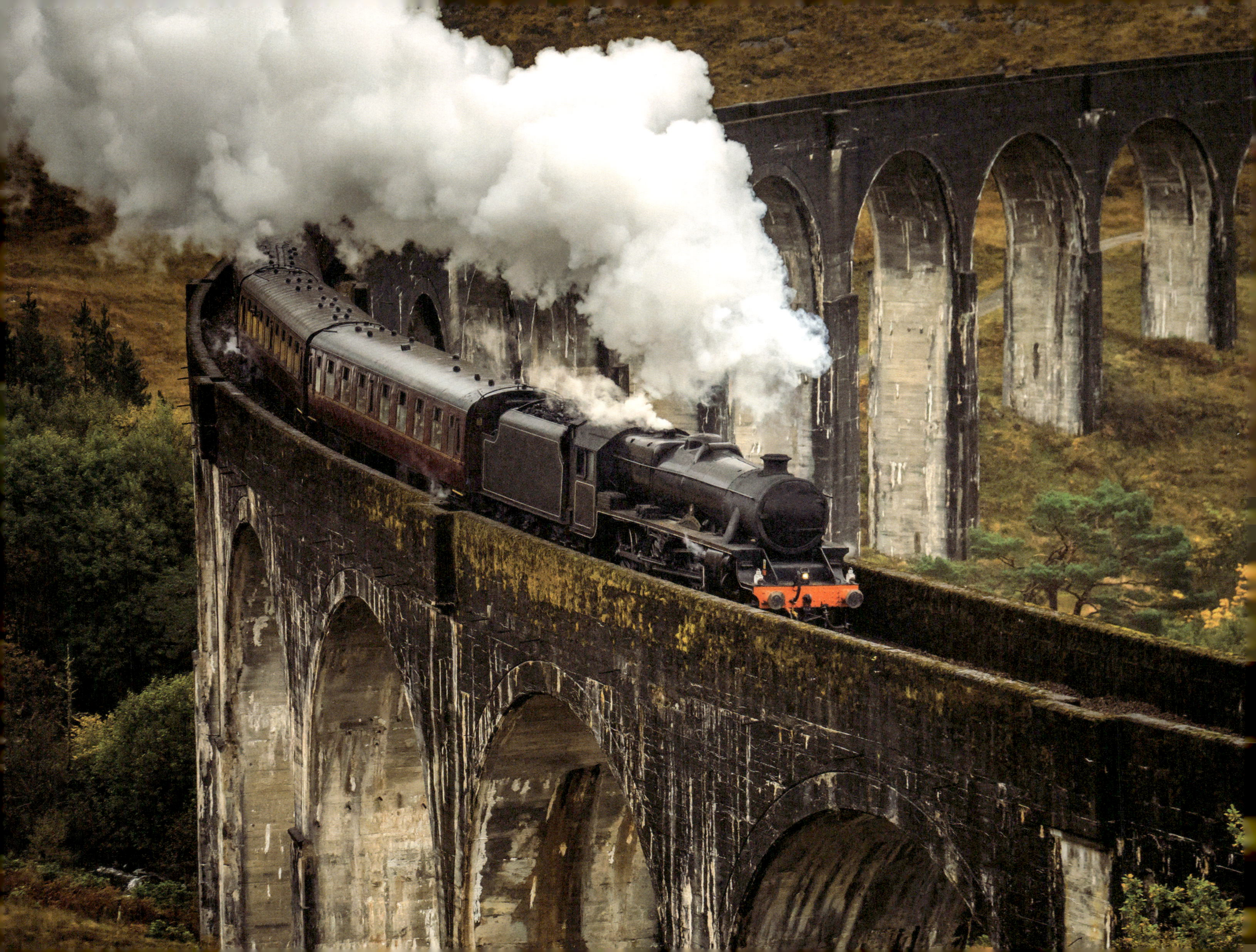

# CONTENTS

*An Introduction to Scotland* . . . . . 6

Aberdeenshire . . . . . . . . . . . . . . 14

Angus . . . . . . . . . . . . . . . . . . . . 30

Argyll and Bute . . . . . . . . . . . . . 36

Ayrshire . . . . . . . . . . . . . . . . . . 52

Clackmannanshire . . . . . . . . . . . 56

Dumfries and Galloway . . . . . . . . . . . 62

Dunbartonshire . . . . . . . . . . . . . 76

East Lothian . . . . . . . . . . . . . . . 80

Edinburgh . . . . . . . . . . . . . . . . . 86

Falkirk . . . . . . . . . . . . . . . . . . 104

Fife . . . . . . . . . . . . . . . . . . . . 108

Glasgow . . . . . . . . . . . . . . . . . 114

Highland . . . . . . . . . . . . . . . . . 126

Lanark . . . . . . . . . . . . . . . . . . 148

Midlothian . . . . . . . . . . . . . . . 152

Moray . . . . . . . . . . . . . . . . . . . 156

Orkney . . . . . . . . . . . . . . . . . . 160

Perth and Kinross . . . . . . . . . . 168

Renfrewshire and Inverclyde . . . 178

Scottish Borders . . . . . . . . . . . 182

Shetland . . . . . . . . . . . . . . . . . 198

Stirling . . . . . . . . . . . . . . . . . 204

Western Isles . . . . . . . . . . . . . . 214

West Lothian . . . . . . . . . . . . . . 220

*Photo Credits* . . . . . . . . . . . . . 224

**Glenfinnan Viaduct in the West Highlands**

# AN INTRODUCTION TO SCOTLAND

## TOP 10 MOST-VISITED SITES IN SCOTLAND

- Edinburgh
- Glasgow
- Ben Nevis (Highland)
- Loch Ness (Highland)
- Loch Lomond (Stirling/Dunbartonshire)
- Stirling Castle (Stirling)
- Skara Brae (Orkney)
- Isle of Skye (Highland)
- Falkirk Wheel (Falkirk)
- Eilean Donan (Highland)

The history of Scotland is both troubled and fascinating. The country has a robust and profound character and culture, in large part due to its Celtic origins and proud history of independence, perpetually fighting against usurping England. Still, Scotland is beautiful all around: as high as Ben Nevis, deep as Loch Ness, lonely as the moors in the highlands, touching as the sound of a bagpipe, or heartwarming as a sip of whiskey, majestic as Edinburgh, and wildly romantic as the islands in the north. In terms of scenic beauty, the country is almost unrivaled in Europe. The wild highlands, the rugged coastlines, and the islands that look like they came from another time all make up Scotland's beauty, keeping millions of visitors returning year after year.

**Top:** Skara Brae is a UNESCO World Heritage Site and one of the four sites that make up "The Heart of Neolithic Orkney."

## HISTORY

Scotland has been inhabited for about 6,000 to 8,000 years, weathering countless successive waves of settlers and invaders in that time. The Celts arrived from the northwest of Europe around 500 BCE; they were later called Bretons by the Roman invaders. These temporary conquerors called the northern lands (above the Forth and Clyde line) Caledonia.

The first thousand years before the Common Era are the history of a state of perpetual war. During this millennium, the peoples of Scotland (Scoti, Picts, Bretons, and Angles) gradually reconciled. By the year 843 BCE, a united Scottish and Pictish kingdom had emerged. In 1018, the southern British were defeated at the Battle of Carham, and the Border was set along the River Tweed. Around 1034, the Bretons of Strathclyde were also added to the greater kingdom, and the shape of Scotland became very similar to that of today.

Following the Norman conquest of England, Norman influences gradually spread throughout

The ruins of Urquhart Castle overlook the dark waters of Loch Ness.

Scotland as well. Anglo-Saxons began settling in Scotland, and feudalism followed close behind; before long, the disparate clans faded in favor of towns and cities. After a crisis of succession in 1290, Edward I of England named John de Baliol King of Scotland; Baliol then allied with France against the English, and Edward I invaded Scotland to proclaim himself king. The Scots rebelled, and this marked the beginning of several battles for independence from England over the next 30 years; it wasn't until 1328 that England finally recognized Scotland as an independent nation. Conflicts with England continued over the next few centuries, only formally coming to an end with the Act of Union in 1707, which marked the inception of the Kingdom of Great Britain.

## CULTURE

Scottish culture is vibrant and distinct. The vitality and creativity of the people of Scotland manifests through a wide range of art forms, far contrary to the stereotype of the rugged and pessimistic Scotsman so often perpetuated. For generations, Scotland has produced writers, painters, sculptors, musicians, composers, and dancers whose talents have received national and international recognition. Some of these arts, such as traditional dance and music, are predominantly Scottish, both in style and inspiration. Others, such as theatre, opera, and painting, incorporate and expand on influences from other parts of the world.

Scotland has a rich heritage of art and culture, and today the traditional and the contemporary, Celtic and diaspora all have their place in the country. Over the years, the composition of Scotland's population has changed with new immigrants from different lands; this situation has led

A bell on the Royal Yacht *Britannia* is inscribed with the coronation date of Queen Elizabeth II, for whom the ship was made.

Two girls compete in the sword dance event at Balquhidder, Lochearnhead, and Strathyre Highland Games, one of many such gatherings every year that feature traditional competitions, such as caber and weight throwing, piping, and Highland dancing.

to an increased variety in Scottish culture, food, and lifestyles, which has only served to enrich the land and life of the people of Scotland.

The instrument most commonly associated with Scotland is undoubtedly the bagpipe, also called the Great Highland Bagpipe. Contrary to popular belief, however, this instrument originated in Middle East Asia and only spread to Europe in the 12th century. The first concrete evidence noting the presence of the bagpipe in Scotland dates to 1396, when references were made to bagpipes being carried into the Battle of the North Inch. By the end of the 16th century, the use of the bagpipe was widespread both recreationally and militarily, as its unmistakable and powerful sound could be heard at considerable distances. These were the Highland war pipes. Bagpipe players, called pipers, played an essential role in Highland clans, so much so that they were often awarded lands to bequeath to their descendants. The playing of the bagpipes soon became intrinsically linked with Scottish culture and was established as a core element of traditional Scottish music. Bagpipes are rarely played with other instruments, but other common instruments used in Scottish folk music include the fiddle, accordion, drum, flute, and harp.

Scotland is one of the cultural capitals of Europe, especially when it comes to the visual arts. The tumultuous history of this country gave birth to countless pieces of powerful and influential art. From the ancient Petrospheres of prehistoric Scotland and the carved Pictish stones of the Middle Ages to the contemporary art being produced today, each era of Scotland's history has produced countless works of note. The 18th and 19th centuries saw the first Scottish artists to be internationally recognized, many leaning towards neoclassicism and Romanticism; this period gave rise to some of Scotland's most renowned artists. Some of Scotland's most well-known visual artists include Henry Raeburn, Ian Hamilton Finlay, James Guthrie, Alison Watt, Allan Ramsay, Gavin Hamilton, David Wilkie, and Margaret MacDonald.

The country is also known for the Scottish Enlightenment, the period in 18th- and early-19th-century Scotland that saw an outpouring of intellectual and scientific accomplishments. The humanist and rational outlook of the Western

**Top:** Casks of whisky age at the Laphroaig distillery on Islay, one of the Inner Hebrides islands. **Bottom:** A street bagpiper entertains pedestrians on Edinburgh's Royal Mile. **Opposite:** The striking Kilchurn Castle in Argyll casts its reflections in Loch Awe at sunset.

> "It is one of the most hauntingly beautiful places in the world, the history is fascinating, the men are handsome and the whisky is delicious."
>
> —J.K. ROWLING

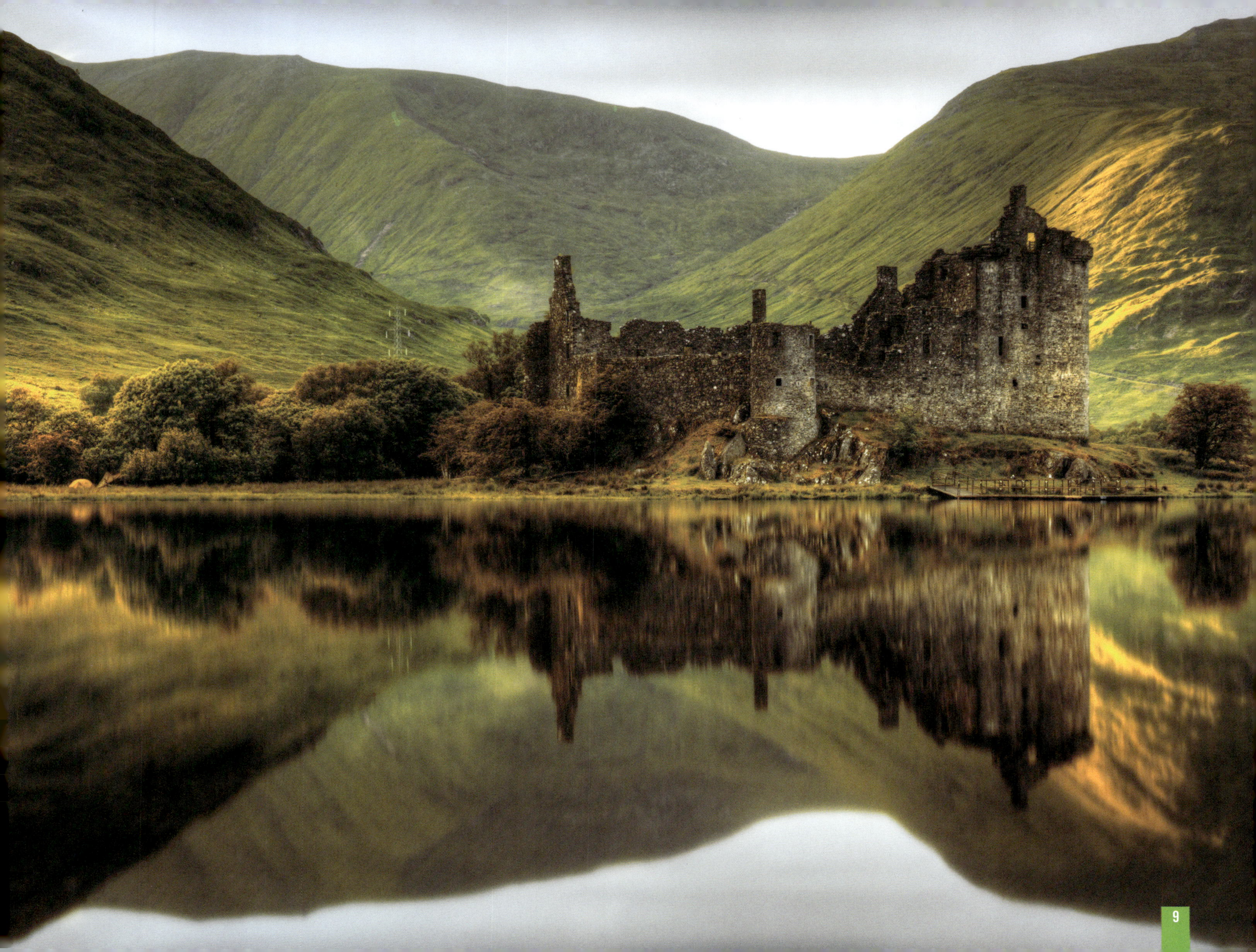

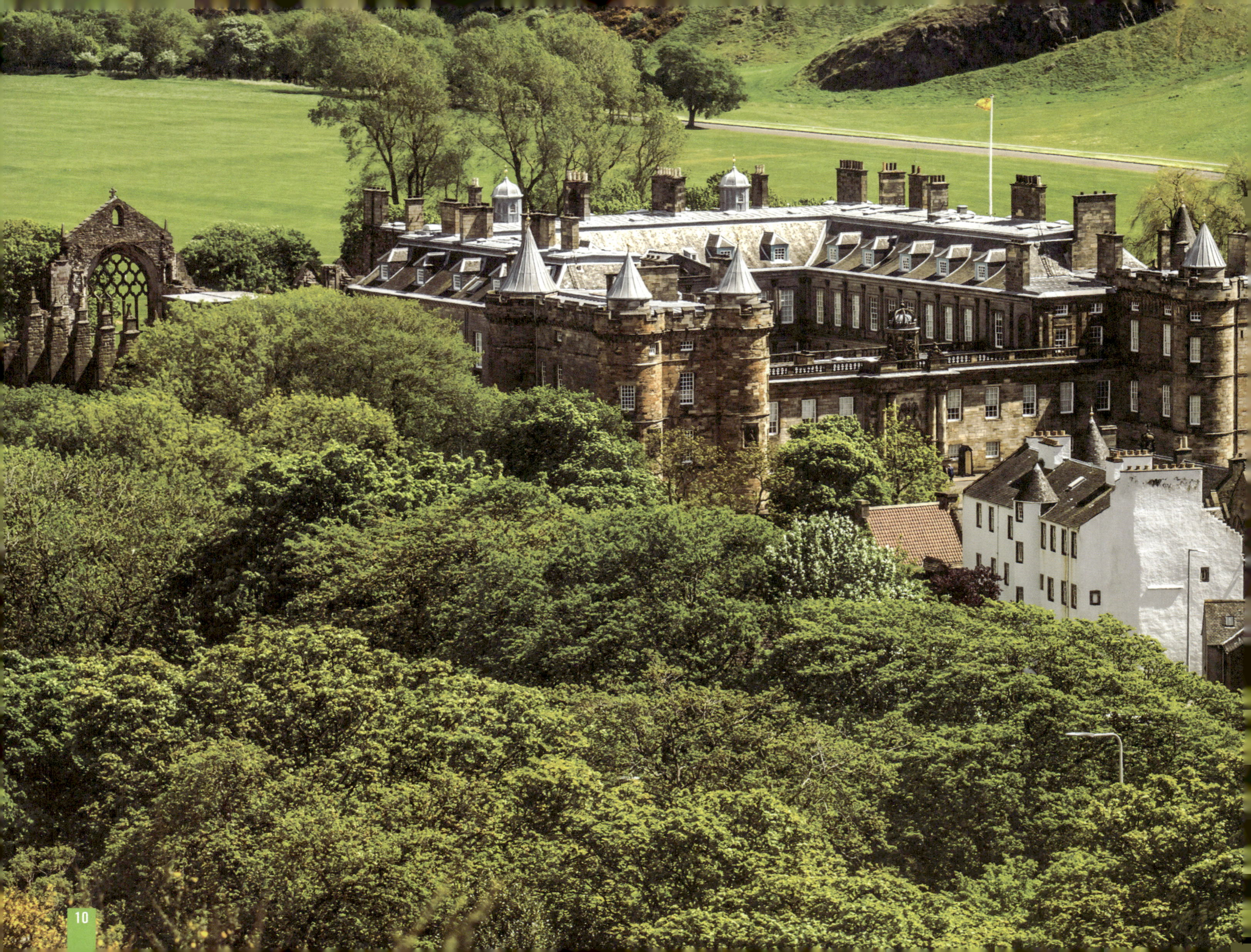

Enlightenment was especially strong in the thinkers of the Scottish Enlightenment, who asserted the importance of human reason combined with a rejection of any authority that could not be justified by reason. Scotland's ancient universities—Edinburgh, St Andrews, Glasgow, King's College, and Marischal College—became centers of empiricism and practicality.

Scotland has also produced some of history's most notable writers. A fully exhaustive list would be impossible to print, but to name just a few: Arthur Conan Doyle, Robert Louis Stevenson, J.M. Barrie, George MacDonald, Kenneth Grahame, Carol Ann Duffy, Walter Scott, and J.K. Rowling all were born in or produced their greatest works while living in Scotland. Edinburgh in particular has deep ties to literature and was named the world's first "city of literature" by UNESCO in 2004.

## GEOGRAPHY AND CLIMATE

Scotland is part of the United Kingdom, occupying approximately a third of its territory, and is located at the north end of the island of Great Britain. In addition, its territory also includes a large number of islands including the Inner and Outer Hebrides, as well as Orkney and Shetland. The entire region of Scotland covers 30,090 square miles, with a total of 6,160 miles of coastline.

Scotland has a temperate, oceanic climate, which can often result in some unpredictable weather patterns. Generally, Scotland receives a good amount

**The Palace of Holyroodhouse, standing at the end of Edinburgh's Royal Mile, is the official residence of the monarchy in Scotland.**

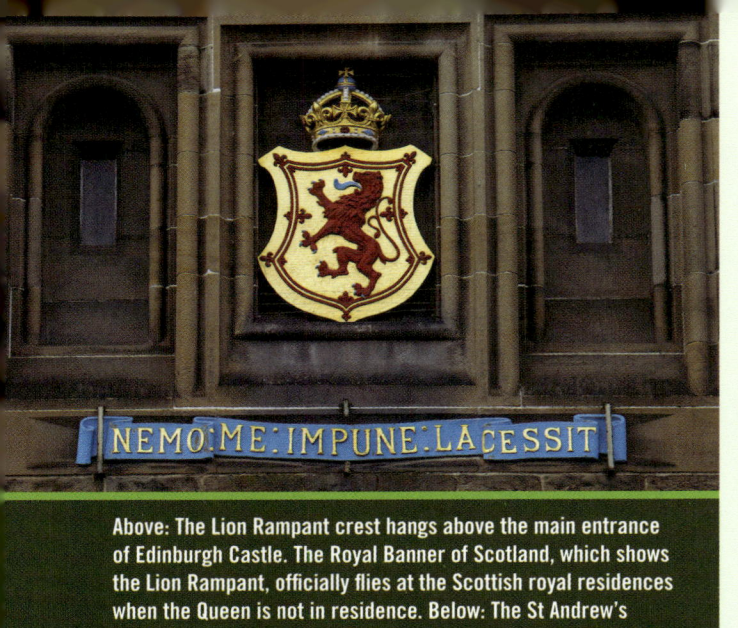

Above: The Lion Rampant crest hangs above the main entrance of Edinburgh Castle. The Royal Banner of Scotland, which shows the Lion Rampant, officially flies at the Scottish royal residences when the Queen is not in residence. Below: The St Andrew's Cross is the national flag of Scotland.

of wind and rain, and overcast skies are common. Summers tend towards cool and rainy, averaging out at 64 degrees Fahrenheit. Scotland's winter temperatures are the coldest in the United Kingdom, but they are still rather mild; temperatures average at 43 degrees Fahrenheit, with rare snowfall.

## PLANNING YOUR TRIP

Planning your trip or tour starts with knowing when best to visit Scotland, depending mainly on the kind of trip you're looking for. Scotland is a wonderful place to visit any time of the year, but as Billy Connolly once said: "there are only two seasons in Scotland, June and Winter." The summer months are perfect for hikes, sightseeing, and excursions into Scotland's many parks and historic landmarks, although Scotland's natural beauty takes on another, unique charm in the winter.

When planning your trip, it's also a good idea to draw up an itinerary ahead of time. It would be impossible to visit all of Scotland's landmarks and attractions in a single trip, but a 10-day-tour of Dumfries and Galloway, a 2-day-trip to Edinburgh, or a 7-day tour of St Andrew, Aberdeen, and the surrounding towns is certainly manageable. Marking your route, rest stops, and points of interest before you leave home is a great way to avoid unnecessary stress upon arrival.

Whether you're interested in breathtaking ocean views, clambering through rugged castles, or exploring the cities and burghs nestled amongst green hills and cattle, there's something for everyone in Scotland. With whisky tours, historic castles, long walks in the woods, incredible ruins, and ancient megalithic structures to explore, even the often-cloudy skies can't dampen Scotland's wild, resilient spirit.

## MAPPING SCOTLAND

Scotland's subdivisions—called thanedoms, sherriffdoms, shires, counties, and council areas, depending on the era—can be somewhat confusing, with many changes over the centuries based on just who was doing the dividing. Malcolm III, who reigned from 1058 to 1093, appears to have introduced sheriffs and sherriffdoms. David I, who reigned from 1124 to 1153, completed this kind of division by converting the existing thanedoms into sherriffdoms. The earliest sheriffdom south of the Forth is Haddingtonshire, which is named in a charter of 1139 as Hadintunschira. It is now generally known as East Lothian. By 1305, in the reign of Edward I of England, there were 23 shires listed, many with the names we know today, and by the 17th century, when the first accurate maps of Scotland were produced, these appeared mostly under recognizable names. These were in use until 1890 and were also called "counties," a term that became interchangeable with "shire."

Today, local government in Scotland is based upon the 32 areas designated as "council areas" in 1996, which sometimes incorporate traditional county names, but frequently have vastly different boundaries. For this book, we will travel through Scotland generally following the council areas.

# THE COUNCIL AREAS OF SCOTLAND

ORKNEY
SHETLAND
WESTERN ISLES
MORAY
HIGHLAND
ABERDEENSHIRE
ABERDEEN CITY
PERTH AND KINROSS
ANGUS
CITY OF DUNDEE
ARGYLL AND BUTE
FIFE
STIRLING
SCOTTISH BORDERS
DUMFRIES AND GALLOWAY

1. NORTH AYRSHIRE
2. SOUTH AYRSHIRE
3. EAST AYRSHIRE
4. INVERCLYDE
5. RENFREWSHIRE
6. EAST RENFREWSHIRE
7. WEST DUNBARTONSHIRE
8. EAST DUNBARTONSHIRE
9. GLASGOW CITY
10. NORTH LANARKSHIRE
11. SOUTH LANARKSHIRE
12. CLACKMANNANSHIRE
13. FALKIRK
14. WEST LOTHIAN
15. EDINBURGH
16. MIDLOTHIAN
17. EAST LOTHIAN

# ABERDEENSHIRE

## TOP SITES IN ABERDEENSHIRE

- Aberdeen Maritime Museum
- Dunnottar Castle
- Footdee
- David Welch Winter Gardens at Duthie Park
- Royal Lochnagar Distillery
- Craigievar Castle
- Duff House and the Bridge of Alvah
- Brig o' Balgownie
- Gordon Highlanders Museum
- Sandend Beach
- Balmoral Castle
- St Mary's Parish Church
- Crathes Castle
- Provost Skene's House
- Kincardine Bridge
- St Machar's Cathedral
- The Tolbooth
- Slains Castle
- Kincardine Castle
- Kincardine O'Neil Memorial

Located in the northeast corner of the country, the county of Aberdeen was once home to the northern Picts, a group of Celtic-speaking tribal people who lived in areas of Scotland during the Early Middle Ages. Remnants of the Picts can be found in Aberdeen to this day, from earth houses to Druidical circles made out of standing stones. Aberdeenshire has seen peaceful and bloody chapters in Scotland's rich past. The county played a vital role in the fighting between the Scottish clans, notably clans Macbeth and Canmore. After the Revolution of 1688, Aberdeenshire enjoyed an era of relative peace, but this was interrupted by events such as the Rising of 1715 and the Rising of 1745. In the same century, the area also witnessed increased prosperity because of improved trade with Germany, Poland, Belgium, Luxembourg, and the Netherlands.

Top: The Aberdeen Fishing Industry Memorial at the Aberdeen Maritime Museum commemorates the men and women who worked in the industry that played such a key role in the city's history.

The Local Government (Scotland) Act 1973 replaced the historic county of Aberdeenshire with the Aberdeenshire Council Area, which includes all of the historic counties of Aberdeenshire and some parts of Kincardineshire. The southernmost of northeastern Scotland's historic counties, Kincardineshire was initially named for the ancient castle of Kincardine, which was used as a stronghold by various Scottish kings. Its coat of arms includes the Crown of Scotland, a ruined castle on the mount, and the Scepter and Sword of Scotland crossed together.

Home to part of the Grampian Mountain Range, Kincardineshire is flat mainly towards the coast with forested hills towards central Scotland. Often called "the end of the Highlands," in reference to the county's lack of mountains and hills, the Mearns was once the site of scores of

Lying where the Dee and Don rivers meet the North Sea, Aberdeen City is known as the "Granite City" for its many gray-stone buildings.

fishing villages. Many rivers are situated around the Kincardineshire area, and among them are Luther water, Burn of People, Burn of Muchalls, and Cowie water.

Much of the traditional shire of Banff, locally called "Coontie o' Banffshire," has also been absorbed into Aberdeenshire. The ancient town of Banff has a long history as a significant northern seaport nestled on Scotland's northeast coastline.

Aberdeenshire is home to Scotland's largest livestock market as well as over 300 castles—including Balmoral Castle, the Queen's summer residence—the densest collection per acre anywhere in the British Isles. It also hosts three of Scotland's oldest colleges: King's College (founded in 1497), Marischal College (1593), and the University of Fraserburgh (1597). Also notable about Aberdeenshire is the Battle of Barra, which was fought at Inverurie in 1308, where the Earl of Buchan defeated Robert the Bruce. And closer to this spot, an army of Hanoverian troops was defeated by the Jacobites in 1745. This central county was the historic seat of the clan Dempster.

Aberdeen City, which is actually designated as its own local government council area, is the third-most populous city in Scotland. Sited between the river mouths of the Dee and the Don and a long, sandy coastline in the North Sea, it has a marine climate. The city is also known for its numerous parks and gardens, and citywide floral displays.

## ABERDEEN MARITIME MUSEUM

Located in the historic heart of Aberdeen near the harbor, this free museum details the city's long relationship with the North Sea. With collections ranging from maritime paintings, shipbuilding, fast-sailing ships, port history, fishing, and the oil industry, this museum ranges

Once a small fishing village, Gardenstown is now full of small creel boats and pleasure craft that bob in the waters beneath the town's buildings, which cling to steep slopes above the harbor.

15

# ABERDEENSHIRE

Above: Picturesque cottage architecture is one of Footdee's tourist lures. Below: A piper decks himself out in full dress to play for visitors to Dunnottar Castle.

> "When I was 12, we went from Glasgow to Aberdeen on a school trip. It was called fresh air fortnight."
>
> —BILLY CONNOLLY

Opposite: A narrow path leads from the mainland to the ruins of Dunnottar Castle, which sit on a rocky headland over the North Sea.

over several buildings, including the former Trinity Congregational Church. The offshore oil rig collection, the uniquely built cruise ship, and countless other exhibits extensively explore Aberdeen's maritime and petroleum industries' historical development. The prototype arts are breathtaking, leaving most tourists marveling at the beauty of the artworks and the stories behind them. If you feel like experiencing a bit of life on the high seas while staying safe on dry land, the Aberdeen Maritime Museum will keep you engaged for hours. Children will especially enjoy directing and diving the remote-controlled submersible ROV model in the Oil exploration exhibit.

## DUNNOTTAR CASTLE

This spectacular oceanside ruin sits atop the sheer cliffs of Stonehaven and has a history reaching as far back as the 9th century. Once home to the powerful Marischal family, this jaw-dropping castle has attracted visitors ranging from renowned photographers to the British royal family. Dunnottar's various structures, which date from the 13th to the 17th centuries, are spread out over a 1.4-hectare headland. From the land approach, the 14th-century keep or tower house is the most prominent structure. The other main buildings are the gatehouse, chapel, and the 16th-century palace that houses the Whigs' Vault, a cellar that was used as a makeshift prison. The steep, crumbling cliff face adds an air of danger to the incredible landscape, as does the narrow path that must be crossed when accessing the castle from the mainland.

## FOOTDEE

This quaint and historic fishing village has roots dating back to the Middle Ages, but it has served to house fishermen and their families in more recent years. The name of the town was originally dedicated to St Fittick, but the pronunciation and spelling was so corrupted over time that it eventually morphed into "Footdee"; it is still called a number of monikers, such as "Foot of the Dee/Fit o the Dee," "Fish Town," and "Fittie" in the Scots language. Footdee displays architecture that has been described as a cross between Neoclassical style and that of a tightly knit fishing community featuring "tarry sheds" made out of driftwood and

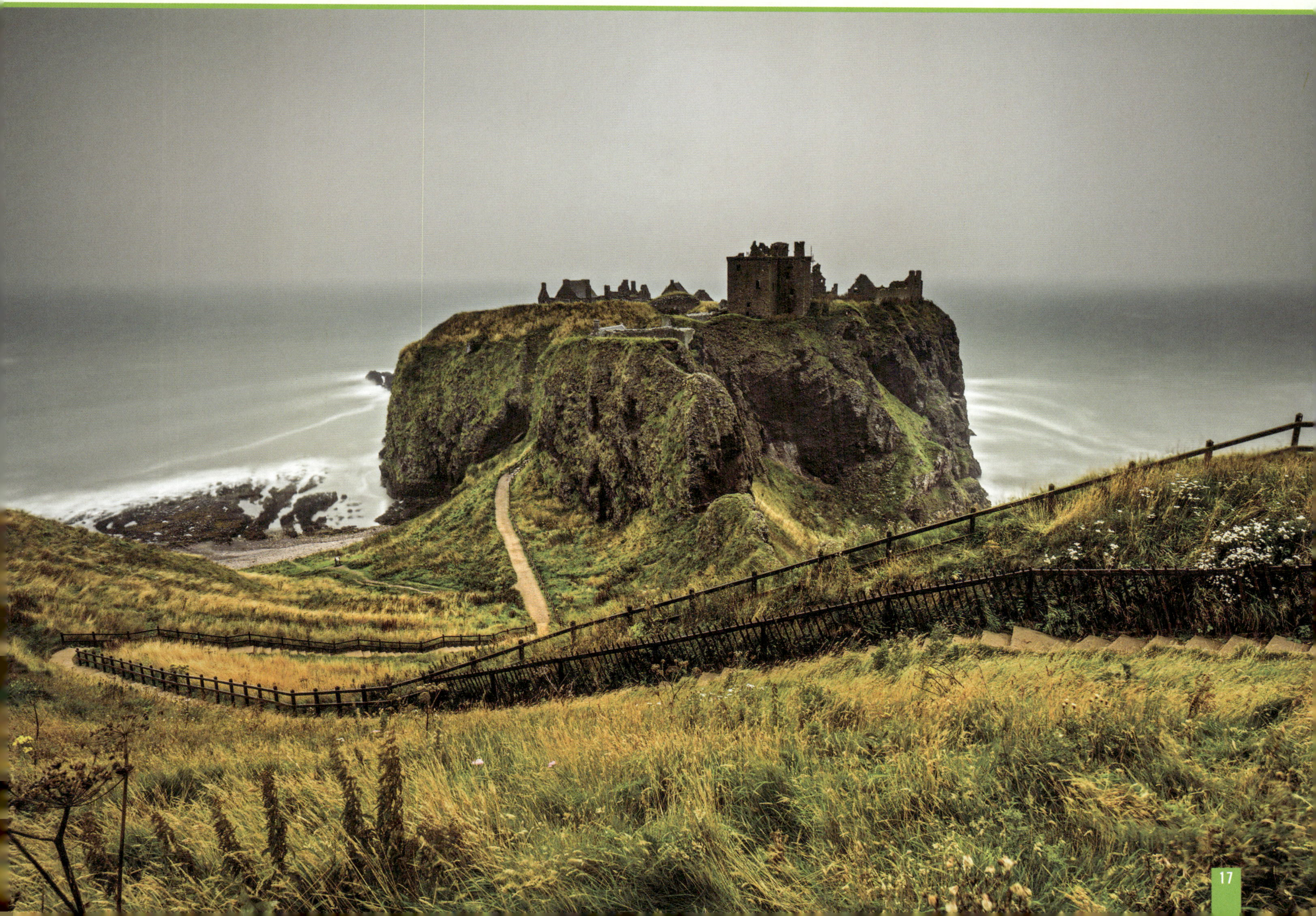

# ABERDEENSHIRE

scavenged materials. The town can be difficult to find even with the help of GPS, but the quaint, homey atmosphere of this quiet fishing town is worth taking a trip to experience.

## DAVID WELCH WINTER GARDENS AT DUTHIE PARK

One of the largest indoor gardens in Europe, the David Welch Winter Gardens at Duthie Park feature rare and exotic plants all year round. The Winter Gardens consist of a series of greenhouses first erected in 1899. Many of these plants would not survive outside the park, as they are not native to Scotland and require specialized care and conditions to flourish. Some notable attractions include the Corridor of Perfume, the Fern, Tropical, and Arid Houses, and the Japanese Garden. This 44-acre park runs alongside the River Dee and has paddle boats and kayaks to offer interested park-goers water play in the boating pond. Railings salvaged from the south side of the major bridge in the middle of the city's Union Street have been repurposed for use in the gardens. The railings are adorned with distinctive metal cats inspired by the city's coat of arms.

## ROYAL LOCHNAGAR DISTILLERY

Once called "New Lochnagar," this single-malt Scotch whisky distillery was renamed after a visit

**Opposite: Autumn hues are the perfect backdrop for Craigievar Castle.**

from the British royal family. According to legend, the first Lochnagar distillery was burned down in 1824 under uncertain circumstances, and a replacement was burned down again in 1841. John Begg constructed the "new" Lochnagar in 1845. When John Begg invited Prince Albert to visit the distillery from nearby Balmoral Castle, the Queen's Highlands house, the Distillery received its Royal Warrant in 1848. The following day, Queen Victoria, Prince Albert, and their three eldest children paid a visit to the distillery. The distillery was therefore dubbed "royal" Lochnagar. Royal Lochnagar offers iconic malts ranging from Talisker to Lagavulin, combining traditional pagoda kiln heads with an open mash tun. This historic distillery is still a front-runner in producing world-class spirits, and their arms are wide open to welcome visitors from anywhere in the world.

## CRAIGIEVAR CASTLE

This enchanting pink castle looks as if it stepped from the pages of a fairy tale and is even said to be the inspiration for the castle motif adopted but Walt Disney. Just outside the town of Alford and 26 miles west of Aberdeen, Craigievar Castle, with its small towers, is an impressive seven stories and features crow-stepped gables, oriel windows, conical roofs, ornamental stone cannons, and decorative zigzag console. First mentions of Craigievar Castle date from 1457, when it was owned by the Mortimer family. Despites it beauty,

**Above: Barrels of whiskey stand at the entrance to the Royal Lochnagar Distillery. Below: A greenhouse of cacti and other succulents is a highlight of the David Welch Winter Gardens.**

# ABERDEENSHIRE

it is a true testament to Scottish practicality. When it was being built, wood was in short supply, so its architects exploited every inch of space under one small roof. A tour here rewards you an authentic castle experience, with no artificial lighting beyond the ground floor. Its impressive collection of artifacts and art include Raeburns, armor, and weapons, and the plasterwork in the Great Hall, the huge Stuart coat-of-arms above the fireplace, and the Renaissance-style carvings on the wall paneling are of note, too. An intricate route of stairways within the tower house include a secret flight of steps that leads to a small room above a window in the Great Hall. You can also take advantage of the woodland trails and lovely gardens that surround the estate.

## DUFF HOUSE AND THE BRIDGE OF ALVAH

This beautiful, fully furnished historic home has seen much throughout its lifetime, including a royal visit from Her Majesty the Queen, and it was even used as a prisoner of war camp. Built in 1730 and still open to the public, Duff House is a Georgian estate house in Banff, in the Banff and Buchan area of Aberdeenshire, and is built of ashlar in three stories on a raised basement with advanced corner towers. This grand house was the former residence of the Earl of Fife's family. The beautiful landscape surrounding the estate includes the Bridge of Alvah, a masterfully crafted stone arch bridge that stretches across River Deveron. The bridge was constructed in 1773 to link the farming communities on both sides of the river and is still under constant use nearly 300 years later. Unusually, a room intended for a toll collector is built directly into the structure of the bridge. A circular path wraps all the way around the grounds of Duff house and crosses the bridge, meandering through forests and farmlands on a route that takes around three hours to travel on foot. Upon returning to Duff House from this long walk, the tea room available to visitors provides refreshments.

**Above: The Brig o' Balgownie spans the River Don. Opposite: The estate lands of the stately Duff House include the bridge and scenic paths.**

## BRIG O' BALGOWNIE

Over a deep pool known as the Black Neuk stands Scotland's oldest bridge, the Brig o' Balgownie. Evidence shows that this structure is the result of rebuilding work in three phases in the early 17th century, but legend has it that it was started in the late 13th or early 14th century and was completed by Robert the Bruce. From its beginnings until the construction of the adjacent Bridge of Don in 1831, it was the main crossing on the River Don. It has

# ABERDEENSHIRE

inspired generations, and English poet Lord Byron, whose mother, Catherine Gordon, was heiress of the Gight estate in Aberdeenshire, cites it in his poem *Don Juan:* "As 'Auld Lang Syne' brings Scotland, one and all/Scotch plaids, Scotch snoods, the blue hills, and clear streams/The Dee, the Don, Balgounie's brig's black wall. . ."

## GORDON HIGHLANDERS MUSEUM

Covering the 200-year history of the Gordon Highlanders regiment of the British Army, this museum explores the history of the aristocrats, students, farmers, fishermen, ghillies, and laborers who made up this group of remarkable men. With exhibits such as 11 original Victoria Crosses, a World War I replica trench, memorial gardens, and an armory, this museum starts its time line in the Napoleonic Wars and travels up to the current day. The wide range of artifacts collected in this museum tells the story of the Gordon Highlanders' efforts in World War I, World War II, and more, with enough information available to impress any student of history. The Gordon Highlanders Museum was one of the named locations chosen for the Aberdeen edition of Monopoly.

## SANDEND BEACH

Located in the small fishing town of Sandend, this beautiful, sandy beach is frequented by families on holiday, local beach-goers, and professionals in the surfing scene. Located off the scenic Moray coast, this beach is about 1.5 hours' drive from Aberdeen City, making it the perfect combination road trip and picnic destination. The beach can also be reached on foot when weather permits, as the route between Portsoy to Sandend Beach is only a few miles long. The pristine sand of this lovingly maintained beach stands out immediately; there is no debris or litter to be seen, and dozens of people can usually be found walking dogs, taking photographs, or just sunbathing in the sand. Close to the beach is the small fishing village of Sandend, where visitors can stop by to shop, get travel information, or have a bite to eat. There are few remnants of World War II structures dotted about Sandend Beach, most notably some surviving pill-box and anti-tank defenses. Several local stalls and shops also offer surfboard rentals and surfing lessons year-round.

## BALMORAL CASTLE

Just 50 miles west of Aberdeen, near the village of Crathie, stands Balmoral Castle,

*Above: A countryside path leads to the pristine Sandend Beach. Left: A moving memorial to the renowned Gordon Highlander Regiment stands in the famous Union Street in Aberdeen City. Opposite: Balmoral Castle is Queen Elizabeth II's private summer residence.*

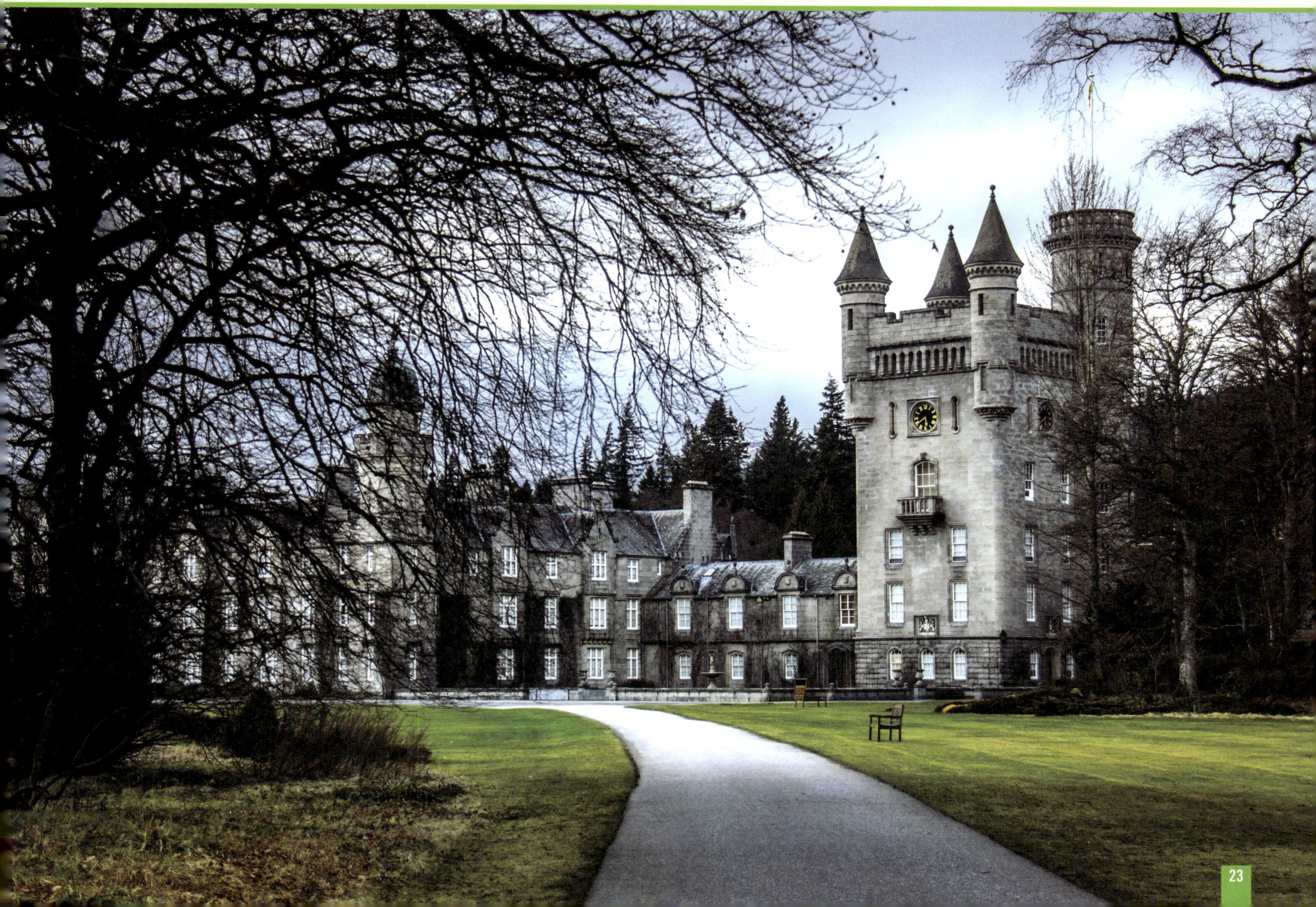

# ABERDEENSHIRE

Top: St Mary's in Banff gives you an opportunity to trace your Scottish genealogy in its ancient churchyard. Bottom: Provost Skene's House is a remnant of Aberdeen's medieval architecture.

Queen Elizabeth II's summer residence in Scotland. The estate was first mentioned in documents in 1484 and is the private property of the Queen. It has been one of the residences of the British royal family since 1852, when architect William Smith designed the castle with advice from Prince Albert. It is now considered an excellent example of Scottish Baronial architecture and is classified by Historic Environment Scotland as a category A listed building. The magnificent castle is well worth visiting on the rare days it's open to the public (and only when the Queen is away). A tour of the interior allows a glimpse of the Ballroom, the only room open to the public, with its stunning paintings and other objets d'art. You can also view a collection of coaches that has come to embody the Neo-Baronial style of the Victorian era. You can also take a relaxing walk in the extensive parkland or explore the incredible scenery aboard a fun Safari Tour that offers opportunities to see local wildlife up close.

While in the area, stop in the nearby town of Braemar, most famous for its annual Braemar Gathering. Known widely as the Highland Games, this uniquely Scottish event has been held here every autumn since 1832. You can also visit the Braemar Highland Heritage Centre, which has exhibits on the history of the games and Scottish traditional sporting.

## ST MARY'S PARISH CHURCH

Whether you would like to attend a service or explore the centuries-old headstones that populate the church's ancient cemetery, the historic St Mary's Parish Church makes for a brief but fascinating stop during a visit to Banffshire. Many visitors come to the church while studying their own genealogy, as many of the headstones come from family lines that can be followed through the generations to the present day. The church is one of the largest in the region, located at the south end of Banff and serving as one of the town's most notable landmarks; the structure of the church has been restored and altered a few times since it was first built in 1790, but has gone unchanged since the 1920s. The architectural design of the church was inspired by Dundee's St Andrew's church, although the towering spire at the forefront of the building was added some 40 years after the main body of the building was constructed.

## CRATHES CASTLE

Set against a backdrop of rolling hills, this castle is a fine example of baronial-style tower house, with its small oriel windows and corner towers. Cragthes Castle traces its beginnings to 1553, but the Burnett family, who lived in the castle for more than 350 years, had roots in the area dating back to 1323 when Robert the Bruce granted them nearby land. Alexander Burnett built the castle in the 16th century as an intricate maze of turrets, towers, oak

Opposite: Crathes Castle includes stunning gardens.

25

# ABERDEENSHIRE

panels, and painted ceilings, many of which survive to this day. A tour inside the castle reveals much of its charms, including amazing 17th-century wooden ceilings in the Room of the Nine Nobles, which depict the ancient heroes Hector, Julius Caesar, and Alexander the Great; three Old Testament characters; and three famous rulers, including King Arthur and Charlemagne. Throughout there are notable works of art, and the castle even claims a resident ghost in the Green Lady's Room. Outside you will find an eight-sectioned walled garden that is a true delight, with imaginative sculpted topiary, beautiful herbaceous edging, and colorfully exotic blooms. The massive yew hedges are thought to have been planted as early as 1702. You can also stop by the castle's visitors center, café, gift shop, an adventure playground, and treetop trekking.

## PROVOST SKENE'S HOUSE

A rare survival of Aberdeen's medieval burgh architecture, Provost Skene's House was built in 1545 and was bought by Sir George Skene, who served as Provost of the city from 1676 to 1685. In 1953, the Queen Mother opened the house to the public as a "Period House and Museum of Local History." The house is much altered, but the rooms have been furnished in the styles of the 17th to early 19th centuries. Highlights of the free

Top: When it was built in the 1930s, Kincardine Bridge was Europe's longest road bridge. Bottom: The simple design of the nave of St Machar's Cathedral is brightened by colorful stained-glass windows.

tour include the carved plaster ceilings Skene most likely commissioned the in the 17th century and a Renaissance-style painted ceiling in an attic gallery. The Costume Gallery presents regularly changing displays of period dress.

## KINCARDINE BRIDGE

The Kincardine Bridge crosses the Fifth of Forth from the Falkirk council area to Kincardine and Fife. It was designed by Sir Alexander Gibbs & Partners, Consulting Engineers and architect Donald Watson. It was built between 1932 and 1936 and was the largest swing bridge in Europe and Scotland's longest road bridge. It was also the first road crossing of the River Forth downstream of Stirling. The swinging central section was used as a passageway until sometime in 1988. While in use, the swinging section of the bridge would raise up to allow larger ships to sail upstream to a small port at Alloa. The Scottish Executive identified the original bridge as being in need of replacement as it was over 70 years old at the time. A new bridge was opened in 2008.

## ST MACHAR'S CATHEDRAL

Located to the north of Aberdeen's city center in the former burgh of Old Aberdeen, stands St Machar's, a Church of Scotland church dating back to the 12th century. Once designated a cathedral, it is now technically a high kirk because it has not been the seat of a bishop since 1690. This now calm and lovely church has had a turbulent history; for example, after the execution of William Wallace in 1305, his body was cut up and sent to different corners of the country to warn other dissenters. It is said that Aberdeen received his left arm and it was buried in the walls of the cathedral.

The earliest parts of the surviving building date to the later 1300s, but the only part now roofed is the eight-bay aisled nave, begun in the late 1300s and roofed in the mid-1400s. It remains in use as the parish church of Old Aberdeen. A tower collapse in 1688 destroyed much of the medieval church, including the transepts, the choir, and the presbytery. You can visit the St Machar's to explore the ruined transepts, which contain some fine late medieval wall-tombs, including an ornate carving and an effigy of Bishop Gavin Dunbar, who died in 1532.

## THE TOLBOOTH

A tourist favorite, the Tolbooth in Aberdeen City is an old prison turned museum. Built between 1616 and 1629 and attached to the Aberdeen Sheriff Court in Union Street, it is one of the city's oldest buildings. The museum traces the grim history of this jail, where an assortment of criminals—so-called and real—were kept. They included 45 women and 2 men accused of witchcraft, and around the year 1630, Marion Hardie suffered a brutal death in front of the public for the crime. After the Battle of Culloden, 96 Jacobite prisoners were held within its walls, and in the mid 1700s,

## MERCAT CROSSES

Diagonally opposite the Tolbooth, stands Aberdeen's Mercat Cross, adorned with a royal white unicorn. Built in 1686 by John Montgomery, the structure includes a center staircase that criers once used to climb to the roof to announce news of newly crowned monarchs to the crowds gathered below. The base of the cross displays portrait medallions showing the heads of the 10 Stuart monarchs from James I through to James VII, Charles I, Charles II, and Mary Stuart. A traveler through the towns and villages of Scotland is sure to come across a few mercat crosses. A mercat cross, the Scots name for "market cross," is found in towns and villages that historically had the right to hold a regular market or fair, a right granted by the monarch, a bishop, or a baron.

# ABERDEENSHIRE

## OTHER TOP SITES

- **ABERDEEN ART GALLERY**
Built in 1884, this gallery houses an exquisite collection of 17th- to 20th-century paintings. Scottish artists with work displayed here include Charles Rennie Mackintosh, William Dyce, Thomas Faed, John Philip, and other representatives of the Glasgow School.

- **UNIVERSITY OF ABERDEEN**
One of the top-rated free sites in the city of Aberdeen is the University of Aberdeen Zoology Museum. This zoo covers everything from protozoa to whales. You can also stop by the King's Museum, which features temporary exhibits of artifacts from various university collections.

- **CRUICKSHANK BOTANIC GARDENS**
Located on the King's College campus, Cruickshank Botanic Gardens include displays of interesting alpine and subtropical collections, as well as a delightful rock and water garden. Also of interest in this peaceful 11-acre site are a sunken garden, rose garden, shrub and herbaceous borders, and an arboretum with a fine collection of more than 2,500 plants.

- **QUEEN MOTHER ROSE GARDEN**
Inside Aberdeen City's Hazlehead Park, you'll find the peaceful Rose Garden, which also features at its center a memorial to those who lost their lives in the Piper Alpha Disaster.

- **PETERHEAD PRISON MUSEUM**
Spanning the prison's 125-year history, this museum offers a self-guided audio tour of "Scotland's Toughest Jail." An audio tour walks visitors through the corridors of the only prison in Scotland where convicts experienced sentences of penal servitude.

- **MUSEUM OF BANFF**
Founded in 1828 by the Banff Institution, this small but carefully curated museum is the oldest surviving museum in Scotland. Today the Museum of Banff offers a display of a vast collection of fascinating artifacts from the Celtic period up to the modern day.

- **TULLIALLAN AND KINCARDINE PARISH CHURCH**
Built in 1833 on the site of a distillery using local Longannet stone, this church sits in the middle of a green grass estate, surrounded by a gravel path and low ashlar walls; a large square tower can be seen rising from the western side of the church roof.

local children were kept here before being transported to America. A tour of the jail includes the Jacobite cell, where visitors can experience an interactive model of Willie Baird, a real prisoner from 1746, tell his sorry tale, and the maiden blade of Aberdeen's mid-16th-century guillotine. The old prison's 17th- and 18th-century cells still hold the original barred windows and doors. With such a gruesome past, it is no surprise it is claimed to be one of the most haunted buildings in Aberdeen and has been the subject of many paranormal investigation teams, such as *James Warrender's: The Ghost Network* and the series *Most Haunted*.

## SLAINS CASTLE

Built by the 9th Earl of Erroll in the 16th century, Slains Castle, also called New Slains Castle, features roofless ruins peering over a cliff toward the North Sea. Slains Castle is often associated with Bram Stoker's *Dracula;* the ruins are a patchwork of mortared granite, red brick from the Middle Ages, and crumbling sandstone, all of which come together to paint a picture of the castle's history. The castle's defenses include the sheer North Sea cliffs, a deep, impassable moat to the west, and a ruined rampart on the south that would have served as the main entrance. The ruins feature well-preserved three- and four-story structural sections, as well as a basement channel that runs the length of the range, especially on the eastern side. Basement kitchens with several fire pits and masonry indentation storage rooms are well-preserved. Internal doorways are mostly well-preserved timber lintel structures, with a few mortared sandstone and medieval brickwork archways thrown in for good measure.

## KINCARDINE CASTLE

This is a private home serving as a hospitality venue for tourists and visitors. Formerly known as Kincardine House, this grand castle sits on a 3,000-acre hillside estate with a stunning view of the Cairngorms National Park and Royal Deeside. It comprises 70 houses, shops, offices and workshops, a quarry, 1,500 acres of forestry, tenant farming, salmon fishing, and gardening. The site was built on an earlier building known as Kincardine Lodge dating back to 1780. The castle served as a hospital in World War I, and then again during World War II.

## KINCARDINE O'NEIL MEMORIAL

This 27-foot-tall granite pillar was originally built in 1922 to commemorate the fallen heroes of World War I, but it was later redesigned to include heroic figures who lost their lives during World War II. Engraved on the body of this monument are 71 names of notable residents of Kincardine O'Neil who were either killed or went missing during the wars. The memorial is surrounded by flowers and well-kept shrubs, as well as the small offerings people often leave at the base of the pillar.

**Opposite:** The sun sets over the stark ruins of Slains Castle.

29

# ANGUS

## TOP SITES IN ANGUS

- Crombie Country Park
- Invermark Castle
- Murton Farm
- Arbroath Abbey
- Pitmuies Gardens
- Glamis Castle

With roots reaching back to Roman occupation, subsequent Pict dwellings, and the Scottish Wars of Independence to reclaim the land taken by the British, Angus has evolved from a linen and jute producing town to an agricultural tourism destination. Nearby hills and glens are popular for avid walkers, and snowy slopes in the mountains attract skiers from all over the world. Angus (formerly known as Forfarshire) is associated with Forfar Bridie, a popular hand-held savory pie originating in the 1850s. With a monthly farmer's market and the annual Forfar Food Festival, there are endless Scottish bites for food enthusiasts and hungry walkers alike to try out.

Angus's story traces back into prehistory; human inhabitation in this area has been dated as far back as the Neolithic period. Angus is rich in archaeological and anthropological artifacts ranging across centuries: an abundance of Bronze Age artifacts and ruins can be found here, for example, and topping the list of this Bronze Age archaeology is a short-cist burial discovered near West Newbigging. The items recovered include pottery urns, a gold amulet, and a pair of silver discs. Researchers have also uncovered Iron Age structures and artifacts in Angus, as well as a wealth of ancient Pictish sculpture stones, which are intricately carved monoliths dating back to the 6th century.

Angus is often considered the birthplace of Scotland because it was here that the declaration that made the country an independent nation was made in 1320. The name *Angus* itself leads back to ancient history, as it comes from an 8th-century Pictish king by the same name who once claimed the area as his territory.

Top: The Peter Pan statue in Kirriemuir commemorates Angus native J.M. Barrie, who created the famous fictional character.

Autumn begins to color the landscape of Crombie Country Park surrounding Crombie Loch.

## CROMBIE COUNTRY PARK

Consisting of 200 acres of gorgeous woodlands surrounding Crombie Loch, Crombie Country Park offers 23 miles of scenic woodland trails as well as a picnic area and playground. Crombie Country Park has a 2.5-mile woodland walk, as well as a number of shorter routes. This large park offers a variety of hikes and pathways for pedestrians and cyclists and a mountain bike mini-cycle track. It has easily accessible ponds, bird shelters, and squirrel feeding areas that are ideal for wildlife enthusiasts and bird watchers. There are also picnic and barbecue areas available. This wheelchair-accessible destination is great for spotting wildlife, ranging from roe deer to woodpeckers, and makes for an excellent sunny day adventure. Anglers can also fly fish for stocked brown trout and geocachers can search out the more than 30 geocache hides in Crombie. Crombie Country Park has something for everyone, but the site is especially popular with cyclists for its 28-mile cycle path and robust mountain biking trails.

## INVERMARK CASTLE

With its first incarnation as a 14th-century keep meant to guard the southern end of the strategic pass leading from Deeside, Invermark Castle is a imposingly tall tower house near Brechin. Its setting is the beautiful mountainous country where Glen Lee and Glen Mark meet to become Glen Esk. With its great height, it truly gives you the sense of just how daunting a building like this would have been to lightly armed attackers. The structure you see now was built around 1526 by the Lindsay family, who made use of the existing keep. Rich in history, Invermark sheltered David Lindsay after he had killed Lord Spynie in Edinburgh in 1607, following a long-standing quarrel, and also James Carnegie, Lord Balnamoon, who was being sought by government troops after the Battle of Culloden in 1746.

## MURTON FARM

Murton Trust offers visitors a farm, a nature reserve, and a tearoom, all of which are open to the public for free. Murton Trust, a charitable organization,

To reach the entrance to the towering Invermark Castle inhabitants used a movable timber bridge or stair. Now barred and well above ground level, the interior is not accessible to visitors.

# ANGUS

The substantial ruins of Arbroath Abbey, founded by William the Lion in 1178, is famously associated with the Declaration of Arbroath.

runs the farm on a donation basis, offering wildlife education and animal sponsorship and adoption. Pop in for one of their house-made scones featured on their rotating seasonal menu or take a stroll amongst the lochs and wetlands looking for wildflowers and waterfowl, or stop and see Dennis and Gnasher, the Kune pigs. You can also expect to observe ferrets, guinea pigs, and other wildlife near the pond. Over 130 different species of birds and wildfowl can be found in the nature reserve, and a large wildflower meadow provides opportunities to examine a wide range of butterflies and insects. This stop along your Scottish journey is especially great for the kids: with sandpits, pedal toys, trampolines, and a host of outdoor games, the little ones are sure to be entertained for hours.

## ARBROATH ABBEY

In 1178 William I, known as William the Lion, asked the Tironensian monks from Kelso Abbey to establish a monastery at Arbroath as a memorial to his childhood friend Thomas Becket, the murdered Archbishop of Canterbury. In 1214, William was buried in front of the abbey's high altar, breaking the tradition of having Scottish monarchs laid to rest in the royal mausoleum at Dunfermline Abbey. Religious life in the abbey continued until the Protestant Reformation of 1560, and parts of the abbey were dismantled in 1580 to build a new burgh church.

"For, so long as a hundred remain alive, we will never in any degree be subject to the dominion of the English. Since not for glory, riches or honours do we fight, but for freedom alone, which no man loses but with his life."

—THE DECLARATION OF ARBROATH, 6 APRIL 1320

Although in ruins, the abbey is still remarkably beautiful and remains an important symbol and landmark. The abbey church at the heart of the monastic complex comprised a presbytery, a monks' choir, two transepts, chapel aisles, and a nine-bay nave with aisles. The presbytery, sacristy and south transept survive to a large extent, but the most complete part of the abbey is its strikingly beautiful twin-towered west front. The abbey's famous "Round O"—the circular window in the south transept gable—became a landmark for mariners. Robert Stevenson, grandfather of the novelist Robert Louis Stevenson, rebuilt it in 1809. Most of the domestic buildings that had been grouped around a small cloister survive only as foundations, except for the abbot's house, which is one of the most complete abbot's residences in Britain, and the gatehouse, the guest house, and a stretch of precinct wall.

The abbey is best known for the Declaration of Arbroath, a document signed in the abbey in which Scotland's nobility proclaimed their independence from England around 1320. In 1951, the abbey again shot to national prominence when, three months after its removal from Westminster Abbey, the Stone of Destiny was found beside the high altar.

## PITMUIES GARDENS

Open through the growing season of April 1 to September 30, these gorgeous grounds consist of mix of garden types. A kitchen garden of vegetables and fruit trees, such as very old apple and pear trees, provides fruit and veg for the house. A "potager" mixes together flowers, herbs, and vegetables with a wooden trellis on which honeysuckle, climbing roses, and shrubs are trained. An archway of clipped silver pear frames a central walkway flanked by a dark red hedge of cherry plum and lined with herbaceous borders leads to a sundial in the formal garden. A series of three rose terraces are linked by stone steps to the central fountain and pond. At the base of the rose garden you will find the splendid Cherry Tree Walk. Long borders of perennials, beautiful old-fashioned delphiniums and roses, as well as paved paths lined with violas and dianthus, are protected by two renowned semiformal wall gardens that adjoin an 18th-century house and steading. The house also has a few notable features that stand out at first glance, including a picturesque turreted doo'cot and a "gothick" wash-house, built more than 200 years ago, that is often mistaken for a chapel. Crocus, snowdrops, and daffodils are among the many springtime blooms. Take a stroll down the Vinny Walk or gaze over the Black Loch for a spectacular outdoor retreat.

## GLAMIS CASTLE

Set in the broad and fertile lowland valley of Strathmore, near Forfar, in the county town of Angus stands Glamis Castle, the ancestral seat of the Earls of Strathmore and Kinghorne since 1372. Glamis Castle is steeped in history: it was

*Above: Hidden in greenery, the turreted doo'cot at Pitmuies Gardens resembles a stone chapel. Below: A wailing Macbeth is one of the wood carvings from the Scottish play scattered within the woodland along the Macbeth Walk at Glamis Castle.*

# ANGUS

the inspiration for Shakespeare's *Macbeth*, the childhood home of the wife of George VI, HM Queen Elizabeth the Queen Mother, and the birthplace of their second daughter, HRH The Princess Margaret.

At Glamis expert guides will help you follow in the footsteps of Mary, Queen of Scots, James V, Bonnie Dundee, the Old Jacobite Pretender to the throne James VIII, and the ill-fated Janet Douglas, as well as, of course, tell the story of the bittersweet life of Mary Eleanor Bowes. The castle is rife with legend, and the most famous is that of the Monster of Glamis, a hideously deformed child born to the family, who was kept in the castle all his life and his suite of rooms was bricked up after his death. Another is that of the "White Lady," thought to be Janet Douglas, Lady Glamis. Whenever the small chapel within the castle is used for family functions, a seat is always reserved for her.

You can also tour the gardens, which are beautiful all year round. Walks take you through a mixture of habitats, ranging from the formal Italian Garden to mixed woodland, such as the Macbeth Walk, which is home to wide variety of flora and fauna. After the tour of the house and gardens, stop in the Glamis Castle Kitchen in the original Victorian kitchen space, which offers tempting fare made from the best of seasonal produce and locally sourced ingredients, some of it coming from the estate's own farms and gardens.

**A statue of King James I of England and King James VI of Scotland overlooks the drive to the sprawling Glamis Castle.**

## OTHER TOP SITES

- **J.M. BARRIE'S BIRTHPLACE**

Visit the childhood of J.M. Barrie, creator of *Peter Pan*, a small whitewashed cottage in Kirriemuir, where Barrie lived with his seven brothers and sisters in two upstairs rooms, while his father toiled in the downstairs weaving workshop. The wash house in the yard was Barrie's first theater—and may even have inspired the Wendy house in *Peter Pan*.

- **TAYSIDE POLICE MUSEUM**

This museum in Kirriemuir charts the history of policing in Dundee City, Perth and Kinross, and Angus. You will find artifacts, documents, and photographs, covering the period from the early 1800s through to the 1980s.

- **BRECHIN CASTLE**

In the ancient city of Brechin standing on a massive bluff of rocks above the River Southesk, you'll find Brechin Castle, where Lord and Lady Dalhousie extend a warm welcome . You can tour the castle and the spectacular gardens at set times each year.

- **DUNNINALD CASTLE AND GARDENS**

Dunninald, just south of Montrose on the Angus coastline, is an 1824 Gothic Revival–style family home with lovely gardens open to the public.

- **RESTENNETH PRIORY**

Restenneth Priory lies at the heart of the old Pictish kingdom. The earliest masonry at Restenneth Priory dates to the 1100s, but its original builders are unknown. Alexander I had the annals of Iona transferred to the priory in the 1100s, and Robert the Bruce buried his young son Prince John here in the 1300s.

- **HOSPITALFIELD HOUSE**

This stunning early Arts and Crafts Scottish Baronial country house in Arbroath was left in trust in 1890 to support artists. Public events, including exhibitions, walks and workshops, and weekly tours take place during the summer.

- **MEFFAN MUSEUM AND ART GALLERY**

This museum and art gallery in Forfar gathers objects, archive materials, and photographs relating to the history of Forfar and reflects both the historical heritage and the contemporary culture of the surrounding area.

# ARGYLL AND BUTE

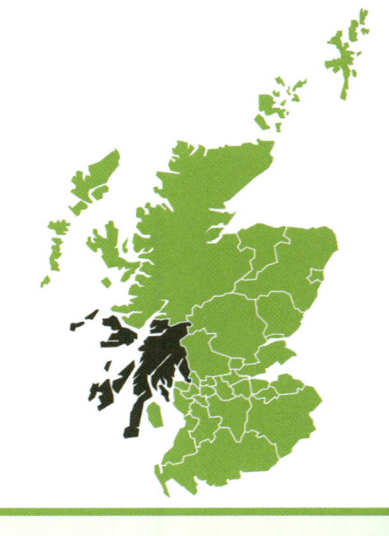

## TOP SITES IN ARGYLL AND BUTE

- Castle House Museum
- Argyll Forest Park
- The Hill House
- The West Island Way
- Inveraray Castle:
- Scalpsie Bay
- St Michael's Chapel Ruins
- Rothesay Victorian Toilets
- Castle Stalker
- St Blane's Church
- Mount Stuart
- Rothesay Castle
- Ettrick Bay Beach
- Kilchurn Castle
- Islay
- Isle of Arran
- Isle of Mull
- Iona

Taking up a relatively small portion of mainland Scotland and an additional seven islands in the Firth of Clyde, the historic county of Buteshire sits nestled on Scotland's rugged southwestern coastline. Bute has been paired with Argyllshire to form the council area of Argyll and Bute. Argyllshire spans 23 inhabited islands—the majority of the Inner Hebrides group, with the notable exceptions of Skye and Eigg—and a large area in the mainland.

Formed in 1326, Argyll has a name with roots in the Old Gaelic *airer Goídel*, which translates to "coastland of the Gaels." Gaelic-speaking Scots invaded Argyllshire in the 2nd century CE from Ireland. Once an agricultural area ruled by Highland lords, today Argyll relies on fishing and tourism as its main industries. Mainland Argyllshire is distinguished by mountainous Highland scenery interspersed with hundreds of small lochs, with a heavily indented coastline containing numerous small offshore islands. These islands present a contrasting range of scenery, from the relatively flat islands of Coll and Tiree to the mountainous terrain of Jura and Mull. For ease of reference, Argyll county can be split into three sections: Northern Mainland, Southern Mainland, and the Inner Hebrides. The Northern Mainland covers two significant peninsulas, Ardnamurchan and Morvern, while the Southern Mainland is much larger than the northern side, and it covers the long Kintyre peninsula. You can see the all the way across the sea to Ireland from Argyllshire's 3,000 miles of coastline on a clear day.

The islands of the county of Bute include Bute, Big and Little Cumbrae, Arran, Holy Isle, Inchmarnock, and Pladda, all of which are accessible by ferry. The historic county of Bute is called *Siorrachd Bhòid*

**Top:** A ferry leaves Rothesay on the Isle of Bute for Wemyss Bay, a village on the mainland coast of the Firth of Clyde.

The ruins of Kilchurn Castle sit on Loch Awe, the longest freshwater loch in Scotland.

in Scottish Gaelic and is also commonly referred to as Buteshire. The county town is Rothesay, located on the Isle of Bute. Bute is notably home to quite a few beautiful beaches, attracting visitors from all over for unparalleled opportunities for wildlife-watching and sunbathing.

Arran, one of Bute's main islands, is roughly peanut shaped, flatter in the south and more mountainous in the north, culminating in Goat Fell, the tallest mountain in Buteshire. The island is separated from the Kintyre peninsula by Kilbrannan Sound. In contrast, Bute Island is much flatter, though still somewhat hilly, especially in the north. Bute is separated from the Cowl peninsula by the narrow Kyles of Bute. A good number of lochs lie in the center of the island, most notably Ascog, Fad, and Quien.

## CASTLE HOUSE MUSEUM

With its immersive historical reconstructions, rich photo archive and memorabilia, and interactive exhibits, the Castle House Museum spans the course of history from Neolithic settlers to the Cold War in the surrounding area of Dunoon. With the Firth of Clyde visible from its extensive grounds, this museum is also home to the famous statue "Highland Mary," after a song composed in 1792 by Scottish poet Robert Burns. Castle House Museum is generally considered a goldmine of local history and knowledge. One notable exhibit includes a video display of photos from the past compared with images from the present day. This detailed video display, the countless unique artifacts gathered here, and the fascinating local historical facts offered by the museum's experts provide an excellent chronology of the area that cannot be found anywhere else.

Above: Traigh Ban Beach lies on the northeastern tip of Iona, one of the islands of the Inner Hebrides. Left: The statue of Highland Mary in Dunoon is dedicated to Mary Campbell, the lover of Robert Burns.

# ARGYLL AND BUTE

## ARGYLL FOREST PARK

Britain's oldest forest park, Argyll Forest Park has attracted nature enthusiasts since 1935. Spanning from the Firth of Clyde to the Arrochar Alps, Argyll Forest Park sits at one end of the Highland Boundary Fault. This beautiful expanse offers five different forests to explore with the family or to wander alone for a quiet afternoon among the trees; it is also an excellent destination for mountain biking, hiking, and wildlife viewing. The park spans about 720 square miles of some of the finest scenery in Scotland. This location encompasses lowlands in the southern part and high mountains in the northern region, as well as several lochs, rivers, forests, and gardens. There are numerous viewpoints and heights that are ideal for a picnic while exploring the grounds. The park also stretches alongside Loch Eck and Loch Fyne, offering many more hidden walks that are certainly worth undertaking.

## THE HILL HOUSE

Located in Helensburgh, this architectural masterpiece was created in 1902 by Charles Rennie Mackintosh in the "Glasgow style" for the publisher Walter Blackie. Built out of a desire to "service the practical needs" of the Blackie family, the Hill House was commissioned to be built by Mackintosh, but some of its most lasting,

**Top:** The Hill House near Helensburgh is a fine example of work by the famous Scottish architect Charles Rennie Mackintosh.
**Bottom:** The popular walking route the West Island Way takes trekkers through the charming landscape of the Isle of Bute.

**Opposite:** A path through Argyll Forest Park offers stunning views.

noteworthy features came from the mind of his wife, Margaret Macdonald. The Hill House is exceptionally well-preserved, with spiraling stairs outside the structure that lead viewers to the roof. It is one of Mackintosh's most famous architectural works, perhaps second only to the former Glasgow School of Art. It was designed too be foremost a home, and apart from the fascinating architectural structure, the superb furnishing and interior design are just as compelling as the structure itself.

## THE WEST ISLAND WAY

The first of its type on a Scottish island, Bute's West Island Way opened in September 2000 as part of Bute's millennium celebrations and offers an easy walk of about 30 miles, passing through seashore, moorland, farmland, and forest. It also affords you great opportunities to watch wildlife. You may be lucky to see a basking shark offshore at the south end, an osprey over Loch Fad near Rothesay town, or a red deer in the north end. This long-distance waymarked path begins at Kilchattan Bay in the south of the island and finishes at Port Bannatyne in the north, having a central point at Rothesay, the main town in Bute. You can complete the hike over two fairly long walking days. The trail is clearly marked, but maps are strongly recommended and can be picked up at the Bute Discovery Centre in Rothesay.

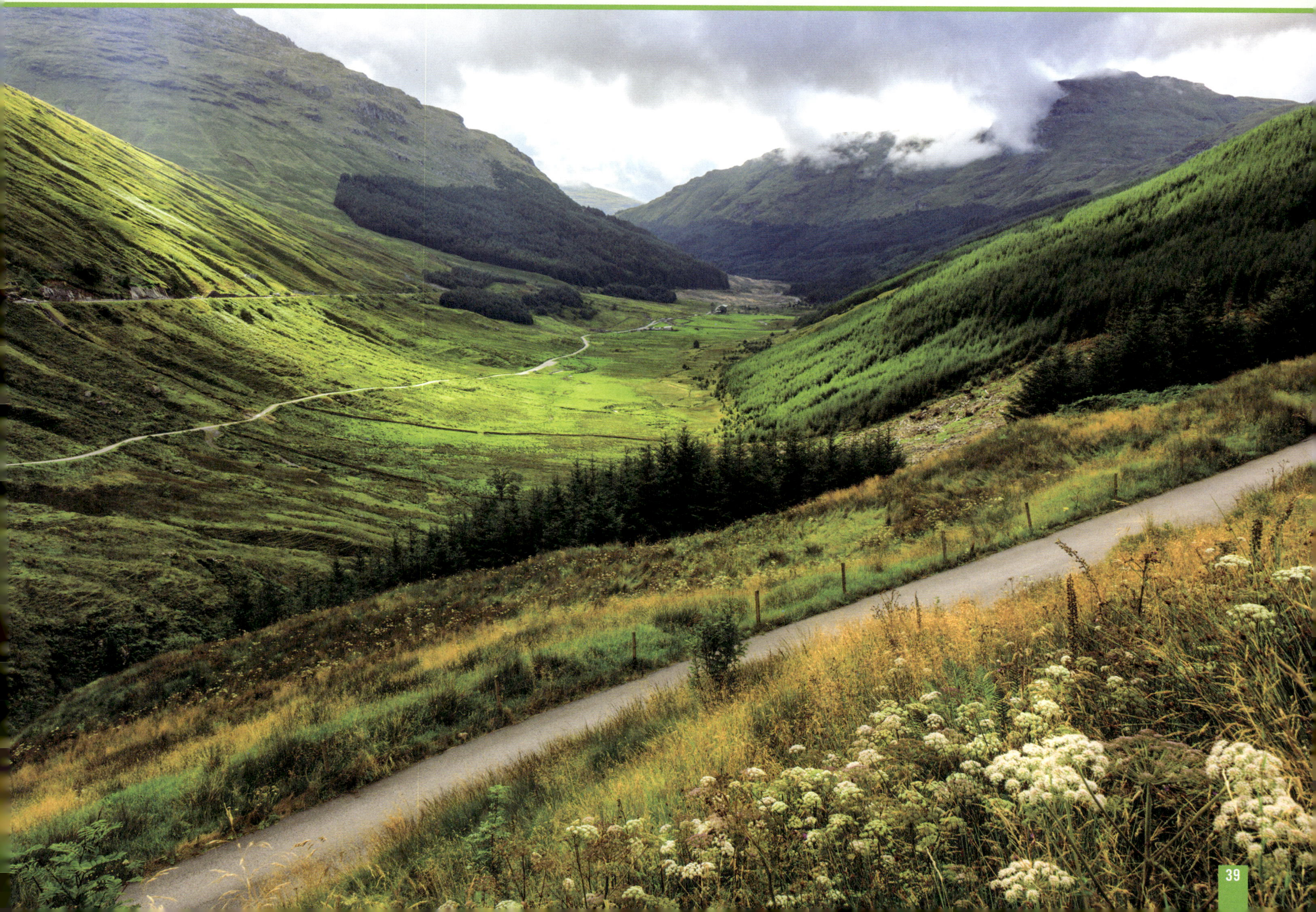

# ARGYLL AND BUTE

## INVERARAY CASTLE:

Once the home of the Duke of Argyll, Chief of the Clan Campbell, Inveraray Castle has been nestled on the banks of Loch Fyne since the 1400s in one form or another—what is visible today was constructed in the mid-1700s by the 3rd Duke of Argyll. With a 16-acre plot of flowers, lawns, and woodlands, the grounds also contain the Doo'cot (Dovecote), Watch Tower, and Frew's Bridge. The large stretch of land surrounding the castle will take close to 10 minutes to walk, and the gardens maintained within Inveraray's walls can be covered in 40 minutes at a brisk pace. Inside the quaint building, there is an armory hall (containing over 1,300 assorted weapons) that happens to be Scotland's tallest chamber; the armory's ceilings are nearly 70 feet high. The castle also displays the Victorian Room, an in-depth exhibition focusing on the life of Queen Victoria's daughter Princess Louise, Duchess of Argyll. Inveraray castle remains the home of the Duke of Argyll and his family today, although the lower floors are open to the public.

## SCALPSIE BAY

Situated on the west coast of the Isle of Bute and once used for military training in World War II, the red-tinged sands of Scalpsie Bay offer amazing views of the Isle of Arran, as well as excellent wildlife-watching opportunities. Scalpsie is a lovely, secluded bay known for its resident herd of grey seals, which can often be found sunning on rocks just offshore at the northwestern end of the bay. The Scalpsie Bay herd consists of approximately 200 seals; visitors have the best chances of spotting them when the tide is out on a sunny day. Overlooking the northwestern end of Scalpsie Bay is a very small Iron Age hillfort occupying the summit of a low hill. This Iron Age hillfort is called Dun Scalpsie, and World War II Home Guard defenses are built into the dun wall. The remains of wooden posts—intended as defenses against potential glider invasions—can still be found embedded in the sand. A little less than half a mile inland, the ruins of a mill constructed in 1497 can be found near Loch Quien.

**A common, or harbour, seal basks on a rock at low tide in Scalpsie Bay.**

## ST MICHAEL'S CHAPEL RUINS

Now roofless, these ruins were built using smooth beach stones and clay. With walls roughly 6 feet thick, this early Christian site was left to crumble on the waterfront hillside with views of Kames and Tighnabruaich on the opposing shore. There is also an archaic burial ground nearby, with the last known burial taking place in 1927. It remains uncertain when the roofless chapel was built, though speculation places the date somewhere between the 5th and 7th centuries. As is a standard feature of many early Celtic Christian churches, this ruin sits within a roughly circular stone-walled enclosure. The stone slab on the eastern end of the

**Opposite:** The charming Inveraray Castle stood in for the fictional Duneagle Castle for the filming of *Downton Abbey*.

# ARGYLL AND BUTE

chapel is believed to have served as the altar, and there are several doorways at the northern wall that support this possibility.

## ROTHESAY VICTORIAN TOILETS

Who knew that toilets could be so beautiful? On the site of a once-booming resort, these elaborately tiled restrooms date back to 1899 and are arguably the most complete Victorian toilets in Great Britain today. The ceramic tiles are formed in a mosaic of the Royal Burgh of Rothesay and are perhaps the most highlighted expression of the luxury of the Victorian Era. These unique toilets are paired with stunning fittings of swirled blue marble, intricately tiled accents, and mosaic floors. Rothesay Victorian Toilets is a reminder of the heady days when the town was a popular destination for day-trippers from Glasgow, who came on regular paddle steamers from the mainland to enjoy an outing by the sea. Today, every part of the fittings, except the cisterns in the toilets cubicles, remains unchanged from the original. Only the men's toilets were constructed in this fashion; a women's restroom was added in 1994, but was designed in standard modern style.

## CASTLE STALKER

Standing on a tidal islet on Loch Laich, an inlet off Loch Linnhe, is the picturesque Castle Stalker. Castle Stalker, in the Gaelic *Stalcaire,* meaning "hunter" or "falconer," is believed originally to have been the site of a small fortified building belonging to the MacDougalls when they were Lords of Lorn and built around 1320. In its long, tumultuous history, it passed through the hands of many families. Its present form, a four-story tower house or keep, is mostly likely the work of Sir John Stewart, the then Lord of Lorn, who built and occupied the castle in the 1440s. At the time of the 1745 Rising, Castle Stalker was held by the Campbells, who resided in it until about 1800. From then on, the castle fell into decay, and around 1840 the roof either fell in or was perhaps removed to avoid a roof tax. In 1908 the castle was regained from the Campbells by Charles Stewart of Achara, who purchased it and carried out some basic preservation work to stem its decay. His successors carried on the work of rebuilding and restoring it as it is today. It is one of the best-preserved medieval tower houses to survive in western Scotland and is a Category A listed building. It stands in the Lynn of Lorn National Scenic Area, one of 40 such areas in Scotland. With its atmospheric island location, it was chosen as one of the filming sites for *Monty Python and the Holy Grail* and also makes a brief appearance in *Highlander: Endgame*. It is privately owned, but limited tours are available each year.

## ST BLANE'S CHURCH

The remains of this ancient chapel have been dated as far back as the 1100s, making it one of Bute's oldest and best-preserved early places of worship. This historic church sits nestled in a valley at the

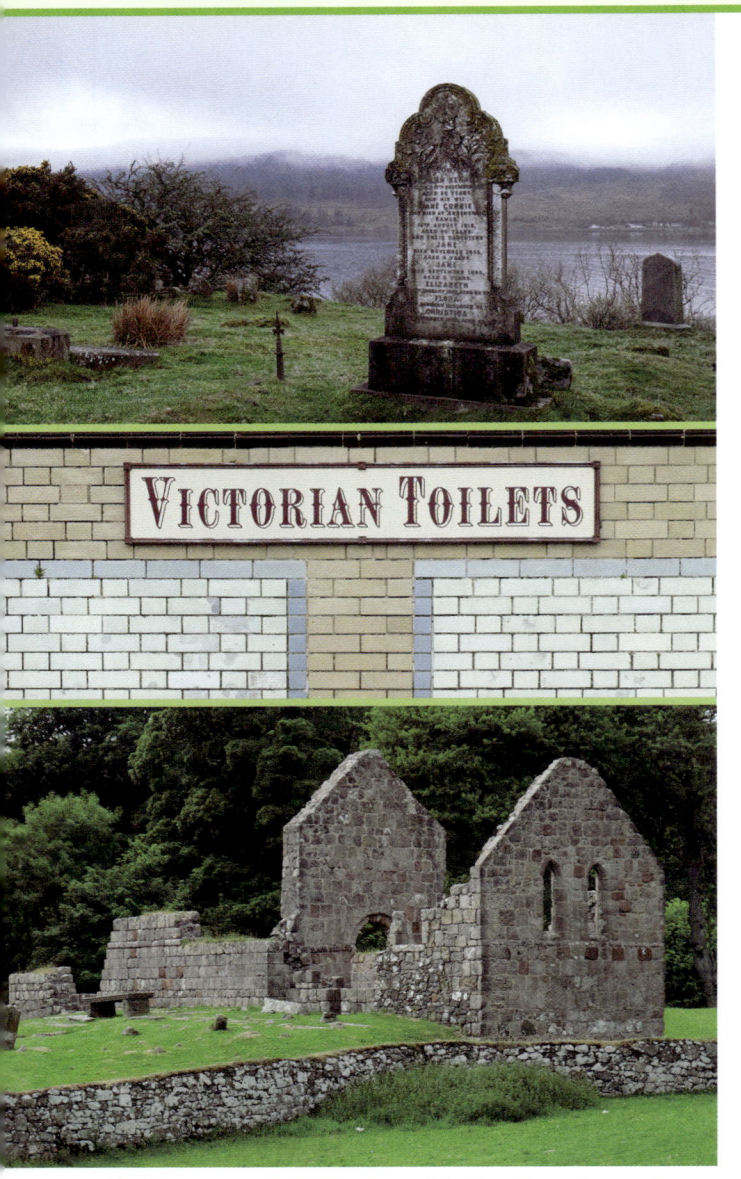

Top: The graveyard at St Blane's contains headstones from various ages. Middle: Each detail of the Rothesay Victorian Toilets on the pier on the Isle of Bute was clearly designed to create an image of luxury for the island's visitors. Bottom: The crumbling ruins of St Michael's Chapel might date back as far as the 5th to 7th century.

Opposite: Castle Stalker sits on a tidal islet in Loch Laich in Argyll.

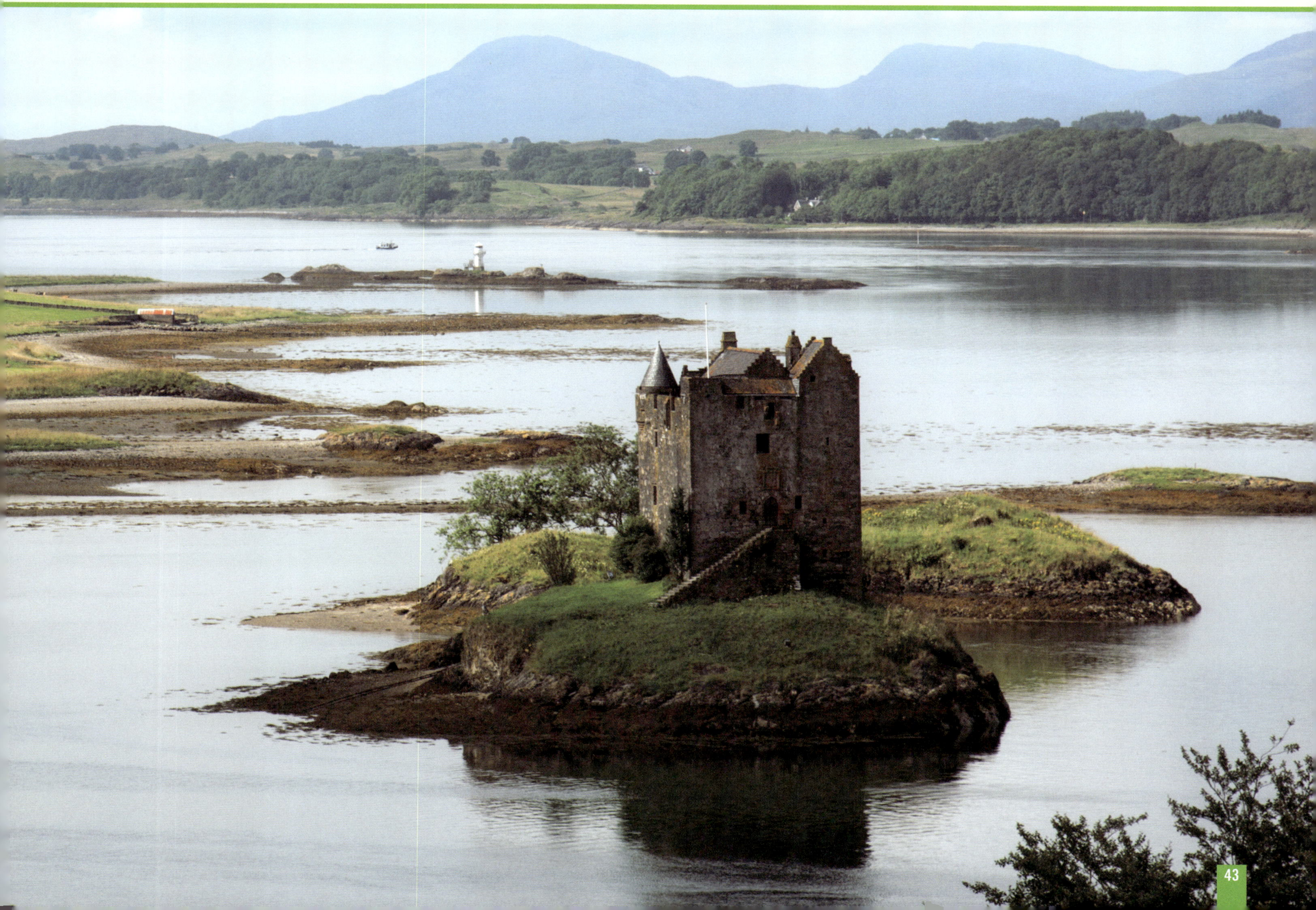

# ARGYLL AND BUTE

*Mount Stuart blends elements of Georgian and Victorian design, resulting in a uniquely lovely country house set in lush green grounds.*

southern end of the Isle of Bute, and its grounds offer gorgeous views of the Isle of Arran off the southern tip, appealing to sightseers and historians in equal measure. The church stands on an even older landmark: a monastery was founded here in around 500 CE but was abandoned and left to ruin after the Viking raids of 790 CE. In the 1300s, the church was expanded to include extensive grounds. Several weathered gravestones can be found in the churchyard, including a distinctive Hogsback gravestone hailing from a time when Bute was part of the Norse North Sea Empire. The remains of a well and the foundations of a manse that was in use until 1587 can also be seen. The church was named after St Blane, a Bishop and Confessor in Scotland who died in 590 CE.

## MOUNT STUART

A remarkable blend of Georgian and Victorian architecture, Mount Stuart is a country house sitting on the east coast of the Isle of Bute. The original house was built in 1719, but a fire severely damaged it in 1877. Despite the exterior damage, most of the contents survived. The wings of the building also survived, and these were incorporated into the house you see today, which was built in the late 19th century. A tour takes you inside the dazzling interior, which was inspired by astrology, art, and mythology and features a map of the stars on the ceiling of the Marble Hall. This house is filled with innovations—from an early telephone system to a Victorian passenger lift, as well as a spiral staircase that leads to what is believed to be the world's first domestic heated swimming pool.

The 300 acres of gardens are as impressive as the house, set against a striking Firth of Clyde backdrop. These gardens can boast of arboricultural and horticultural collections of global significance. Each season brings something special to admire, from spring's rhododendron and magnolia blooms to autumn's golden birch and maple trees. Exotic plant life flourishes, adding an unexpected hint of the tropical, while winding woodlands stretch right down to the shore. There is also a Victorian rock garden, an arboretum with trees dating back to the estate's early days, and a pinetum, home to more than 800 towering conifers.

## ROTHESAY CASTLE

This ruined castle in Rothesay on the Isle of Bute has been described as "one of the most remarkable in Scotland," both for its long history dating back to the beginning of the 13th century and its unusual circular plan. The castle comprises a huge curtain wall that had been strengthened by four round towers after the Norse siege of 1263 and 6th-century forework, all surrounded by a broad moat. Built by the Stewart family, it survived Norse attacks to become a royal residence. Its close links with the Stewarts—both while they were hereditary high stewards and, from 1371, a royal dynasty. To this day, the heir to Great Britain's throne still has the title Duke of Rothesay.

Though falling into ruin after the 17th century, beginning in 1871, the castle was repaired by the 3rd Marquess of Bute before passing into state care in the 20th century. Today, a tour takes you inside the great hall in the gatehouse, restored in 1900, to see displays about the castle and its royal owners, and you can stroll around the moat to view the stone curtain wall in all its glory, while also meeting the castle's resident ducks. You can also take in the impressive views over the town and back toward the mainland from the top of the walls.

## ETTRICK BAY BEACH

This mile-long sandy beach lies along the clear blue waters of Ettrick Bay. Close to Rothesay, the Ettrick Bay Stone Circle, a nearby bird habitat, and the Ettrick Bay Tearoom, this gorgeous attraction offers a lot, especially on a clear day with breathtaking views of the Isle of Arran. The bay faces the Kyles of Bute, a narrow sea channel that separates the northern end of the Isle of Bute from the Cowal peninsula. Ettrick Bay is bounded by a coarse sandy beach, which is popular with tourists

Top: The moat surrounding Rothesay Castle catches its reflection.
Bottom: The island of Arran looms in the background as a derelict fishing boat lies beached in the sands of Ettrick Bay Beach.

# ARGYLL AND BUTE

Above: A shaggy-haired Highland cow grazes on a hill above the Mull of Oa on Islay. Below: A giant pot still greets visitors to the Ardbeg Distillery in Port Ellen.

and locals alike. During low tide, the water's edge can be up to 1,600 feet from the high-tide mark. Several rivers flow into the bay, including the Glenmore Burn, St Colmac Burn, Ettrick Burn, and Drumachloy Burn. At the north end of the bay, mainly occupied by rocky outcrops, lies Kildavanan Point. Far at the south end of the bay is the outcrop called Island McNeil, which formed part of the outer boundary of the bay.

## KILCHURN CASTLE

One of the most photographed sites in Scotland, Kilchurn Castle looks out over the waters of Loch Awe. The building has been a fortress, a residence, and a garrison stronghold, and it contains the oldest-surviving barracks on the British mainland. An imposing five-story tower house stands over a lower hall, courtyard, and barracks. Built in the mid-1400s, it remained the base of the mighty Campbells of Glenorchy for 150 years. After the first Jacobite Rising of 1689, Kilchurn was converted into a garrison stronghold but was abandoned by the end of the 1700s. These days you can tour the grounds of this beautiful castle.

## ISLAY

Known as the "Queen of the Hebrides," Islay lies in Argyll just south west of Jura and around 25 miles north of the Northern Irish coast. Port Ellen is the main port. Modern Islay's economy relies on agriculture and fishing, whisky distilling, and, of course, tourism. More than 45,000 summer visitors arrive each year by ferry and a further 11,000 by air to take in the stunning scenery, fascinating history, unparalleled bird watching, and world-famous whiskies. As much a driver of the economy, there are also some of the top tourist destinations, featuring various shops, tours, and visitor centers. The whisky makers in the south of the island produce malts with a very strong peaty flavor—these are Ardbeg, Lagavulin, and Laphroaig. On the north of the island, the Bowmore, Bruichladdich, Caol Ila, Bunnahabhain, Ardnahoe, and Kilchoman distilleries produce whisky that is substantially lighter in taste. Bowmore, with its record dating to 1779, is the oldest legal distillery. It is in the island's capital of Bowmore, where you can also see the distinctive round Kilarrow Parish Church. The distillery of Lagavulin officially dates from 1816, which consistently receives accolades for its Islay single-malt Scotch whisky. You can visit this distillery situated in a small bay near the south coast of Islay near the ruins of Dunyveg Castle. Named after the area of land at the head of Loch Laphroaig on the south coast of the island of Islay, the Laphroaig Distillery was established in 1815. Take a tour here to sample what has been called the most richly flavored of all Scotch whiskies. When not touring one of the many distilleries, Islay visitors can enjoy golfing on the 116-year-old Machrie golf course or walk or cycle the 130 miles of coastline.

The Lagavulin Distillery, one of the islands' many whisky makers, sits on the coastline of Islay.

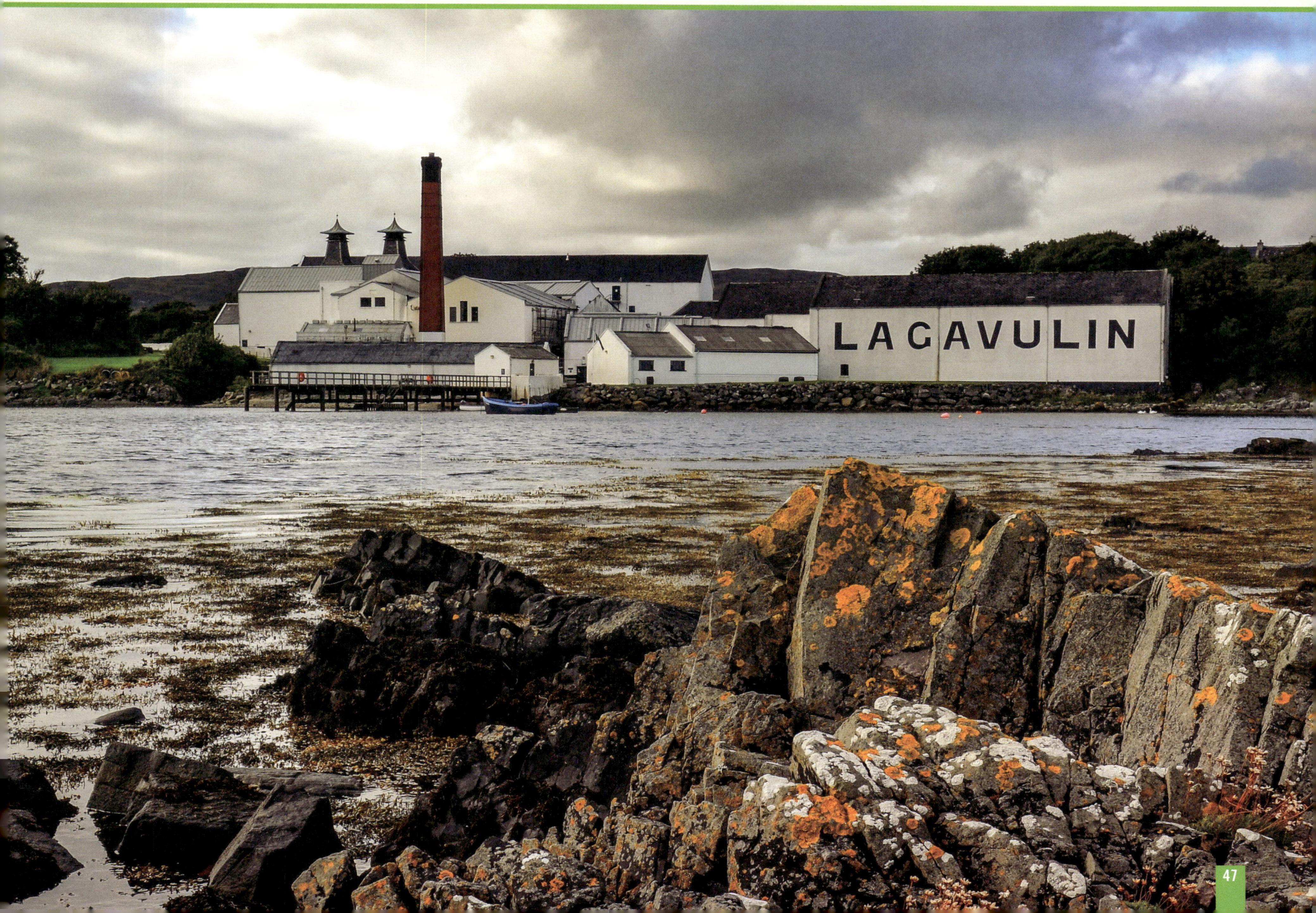
LAGAVULIN

# ARGYLL AND BUTE

"Arran of the many stags
The sea strikes against her shoulders,
Companies of men can feed there
Blue spears are reddened among her boulders.
Merry hinds are on her hills,
Juicy berries are there for food,
Refreshing water in her streams,
Nuts in plenty in the wood."

—*AGALLLAMH NA SENORACH*, AN ANCIENT IRISH POEM

**The rich archaeological landscape of Machrie Moor includes stone circles and standing stones dating to between 3500 and 1500 BCE.**

## ISLE OF ARRAN

Arran, one of the main islands of Bute, is the largest island in the Firth of Clyde. It is a popular tourist destination, often referred to as "Scotland in miniature" due to its wide variety of scenery, historical sites, and geographical features. Though culturally and physically similar to the Hebrides, it is separated from them by the Kintyre peninsula. Since the early Neolithic period, Arran has been home to humans, and numerous prehistoric remains have been found, including the Machrie Moor Standing Stones. From the 6th century onwards, it was turned into a religious center by peoples from Ireland. In the troubled Viking Age, it came under Norse rule, until it was absorbed by the kingdom of Scotland in the 13th century. The 19th-century "clearances" led to significant depopulation and the end of the Gaelic language and way of life. The economy and population have recovered in recent years, mostly due to tourism. Visitors can enjoy miles of coastal pathways, numerous hills and mountains, forested areas, rivers, small lochs, and beaches, with the standouts being Brodick, Whiting Bay, Kildonan, Sannox, and Blackwaterfoot. Popular walking routes include climbing to the summit of Goat Fell and the Arran Coastal Way, a trail tracing the island's coastline. If you love history, you will appreciate Brodick Castle outside the port of Brodick, which is a grand baronial castle that offers an interactive visitor experience, including a Victorian arcade, mood lighting, and evocative sounds, as you view an impressive collection of period furniture, silverware, porcelain, paintings, and sporting trophies. The site also features formal gardens on the Silver Garden Trail and Plant Hunters' Walk and woodland trails with ponds and waterfalls. Kids, will love the Isle Be Wild adventure play area and the Fairies and Legends Trail. Along with a number of golf courses, the island is the site of the Arran Distillery, which is open for tours.

## ISLE OF MULL

The second-largest island of the Inner Hebrides, the Isle of Mull falls within the council area of Argyll and Bute. Its gorgeous coastline stretches almost 300 miles long, and with tourists flocking to take advantage of all it offers, the population of Mull and neighboring Iona and Ulva probably doubles in

**Opposite:** Perched on the sea cliffs of the Isle of Mull, the 13th-century Duart Castle is the ancestral seat of Clan MacLean.

# ARGYLL AND BUTE

## OTHER TOP SITES

- **BUTE MUSEUM**
With archaeological, natural history, and geological exhibits, this museum makes an excellent pit stop for travelers hoping to get their bearings for the local landscape. One of the most remarkable things in this museum is potentially the first evidence of human life in Scotland, as shown in a fine collection of Mesolithic microliths that were found in the south of the island.

- **ARDENCRAIG GARDENS**
Designed as an extension of the nearby Ardencraig House, this walled garden in Rothesay boasts extensive flowerbeds, as well as a few aviaries hosting several species of foreign birds, making it a very popular site for birdwatchers and nature enthusiasts.

- **OBAN DISTILLERY**
On the west coast port of Oban, you will find the Oban Distillery, which was established in 1794. With only two pot stills, it is one of the smallest in Scotland, producing a whisky that has been described as having a "West Highland" flavor that falls between the dry, smoky style of the Scottish islands and the lighter, sweeter malts of the Highlands.

- **GLEN SCOTIA DISTILLERY**
With fermenters, a stillroom, and a dunnage warehouse dating back to the 1830s, Glen Scotia Distillery resides in Campbeltown, a town that was once known as the whisky capital of the world. At the height of Campbelltown's whisky production in the 19th century, the town was home to 21 distilleries, but today Glen Scotia is one of Campbell's only three remaining distilleries. This small-batch distillery uses malted barley from the east of Scotland and has gained notoriety worldwide for its high-quality products and storied history. The distillery—often referred to as "The Scotia" or "Old Scotia" by locals—offers daily tours and tastings, as well as a Victorian-tiled shop.

- **KINGARTH STANDING STONES**
Though Bute has no shortage of mysterious and ancient standing stones, perhaps one of the simplest examples stands at Blackpark Plantation. What used to be a collection of seven standing stones has fallen to just three over the years, but shaded beneath the dark forest in a small clearing, these stones still maintain their atmospheric integrity.

the summer. Tobermory, where most of the island's residents live, is surrounded by the Sound of Mull in the north, the Firth of Lorn in the south and east, and the Atlantic Ocean in the west. The brightly colored shops and restaurants give the town a unique character. Sites of note in the town include the Tobermory Clock Tower, the Tobermory Scotch whisky distillery, and the Isle of Mull Brewery. For birdwatchers, Mull is a fascinating destination, as it is home to over 250 different bird species, including the white-tailed eagle. Boat tours around the island offer glimpses of minke whales, porpoises, and dolphins. For hikers, Ben More, the highest peak in the Inner Hebrides, offers an invigorating day out. Situated in the south of the island, above the shores of Loch na Keal, the approximately 4-hour walk from sea loch to summit follows farm tracks, the side of a stream, and up scree slopes to the top. From the summit on a clear day, you can enjoy breathtaking views of the Sound of Mull, Staffa, the Ross of Mull, and Iona in the distance. Standing on a cliff top above the Sound of Mull, is Duart Castle, the base of the Clan Maclean for more than 400 years. A visit here will allow you to take in views from one of the most spectacular positions on the west coast of Scotland.

Off the west coast of Mull is Ulva, a community-owned island. It known for its wildlife, which includes deer, buzzards, golden eagles, and sea eagles. Off the southwest coast of Mull are the uninhabited Treshnish Isles, an archipelago of small islands and skerries that is home to breeding seabirds, Atlantic grey seals, and ruined castles. Staffa, lying between Mull and Iona, is a tiny island, but during the summer, boats from Oban and Fionnphort allow visitors to view the migratory puffins that settle on the island.

## IONA

In 563, after his exile from Ireland, Saint Columba founded a monastery on Iona. From here, he and his 12 companions set to convert pagan Scotland and much of northern England to Christianity, which gave rise to Iona's fame as a place of learning. Known as a holy island, several kings of Scotland, Ireland, and Norway came to be buried here, including Scotland's kings Donald II, Malcolm I, Duncan I, Macbeth, and Donald III. Many believe that at least a part of the *Book of Kells* was produced on Iona toward the end of the 8th century. In the 18th century, visits from Samuel Johnson and James Boswell brought the island even greater fame, when both men wrote travelogues of their journeys. The small island now brings some 140,000 visitors to its shores each year aboard ferries from Fionnphort on Mull. Iona differs much from neighboring Mull; there are no tall mountains here, but there are some lovely white beaches. Interesting sites on Iona are Iona Abbey—which is home to the St John's Cross—the Iona Nunnery, St Martins Cross, and several other Celtic high crosses.

**Opposite:** The colorful waterfront of Tobermory delights thousands of visitors each year.

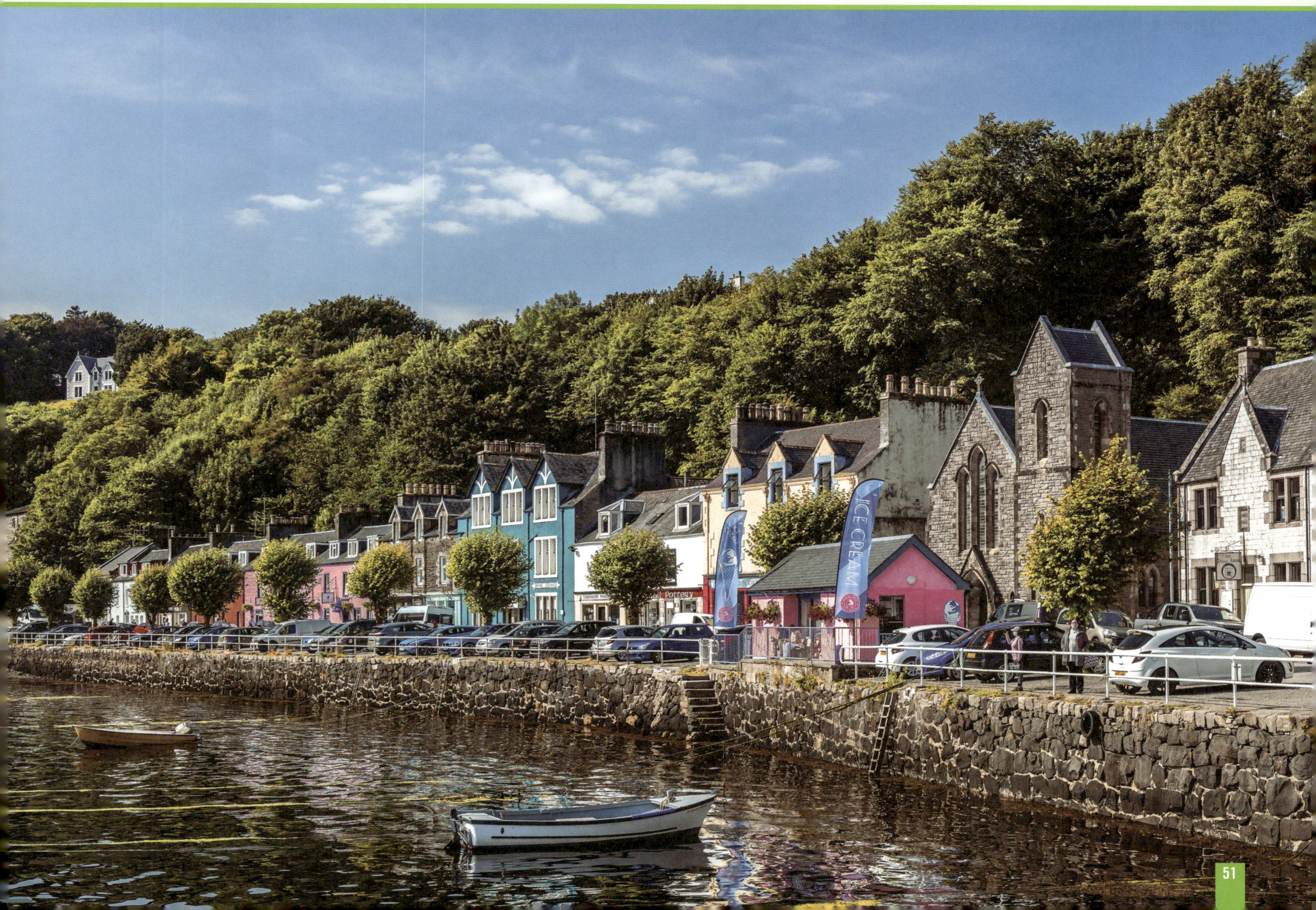
ICE CREAM

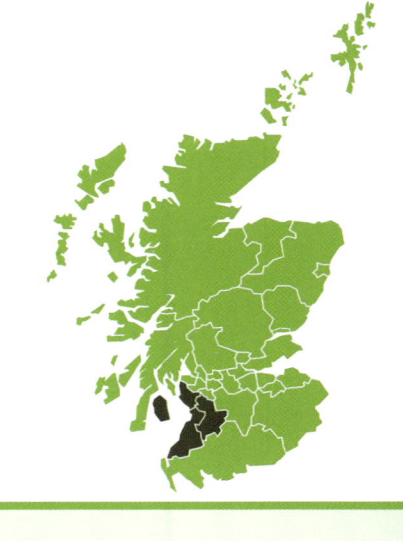

# AYRSHIRE

## TOP SITES IN AYRSHIRE

- Robert Burns Birthplace Museum
- Greenan Castle
- Dean Castle Country Park
- Dumfries House
- Culzean Castle and Country Park
- Rozelle Park

Located on the bonny shores of the Firth of Clyde in southwest Scotland, Ayrshire is home to some of the most fertile lands in the country. Ayrshire's fields are utilized to produce everything from strawberries, potatoes, and root vegetables to cattle and pork. The town of Ayr was named for the river that runs through it. It is home to nine historical churches dotted across its verdant landscape.

The historic county of Ayrshire has been divided administratively into South, East, and North regions. These geographical divisions notwithstanding, many visitors and locals instead identify the county's regions with more natural geographic divisions like the coast, the islands, and the inland areas. Ayrshire is predominantly a flat region with large expanses of low, smooth hills. The low hills area forms part of the Southern Upland geographic region of Scotland. South Ayrshire shares with the Galloway counties some rugged hill country locally known as the Galloway Hills, while North Ayrshire is home to the largest towns and the bulk of the county's population. Ayrshire is one of Scotland's most agriculturally fertile regions; in fields near the coast, potatoes are grown using seaweed-based fertilizer. Ayrshire is also home to Glasgow Prestwick International Airport, which was frequently used as a rest stop for US military personnel traveling to military bases in Germany. The US military influence bolsters Ayr's aviation industry, and its lowlands also offer outstanding golfing grounds and make excellent runways. For fans of music, Ayrshire has a strong musical history, and is notably the only place in Great Britain visited by the King of Rock and Roll himself, Elvis Presley.

**Top:** The famous late-medieval Brig o' Doon over the River Doon at Alloway features in the Burns poem *Tam o' Shanter*. It is close to the Robert Burns Birthplace Museum and is a well-known attraction.

Dean Castle was once the stronghold of the lords of Kilmarnock after Robert the Bruce granted the land to Sir Robert Boyd for his services at the Battle of Bannockburn.

## ROBERT BURNS BIRTHPLACE MUSEUM

This museum is home to more than 5,000 artifacts about Scotland's national bard, Robert Burns. Tourists can visit the cottage where Burns—affectionately called "Rabbie" by locals—was born and spent his formative years and the monument that was erected in 1823 to commemorate Burns's life and influential works. The cottage, which is part of the museum, was built by his father, William Burnes in 1757, and Burns was born there in 1759. The journey of the museum weaves through the village, along the Poet's Path, taking tourists from historical buildings to landmarks known to Burns. Spending some time in the Robert Burns Birthplace here will open your eyes and ears to an enduring hero of Scotland's literary heritage. Explore the surrounding gardens and snag a bite at the café or take a walk over the nearby Brig o' Doon. The fascinating displays in the museum and Burns Cottage include plenty of hands-on and interactive activities, including some of Burns's original hand-written manuscripts.

## GREENAN CASTLE

Resting above a sheer seaside cliff, Greenan Castle has existed on a fortified plot since the 12th century, first as a promontory fort and then as a motte-and-bailey. The castle is located southwest of Ayr and was built by the Lords of the Isle, who later passed it into the hands of the Kennedy family. All that remains of this ancient castle is the base of the tower house. Near the tower are remains of a walled courtyard and outbuildings, perhaps what were once stables, and a kitchen block, as the small tower has no kitchen within its walls. It was from the courtyard that Sir Thomas Kennedy rode off with his servant on the 12th of May 1602 to Edinburgh; he was ambushed and murdered on the way, and the castle was passed down through members of the clan over the years. By the time Greenan Castle became the property of the Earl of Cassilis in 1766, any residential use of the grounds had long since ceased. Today Greenan Castle has become one of Ayrshire's most significant historic ruins, attracting the interest of both scholars and tourists.

The ruins of Greenan Castle perch precariously close to the crumbling edge of the cliff face over Greenan Bay

53

# AYRSHIRE

Top: A fountain decorates the grounds of the elegant Dumfries House. Bottom: The Rozelle Remembrance Woodland at Rozelle Park was created as part of the World War I centenary commemorations.

## DEAN CASTLE COUNTRY PARK

Sprawling over 200 acres in East Ayrshire, the Dean Castle Country Park is nestled in the heart of Kilmarnock. The castle was the home and stronghold of the Boyd family for more than 400 years. The Keep, dating to around 1350, houses outstanding displays that tell the story of the Boyd family and medieval life, as well as a stunning collection of arms and armor and early musical instruments. The Rural Life Centre gives you the opportunity to learn about sustainable living, while also offering beautiful woodland walks and the chance to spot some local wildlife along the way. Children can meet farm animals at the Urban Farm, and after a fun day exploring all the grounds have to offer, you can pick up a souvenir from the gift shop or relax in the café while enjoying views over the country park. Fans of *Outlander* might recognize the castle and surrounding area, which was used as a filming location for the hit TV series. The Country Park also has an extensive events program throughout the year, from pond dipping and nature walks to harvest festivals and more.

## DUMFRIES HOUSE

One of Britain's most beautiful stately homes, Dumfries House is a Palladian country house that features the architecture of Robert Adam and the furniture of Thomas Chippendale and other leading 18th-century Scottish cabinet makers. Built between 1754 and 1759, it consists of a three-story central block connected to smaller pavilions by linking wings. In the late 20th and early 21st century then owner, the 7th Marquess of Bute, the racing driver known as John Bute, faced crushingly heavy death duties, so he twice offered the property to the National Trust. When those plans fell through it was the intervention of HRH the Prince of Wales in 2007 that saved the house and its original contents—which include nearly 10 percent of Chippendale's surviving work. Since then Dumfries House has been fastidiously restored to its original splendor and opened to the public for guided tours in which experts point out the stunning interiors of this once-again resplendent stately home.

## CULZEAN CASTLE AND COUNTRY PARK

Set in a glorious 260-hectare grounds, Robert Adam's masterpiece rises above the South Ayrshire cliffs just west of Maybole. Once the home of David Kennedy, 10th Earl of Cassillis, this opulent estate features a world of woods, beaches, secret follies, and play parks. A visit here takes you through stands of conifers and beech, miles of sandy coastline dotted with caves, a deer park, the Swan Pond, and flamboyant formal gardens. Among its 40 building is an ice house and fruit-filled glasshouses. Inside is the can't-miss centerpiece of the castle, the dramatic Oval Staircase, as well as an extensive collection of flintlock pistols and military swords. Children will have fun running wild in the Adventure Cove and Wild Woodland play areas. You can also

**Culzean Castle is an ornate Neoclassical mansion set in stunning gardens overlooking the cliffs of Ayrshire.**

stop by the Home Farm Kitchen and Home Farm Shop, the Aviary Kiosk, and even pick up a tome or two at the Second-hand Bookshop.

## ROZELLE PARK

This historic estate in Ayr features an original mansion from the 1760s, as well as an art collection and gallery, a tearoom, green playing fields, and scenic walking paths. Rozelle Park spans an area of 37 hectares in South Ayrshire, which has a varied wealth of flora and fauna. It was initially only a cultural and recreational ground, but today it combines mature woodland, rhododendron walks, parkland, and ornamental ponds to produce a rich and varied landscape. It is also the yearly host for the Ayr Flower Show, Scotland's premier horticultural event, as well as the Holy Fair. The Ayrshire Yeomanry Museum can also be found here, displaying a cross-section of what life was like in this area centuries ago. A series of sculptures by the world-famous sculptor Henry Moore are also arranged throughout, as well as the Maclaurin Art Gallery's collection of traditional and modern works by commissioned artists and works purchased by the Maclaurin Trust. Rozelle Park is a peaceful hidden gem for art lovers and nature enthusiasts alike.

## OTHER TOP SITES

- **HEADS OF AYR FARM PARK**

The Heads of Ayr Farm Park has been a beloved day-trip location for Ayrshire locals and visitors alike since 1993. With attractions including bumper boats, a sandpit, trampolines, a playpark, an "adventure barn", and even quad biking, there is something to keep the kids entertained year-round. Aside from housing rabbits, guinea pigs, and the like, this long-running, well-loved park also offers more exotic animals—including camels, tapirs, llamas, and monkeys—within its Animal Zone.

- **SCOTTISH MARITIME MUSEUM**

With two sites in Irvine and Dumbarton in North Ayrshire, this museum holds an important nationally recognized collection, encompassing a variety of historic ships, artifacts, shipbuilding machinery, machine tools, and fascinating personal items.

- **BELLEISLE CONSERVATORY**

With a rich history reaching back to 1879, the first iteration of this conservatory was built for William Smith Dixon, an ironmaster from Govanhill. The conservatory has been often rebuilt and maintained over the years and now contains orchids, cacti and succulents, alpines, and various other colorful, exotic plants. The Victorian walled garden and conservatory offers one of Scotland's greatest collections of plant life, as well as a carefully manicured golf course that spans a remarkable area of the grounds.

# CLACKMANNANSHIRE

## TOP SITES IN CLACKMANNANSHIRE

- Dollar Glen
- Castle Campbell
- Japanese Garden at Cowden
- Clackmannan Tower
- Alloa Tower
- Gartmorn Dam Country Park and Nature Reserve
- Ochil Hills

Clackmannanshire, also called *Siorrachd Chlach Mhannainn"* in Scottish Gaelic, is often referred to as "The Wee county" because of its small size. Officially the second-smallest county in Scotland, Clackmannanshire is bordered by Stirling, Fife, and Perth and Kinross and is located in the eastern half of Scotland.

The name *Clackmannanshire* comes from the Scottish Gaelic word *"chlach,"* or "stone," and the Brythonic name of the Iron Age tribe of Manaw, which lived in the region for some time. It is sometimes colloquially called "Clacks" as a term of endearment. This historic county originally became known for the weaving mills powered by the Hillfoots burns. While the county's economy once revolved around shipbuilding, mining, glass manufacturing, and brewing, Clackmannanshire's primary industries today are service industries and tourism. The old county town, Clackmannan, is named after the ancient stone associated with the pre-Christian deity called Manau or Mannan. Today, the stone rests on a larger stone beside the Tolbooth Tower, which dates from 1592, at the top of Main Street.

Clackmannanshire has a population of just 51,400, around half of whom live in Alloa, the main town and administrative center. The Black Devon River flows past the town of Clackmannan to join the Forth near Alloa. This confluence at one time included a small pier for portage to Dunmore pier on the south shore and anchorage of smaller sailing ships. Other, grander cargo ships were scheduled to dock at Dunmore pier on the opposite banks of the Forth. In the center of the county of Clackmannan is Gartmorn Dam Country Park; there are several other small patches of forest in

**Top: Alloa Tower once guarded the north shore of the Firth of Forth.**

An arched footbridge spans a pond filled with water lilies in the tranquil Japanese Garden at Cowden in Dollar.

the southeast of the county, but Gartmorn Dam Country park is far and away the most impressive nature reserve in the county. The Ochil Hills dominate the northern third of the county, where Ben Cleuch, the highest point in Clackmannanshire, can be found.

 Clackmannanshire has a motto: "Look Aboot Ye," which replaced its previous slogan, "More Than You Imagine." According to legend, Robert the Bruce, the king who freed Scotland from English rule, misplaced his gauntlets when visiting Clackmannanshire; when he asked where he might find them, he was told to "look aboot ye," giving birth to the motto.

## DOLLAR GLEN

Often associated with Castle Campbell, this network of woodland paths is home to exciting geology, verdant wildlife habitats, and cascading waterfalls. With an array of visible wildlife, including brown long-eared bats, two kinds of woodpeckers, and pied flycatchers, there is always some natural marvel to behold at Dollar Glen. Tucked at the foot of the Ochil Hills with Castle Campbell towering high above, the glen is less than an hour's drive from the cities of Edinburgh and Glasgow, making the site an ideal location for a family stroll. Long, winding paths cut through the glen, taking visitors past deep gorges and high waterfalls amid wildly abundant plant life. Dollar Glen features a range of wildlife habitats and essential geological landmarks, which led to it being designated a Site of Special Scientific Interest. Fun fact: there are 190 species of lichen in Dollar Glen, and over 100 different kinds of moss.

## CASTLE CAMPBELL

Originally belonging to a powerful family in medieval Scotland primarily associated with the Highlands, this Lowland castle dating back to the 1400s rests high above the lush and verdant Dollar Glen. This impressive structure and its surrounding grounds make for an excellent journey back in time with spectacular views over

A waterfall squeezes it way over a hill where the Burn of Sorrow drops down through a narrow gorge in Dollar Glen.

# CLACKMANNANSHIRE

miles of the Lowlands. As one of Scotland's best preserved tower houses, Castle Campbell offers a nearly unparalleled view into what life might have been like 600 years in the past. There is a beautiful grassed terrace in the front of the castle, although the uneven cobbled pathways and castle interior may not be wheelchair accessible. Castle Campbell was once the residence of the powerful Campbell earls of Argyll. The castle also has some historical connections with prominent figures, such as John Knox and Mary, Queen of Scots. An open-air walkway called the loggia, designed with inspiration from Italian and Spanish architecture, is another great way to take in the estate.

## THE JAPANESE GARDEN AT COWDEN CASTLE

Designed in 1908 by Taki Handa for Ella Christie, this Japanese Garden at Cowden was built on the heels of the adventurous Christie's travels through China, Korea, and Japan. The garden offers some fascinating insights into Christie's unique character and life story, as well as interesting information about the creation and design of the garden itself. After 1955, it had been closed to the public and fell into dereliction. It has now undergone restoration, and you are welcome to wander the trails or spend an afternoon relaxing by the pond under the shade of a beautifully constructed gazebo. This lovely garden consists of several acres of serene Japanese-influenced landscape, unique non-native plants, and a perimeter path around the small loch. In addition, there are about 20 acres of woodland trails to explore and enjoy. The garden also has a gift shop where you can buy some exotic plants of your own.

## CLACKMANNAN TOWER

Dating back to the 1300s, Clackmannan Tower was built by a descendant of Robert the Bruce. This stand-alone tower house, built atop a hill in a distinctly imposing position, might have once been the site of a royal residence from the 11th century. Clackmannan Tower is a soaring five-story structure and is considered to be one of Scotland's most impressive tower houses. At the beginning of its construction, King's Seat Hill provided this strategic site in the control of the Forth. It was generally believed the site was sold with its hunting lodge to Robert to keep it in the family without it continuing as a royal burden. Clackmannan Tower remained the home of the Bruce clan for centuries, until it was abandoned in the late 1700s. Several notable figures lived in and visited the tower over the years: Katherine Bruce, for instance, was once visited by the famed Scottish poet Robert Burns toward the end of her life. The first construction was the great rectangular tower, made from cut blocks of pink sandstone, but a taller square tower was added in the 15th century. To this day, fragments of the outer walls, a garden terrace, and an ancient bowling green are still visible.

## THE TOWERS OF CLACKMANNANSHIRE

Tall tower houses dot the Clackmannanshire landscape. These structures, dating from the late 14th and 15th centuries, were built by aristocrats who needed to be near the royal court in Stirling, partly for defense, but mainly as a way of showing off their status, wealth, and style. Each has its own fascinating history, whether they withstood attack or hosted illustrious visitors. By the later 16th century, however, towers were going out of fashion, giving way to "modern" houses, such as Menstrie Castle and Old Sauchie House. To get the full effect of them, try the Clackmannanshire Tower Trail, which takes you on a tour of Clackmannanshire's four medieval towers—Alloa Tower, Castle Campbell, Clackmannan Tower (above), and Sauchie Tower—and Menstrie Castle, with information panels at all five sites.

**Opposite:** The ruins of medieval Castle Campbell stand high above Dollar Glen.

# CLACKMANNANSHIRE

Swans take an early-evening swim on Gartmorn Dam.

## OTHER TOP SITES

- **TOLBOOTH CROSS AND THE STONE OF MANNAN**
Built in the late 16th century, the Tolbooth in Clackmannan began life as a place to hold prisoners when the local sheriff was no longer inclined to hold them in his own dwelling house. All that remains now is the belfry tower. Beside this is the ancient standing Stone of Mannan, associated with two stories: one of the sea god Mannau, the other concerning Robert the Bruce's lost glove (or "mannan"). Nearby is the Mercat Cross, a solitary pillar bearing the arms of the Bruce family.

- **TILLICOULTRY GLEN PATH**
Located above Tillicoultry village, the path borders a large quarry that supplied surfacing for paths and roads. The fast-flowing water of Tillicoultry burn once powered eight textile mills using a dam and lade (water channel) system. The remains of burn-side sluices and the old wooden dam can still be seen. At the top of glen to the west of the burn there once stood a Pictish fort. In spring listen for woodpeckers as they try to attract a mate.

## ALLOA TOWER

The largest surviving keep in all of Scotland, Alloa Tower affords visitors a magnificent view from the top, which spans nine counties on a clear day. The tower was originally built in the 14th century to guard the strategically important ferry crossing at the River Forth. It is the ancestral home of the Erskine family, the Earls of Mar and the Earls of Kellie, all of whom were key figures in Scotland's turbulent history through the centuries. Tours are offered at the tower to guide you through the complex. Alloa Tower retains many of its medieval features, including the stone well on the first floor built into the tower walls, the magnificent beamed ceiling in the solar, and the dungeon, which is thought to be even older than the tower itself. The tower also contains a magnificent Italianate staircase and a unique, carefully curated art collection, as well as some highlights of 18th-century interior design and furniture.

## GARTMORN DAM COUNTRY PARK AND NATURE RESERVE

This 370-acre park is home to a 170-acre reservoir, held in place by Gartmorn Dam—a great, centuries-old structure that marked the catalyst for nearby Alloa's industrial development when it was first constructed. Whether you are interested in the history or the wildlife of Gartmorn Dam, a simple walk along the dam or a taste of their "Dam Good Coffee," Gartmorn Dam Country Park and Nature Reserve is definitely worth a visit. Mining started in this area in the early 1700s; at that same time, a weir was built, along with a 2-mile lade dugout with a dam to hold back the huge artificial body of water. The strong current of the water was enough to power three mines and nine mills in its heyday. The industrial use of the dam came to a stop in the 1920s, however, and the reservoir and its surrounding countryside were turned into a nature preserve. Today, the Gartmorn Dam Country Park and Nature Preserve is a haven for local wildlife; lush forests and thriving fauna can be seen everywhere one looks, as well as some fascinating remnants of the original industrial fittings of the dam that can still be found scattered throughout the park.

## OCHIL HILLS

With few major roads crossing these lovely hills, they are perfect for a long hike or country ramble. The Ochil Hills stand north of the Forth valley, straddling Alloa, Stirling, Kinross, and Perth. You can also visit the Ochil Hills Woodland Park, which was originally planted as an informal garden for a grand 17th-century house set in a woodland park that is believed to be one of the oldest plantations in Scotland. The house collapsed during World War II, but the grounds are now open to the public. As well as scenic walks, the park has a children's play area, picnic sites, and display boards.

**Opposite:** An old farm track winds its way through the Ochil Hills.

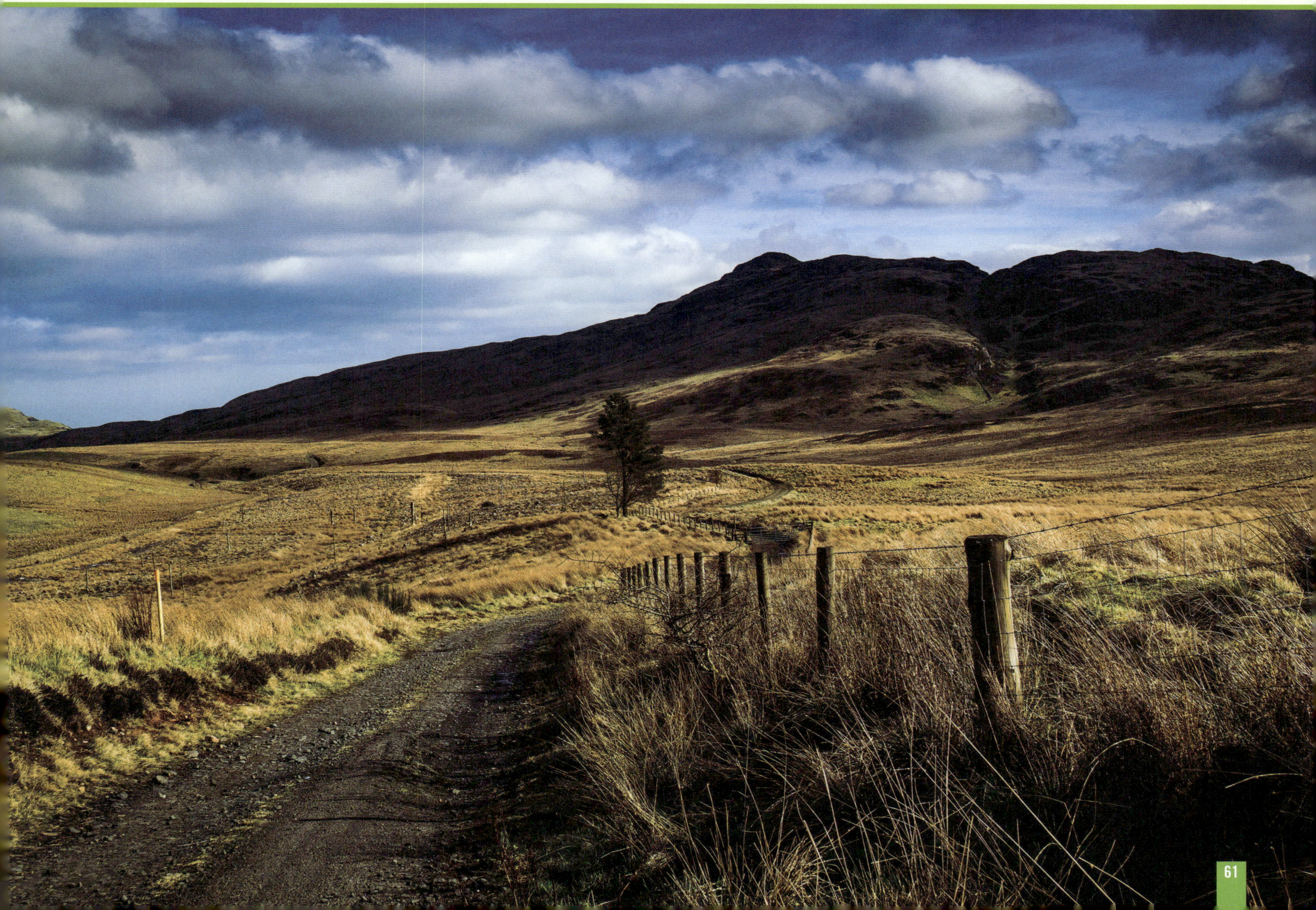

# DUMFRIES AND GALLOWAY

## TOP SITES IN DUMFRIES AND GALLOWAY

- Robert Burns House and Burns Mausoleum
- Caerlaverock Castle
- Dumfries and Galloway Aviation Museum
- The Bookshop
- Dumfries Museum and Camera Obscura
- Crook of Baldoon
- Cairn Holy Chambered Cairns
- Torhouse Stone Circle
- Wigtown Martyrs' Monument
- Drumlanrig Castle
- Threave Castle
- Broughton House and Garden
- Kirkcudbright Galleries
- Famous Blacksmiths Shop at Gretna Green
- Orchardton Tower
- The Stewartry Museum
- Southerness Lighthouse

Located in southern Scotland along the River Nith, the historic region of Dumfries is nicknamed "Queen of the South." Folks who hail from Dumfries are known as "Doonhamers," a term that originated from the phrase "Doonhame," or "down home," as a reference to those who make the commute to Glasgow for work. One possible origin for the name is the Scottish Gaelic *Dún Phris,* which means "fort of the thicket." The remnants of the Roman occupation can still be found in Dumfries in weapons, coins, sepulchral remains, and ancient roads. Once a booming market town and port, the former royal burgh of Dumfries now relies primarily on agriculture and forestry for its revenue. According to some legends, the 10th recorded battle of King Arthur may have taken place near Dumfries.

**Top: The Robert Burns House in Dumfries has been preserved as a museum dedicated to the final years of the poet's life.**

The county of Dumfries has three subdivisions: Annandale, Eskdale, and Nithsdale, and it combines with Galloway to form the council area of Dumfries and Galloway. This council area also takes in the historic counties of Kirkcudbrightshire and Wigtownshire.

Kirkcudbrightshire was once home to a tribe of Celts called Novantae, who remained unaffiliated and undominated for a remarkable stretch of Scotland's history. Unlike many of the other historic counties of Scotland, this region held onto its own set of laws well into the 14th century, when John de Balliol eventually managed to introduce Norman practices into the county. Once the site of significant contraband trade in the 19th century, today Kirkcudbrightshire is known as the "Artists' Town" for its Professional Artists Collective at the town center, roughly six miles from the Irish Sea. The landscape of

Cows graze in the bright green fields high above Sandyhills Beach on the Solway Firth.

this historic county features dense forests, high mountains, and steep cliffs lining the edge of the coast.

Located on the southwest tip of the Machars peninsula, the historic county of Wigtownshire is popularly referred to as "The Shire." Within the county, the town of Whithorn can boast of the first recorded Christian church in Scotland, named the "Shining House," or "Candida Casa." The Machars is rife with prehistoric remains, notably including the Neolithic Torhouse Stone Circle. Predominantly rural and sparsely populated, this peaceful area offers spectacular coastal views, as well as rolling green hills. The former royal burgh of Wigtown has been known as "Scotland's National Book Town" since 1998 and features numerous second-hand book shops, as well as an annual book festival; within its town limits live over a quarter of a million books.

The climate of Dumfries and Galloway is mild, and the annual rainfall is relatively minimal compared to other regions of Scotland. Many notable archaeological artifacts and structures have been discovered here over the years, including several stone circles, Pictish carved stones, the remnants of ancient hillforts and camps, and an ancient Anglo-Saxon cross that tells the story of the Crucifixion in intricately carved runes. Dumfriesshire was once the original breeding place of the Dumfriesshire Black and Tan Foxhounds, thought to have been initially descended from the Bloodhound, Grand Bleu de Gascogne, and English Foxhound.

## ROBERT BURNS HOUSE AND BURNS MAUSOLEUM

On Burns Street in Dumfries, you will find the simple red sandstone house in which Scotland's national bard spent his last years. Burns

The Burns Mausoleum in the churchyard of St Michael's Church in Dumfries has become a shrine to the legacy of poet Robert Burns.

63

# DUMFRIES AND GALLOWAY

enthusiasts from all around the world have long made this a place of pilgrimage, with many famous visitors including the poets Wordsworth, Coleridge, and Keats. The house still has the atmospheric feel of the Burns family home, retaining most of its original features, such as the kitchen, scullery, bedroom, and study. In the parlor you can view many interesting artifacts, such as original manuscripts and personal belongings. In the study is his desk and chair, where he created some of his finest works. He died here in 1796 at the age of just 37 and was buried in the churchyard of St Michael's, only a short walk away.

Burns had originally been buried in the northeast corner of the churchyard, but devoted fans began to feel that his existing grave wasn't worthy of Rabbie's genius. A fund-raising campaign, with Sir Walter Scott as a key figure, eventually resulted in the construction of the Burns Mausoleum. In 1817, Burns' remains were disinterred from his original burial place, along with those of two of his sons, who had died at the ages of 9 and 2, and then re-interred under the floor of the new mausoleum. His wife, Jean Armour, was buried in the mausoleum on her death in 1834, as was his son Robert, who died in 1857.

## CAERLAVEROCK CASTLE

With a turbulent history of being caught in the middle of border conflicts between England and Scotland, this picturesque castle features a moat, high battlements, and a two-towered gatehouse. It was first built in the 13th century and is located on the southern coast, 7 miles south of Dumfries, on the edge of the Caerlaverock National Reserve. Caerlaverock became the stronghold of the family from the 13th to the 17th century, when the castle was abandoned, though it was later besieged by the English during the wars of Scottish independence and went through years of reconstruction from the 14th century to the 15th. In the 16th century, this castle was besieged for the last time, and then demolished and rebuilt several times over the years. The castle, however, retains the typical triangular plan first laid out in the 13th century. The structure still standing today was rebuilt in the 17th-century out of red sandstone. Likely in part due to its striking appearance, Caerlaverock Castle has been featured in several films, including the romantic comedy *Decoy Bride*.

**The control tower at the Dumfries and Galloway Aviation Museum is a rare example of a tower dating back to World War II.**

## DUMFRIES AND GALLOWAY AVIATION MUSEUM

Located two miles northeast of the center of Dumfries, the Dumfries and Galloway Aviation Museum features indoor and outdoor exhibits in the form of a host of vintage airplanes, a gift shop, and

# DUMFRIES AND GALLOWAY

*Spiraling stone books frame the entrance to The Bookshop in Wigtown, Scotland's National Book Town.*

a small café. This independently owned museum covers RAF Dumfries and the Bomber War and the Home Front, and it is the only dedicated Airborne Forces collection in Scotland. The museum was created with the purpose of salvaging wreckage from World War II aircraft crashes and is located in and around the WWII-era watch tower at the former RAF Dumfries. It was first opened to the public in 1977 after a year of gathering and restoring wrecked aircraft and began receiving donations soon after that. Today, the museum features several aircraft, informational exhibits, and artifacts and memorabilia dating back to the war years.

## THE BOOKSHOP

Everyone who has read Shaun Bythell's *Confessions of a Bookseller* knows that The Bookshop is a sort of celebrity. This famous bookstore has been thriving for more than 50 years in Wigtown, Scotland's National Book Town, and contains nearly a mile of shelves lodging around 100,000 volumes making it Scotland's biggest used-book shop. Inside, there are nine separate rooms to explore, lined with books on every imaginable topic. There is also a cozy children's section, complete with several sofas and plenty of stepladders to help reach those high-up tomes. This antiquarian section is also home to some of Scotland's rarest and most sought-after books, as well as the Captain, a cat who has lived in the store for the last decade.

## DUMFRIES MUSEUM AND CAMERA OBSCURA

With a stunning spiral staircase leading to its top story, this 18th-century windmill-turned-museum spans history beginning with prehistoric fossils of dinosaur footprints to stone carvings from Scotland's earliest Christians. Located within the heart of Dumfries proper near the River Nith, this museum makes for an excellent stop while exploring the surrounding area. It is the largest museum in the region and is also home to the world's oldest working camera obscura. The museum's collections cover materials relating to the region's natural history and human prehistory, ranging from geology to dress, folk material, archaeology, and early photographs. Notable artifacts include a Bronze Age cist burial, including the remains of a 35-year-old man; a replica of the very first bicycle as designed by Kirkpatrick Macmillan; the photographic archive of Dr Werner Kissling; and the personal belongings of Thomas Carlyle.

## CROOK OF BALDOON

The Crook of Baldoon is a 196-hectare nature reserve located in Wigtown. Home to thousands of golden plovers, lapwings, red knots, oystercatchers, wigeons, curlews, pintails, and dunlins, this site

Opposite: The world's largest camera obscura is part of the Dumfries Museum, housed in an old windmill.

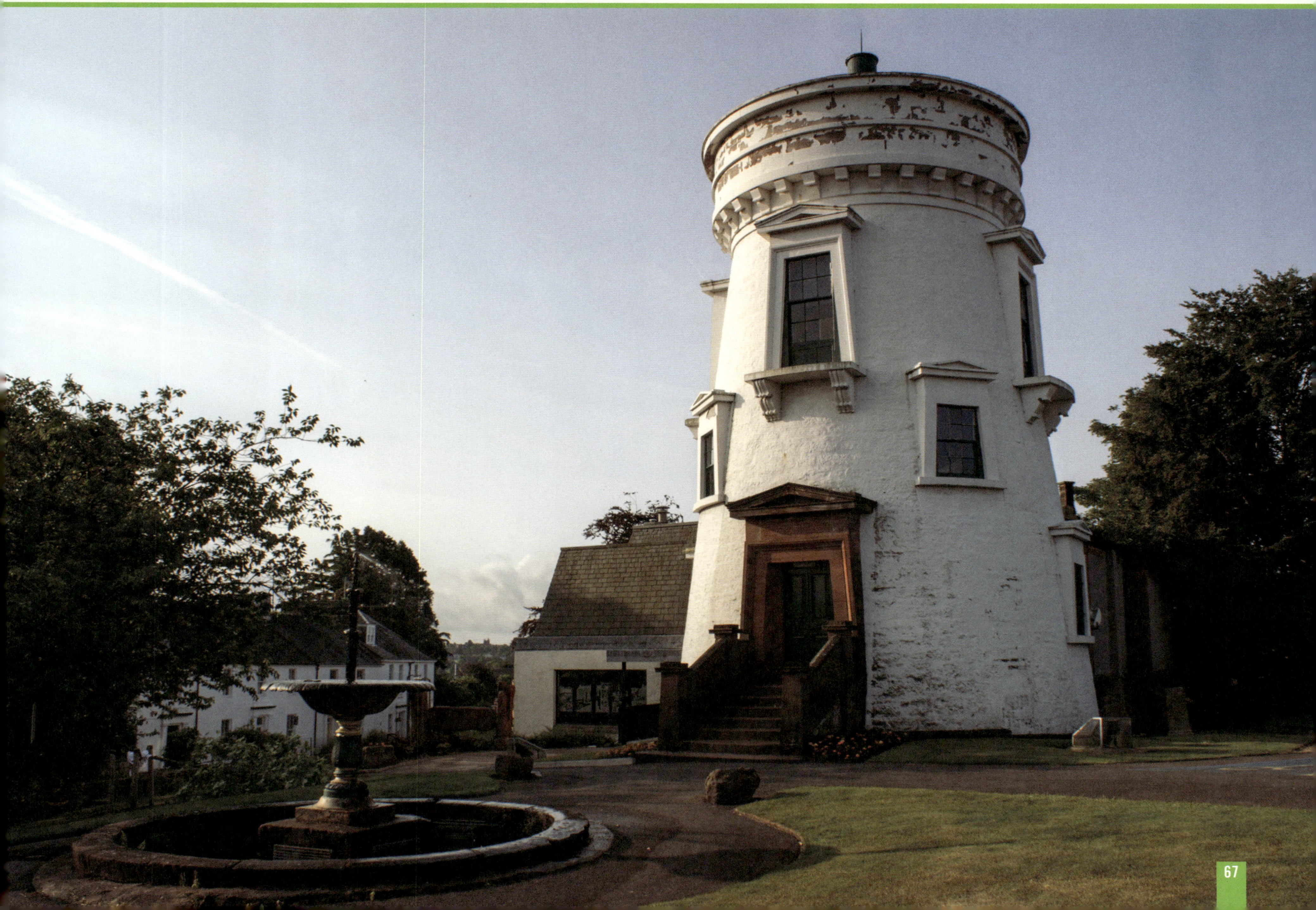

# DUMFRIES AND GALLOWAY

is an ideal place for bird-watching. With its wet grassland and rich wildlife, the reserve also sees a good number of winter visitors, such as shelducks, whooper and mute swans, and a staggering number of geese. The Galloway Hills and Cairnsmore of Fleet fill in as a background to the saltmarsh and mudflats abounding with wildlife. This Crook of Baldoon is the newest reserve managed by the Royal Society for the Protection of Birds, and since buying the reserve, the RSPB has restored a good deal of farmland and a willow crop to the wet grassland spanning the reserve. A nearby parking lot can be found at the entrance to a walking trail that stretches from coastline as far as the river at Wigtown.

## CAIRN HOLY CHAMBERED CAIRNS

Located not far east of the village of Carsluith, the Cairn Holy Chambered Cairns sit on a hillside overlooking Wigtown Bay. Cairn Holy I and Cairn Holy II, are impressive survivals of the 4th millennium BCE, particularly Cairn Holy I, the more elaborate of the two, with its concave facade of tall pillar stones. Cairn Holy II is said to be the tomb of Galdus, a mythical Scottish king. Both are known as Clyde cairns, a type of tomb characteristic of southwest Scotland. The tombs are now open to the sky, their covering stones long ago robbed to build field dikes. In 1949 the site was partially excavated. Little human remains were found, but there were some surprising artifacts, including a flake of pitchstone from the island of Arran in Cairn

**Top:** Cairn Holy II once contained two burial chambers. **Middle:** The Torhouse Stone Circle probably dates back 4,000 years. **Bottom:** A memorial to the Wigtown martyrs sits near the site of their deaths.

Holy I's forecourt, fragments of pottery from a bowl made in the English style, Beaker pottery dated to centuries after the tombs' original construction, and part of a ceremonial axe made of jadeite, found in Cairn Holy I's outer chamber. These finds are now housed in the National Museum of Scotland.

## TORHOUSE STONE CIRCLE

The Torhouse Stone Circle, also known as Torhousekie, is a stone circle made up of 19 granite boulders on the land of Tollhouse, 3 miles west of Wigtown. The stone circle stands in a rich prehistoric landscape of the Bladnoch Valley. Local folklore maintains that the three large stones in the center of the circle once contained the tomb of Gauldus, a legendary Scottish king. It is uncertain when exactly the stone circle was constructed, but experts believe the structure dates back as far as 4,000 years ago. Bladnoch Valley itself is home to several other ancient structures, including five other standing stones and a series of burial cairns nearby.

## WIGTOWN MARTYRS' MONUMENT

This site commemorates the life of the Scottish Covenanters who were killed in 1685 for disobeying King Charles II. Margaret McLachlan was 68 years old and Margaret Wilson was 18 at the time of their execution; the two women were members of a

**Opposite:** The great stone slab resting on the two taller end slabs probably once formed the roof of Cairn Holy I.

# DUMFRIES AND GALLOWAY

17th-century religious and political movement that supported the Presbyterian Church of Scotland. When discovered and arrested, the women were consequently sentenced to be tied to stakes in the tidal channel of the river Bladnoch near its entrance to Wigtown Bay to be drowned by the incoming tide. Supposedly, the true plan was to allow the older woman to drown to frighten the younger woman into changing her ways, but unfortunately neither survived. There are two gravestones nearby to memorialize them, as well as an inscribed stone near the site of their deaths at the river's edge.

## DRUMLANRIG CASTLE

Sometimes called the "Pink Palace" due to the pale red sandstone from which it was built, this castle is considered one of the finest surviving examples of Scottish 17th-century architecture. It is located in the Queensberry Estate in Dumfries and Galloway and is open to the public at set times. This Category A listed castle served as the Dumfries home of the Duchess and Duke of Buccleuch and Queensberry while they traveled in this county; it was constructed between 1679 and 1689 from the unique pink sandstone that this region of Scotland is known for. In 1984, aerial photography revealed the outline of a substantial Roman fort about 350 yards to the southeast of the castle; this remarkable fort was partially excavated in 2004 by the *Time Team* television program. With luxurious interiors and manicured grounds, the dignified Drumlanrig Castle is home to period pieces, tapestries, and artwork that include Rembrandt's *An Old Woman Reading* and Da Vinci's *Madonna of the Yarnwinder*, which was stolen in 2001 but returned the same year after it was located in Glasgow.

**Opposite: The pink sandstone of Drumlanrig Castle is complemented by the lush greenery of the castle's garden setting.**

## THREAVE CASTLE

Built on an island in the River Dee by Archibald the Grim in 1369, Threave Castle served as a stronghold for the "Black Douglases," who were also the Earls of Douglas and Lords of Galloway, until their fall in 1455. It became a royal castle in the 16th century under Lord Maxwell and did not see serious combat until the Bishops' Wars of 1638–40. The Maxwells supported Charles I and installed a garrison at Threave. The army of the Covenanters, opposed to the royalist cause, laid siege to the castle in 1640 for 13 weeks, before the garrison surrendered. The Covenanters ordered the castle to be dismantled and the materials to be disposed of. Despite being only partially dismantled, the castle remained largely unused until given into state care in 1913. The site also harbors a tower house and an L-shaped artillery house and is now maintained by Historic Environment Scotland and open to the public all year round. It is only accessible via boat; there is a brass bell with a rope pull to notify the boatman as soon as you arrive at the jetty. You can board a boat

**Above: A bell hangs ready at the jetty to alert the boatman of visitors' arrivals at Threave Castle. Below: The ruins of Threave Castle still stand tall on a small island in the River Dee.**

# DUMFRIES AND GALLOWAY

from the Threave Estate, owned by the National Trust for Scotland and operated as a nature reserve and wildlife shelter for bats and ospreys.

## BROUGHTON HOUSE AND GARDEN

This iconic 18th-century house in the heart of Kirkcudbright features a carefully maintained Japanese-inspired garden, as well as a dazzling collection of unique paintings, photographs, and sculptures. In the gallery is a frieze designed to imitate the Elgin Marbles from the Parthenon. Since 1997 it has been maintained as a living museum of painter Edward Atkinson Hornel's work, managed and taken care of by National Trust for Scotland. The house served as both the home and studio space of Hornel for 30 years until his death in 1933, and it is now home to Hornel's extensive reference library of about 15,000 books, including a 2,500-volume collection of works by or about Robert Burns. Today, thanks to this collection, Broughton House and Garden is home to one of the world's most extensive collections of Burns's works. The library also holds Hornel's personal belongings, his archive of newspaper clippings, letters, and other materials. The studio is kept exactly as it would have looked when the artist was at work. The gardens covering an area of roughly 2 acres adjacent to the estate were designed and cultivated by Hornel and his sister.

## KIRKCUDBRIGHT GALLERIES

A warm welcome always awaits in Kirkcudbright Galleries, a relatively new gallery of great national significance. Visitors arriving during the national touring exhibition will be stunned by the vast collection of artworks and paintings on display. The gallery was created for the purpose of celebrating Kirkcudbright's unique and vibrant artistic heritage, and it holds some of the very best collections available of the works of Edward Atkinson Hornel, Jessie Marion King, John Faed, Robert Sivell, and Samuel John Peploe. The gallery also features a great deal of contemporary work and focuses on more than just paintings; expect to find jewelry, craftwork, furniture, books, silverware, and even furniture on display, with new pieces rotating in and out of the gallery with every season.

## FAMOUS BLACKSMITHS SHOP AT GRETNA GREEN

The infamous site of hasty elopements, the small parish of Gretna Green sits just on the Scottish side of the borders of Scotland and England. Built here in 1713, the Famous Blacksmiths Shop, the first stop in Scotland, stands at the junction of five old coaching roads that had been well-used by travelers passing in and out of the country for hundreds of years. In 1754, the first batch of runaway couples

**Top:** Broughton House and Garden sits in the old High Street in Kirkcudbright. **Bottom:** A sculpture of clasped hands stands in the courtyard at the Famous Blacksmiths Shop in Gretna Green. This town on the border was made famous in the 18th century as a destination for runaway marriages.

seeking marriage outside of the restrictions of England and Wales, began converging on Gretna Green because Scottish marriage law allowed for "irregular marriages," meaning that if a declaration was made before two witnesses, almost anybody had the authority to conduct the marriage ceremony. It became a tradition for a blacksmith to meet the couples at the crossroads and conduct the ceremonies over the now world-famous marriage anvil, with his wife and sympathetic locals standing as witnesses. The blacksmiths in Gretna became known as "blacksmith priests" and "anvil priests," culminating with Richard Rennison, who performed 5,147 ceremonies. The local blacksmith striking his anvil became lasting symbols of Gretna Green weddings—forging together the lives of the two lovers in an unbreakable bond. You can now visit the Famous Blacksmith Shop and shopping village, and even have your own wedding there.

## ORCHARDTON TOWER

Orchardton Tower in Kirkcudbrightshire is located 4 miles south of Dalbeattie. This free-standing cylindrical tower house is the only one of its kind in Scotland. It used to be the fortified home of John Cairns, who acquired the land around 1455 and built this unique tower 200 years after such structures had gone out of fashion. A set of incredible clockwise narrow steps leads to the top of the tower, which was solely reserved for living quarters, and the view from the top of the stairs

*Winding stone steps leads up into the ruins of Orchardton Tower.*

# DUMFRIES AND GALLOWAY

is amazing. The present entrance was constructed in the 17th or 18th century and had a new door formed from an existing window and a permanent stone staircase constructed. While parts of the tower may have fallen to ruin over the centuries, it is still a beautiful and fascinating site to explore.

## THE STEWARTRY MUSEUM

Founded in 1879, this museum was originally housed on the top floor of Kirkcudbright town hall before it was later upgraded in 1893. The Stewartry Museum Association maintained the museum until 1990, when control of both the museum and the building passed to the Stewartry District council. It offers an essential collection related to the human and natural history of Kirkcudbrightshire. In a setting soaked in old world charm, you can learn about the social history of the 18th and 19th centuries. The museum and its companion art venue, Kirkcudbright Galleries, houses two nationally recognized collections of art and archaeology. Notably, the museum houses one of the oldest surviving sports trophies in the United Kingdom: the Siller Cup. Objects illustrative of the folklore, traditional crafts, and agricultural life of the area are also displayed here. The museum's archaeological collections include significant Mesolithic and Neolithic artifacts, such as barbed arrowheads, ax heads, and other fragments collected from the early medieval era, as well as a respectable collection of Viking weaponry.

## SOUTHERNESS LIGHTHOUSE

Toward the southeast point of the village of Southerness overlooking the Solway Firth stands the Southerness Lighthouse, one of the oldest lighthouses in Scotland. It was commissioned by the local council in 1749 to aid the safe passage of ships through the Firth towards the Nith Estuary, which was an important shipping route for cargo boats coming from Liverpool and Ireland carrying goods to the local area and beyond. The nearly 60-foot-high lighthouse is no longer in operation, but it is still a fascinating landmark set in a beautiful location. The lighthouse is often open to the public in high season, giving visitors who brave the climb to the top fabulous views of the surrounding scenery.

## OTHER TOP SITES

- **MORTON CASTLE**

It may be a bit difficult to locate, but this castle, majestically situated on a promontory surrounded by steep drops to Morton Loch, is well worth a look. One of Scotland's most enigmatic castles, Morton Castle was most likely built in the late 1200s or early 1300s as a rare hall-house.

- **MOAT BRAE HOUSE AND GARDEN**

The grounds of this Georgian townhouse in Dumfries is the inspiration for J.M. Barrie's Neverland and the place where *Peter Pan* began. Saved from demolition and restored, Moat Brae now houses Peter Pan's Enchanted Land and a National Centre for Children's Literature and Storytelling.

- **CREETOWN GEM ROCK MUSEUM**

This award-winning museum is home to one of the finest private collections of fossils, gemstones, and crystals in all of Scotland.

*The 18th-century Southerness Lighthouse keeps its solitary vigil over the Solway Firth.*

# DUNBARTONSHIRE

## TOP SITES IN DUNBARTONSHIRE

- Geilston Garden
- Overtoun House
- Dumbarton Castle

The small counties of West and East Dunbartonshire are nestled in the heart of mainland Scotland. The county name *Dunbartonshire* is taken from the name of the town Dumbarton, from the Scottish Gaelic *Dùn Breatann,* or "fort of the Britons," though some people call it by its interchangeable name of Dumbartonshire. Dunbartonshire was a historic and registration county and also a lieutenancy area that has been a part of the historic district of Lennox, a duchy in the peerage of Scotland related to the duke. Its history goes back at least as far as the Iron Age and into the early Roman settlements.

Once known for whisky distillation, shipbuilding, and glassmaking, the town of Dunbarton is now just as popular as a commuter town for Glasgow.

Top: Competitors row their skiffs out into the River Clyde estuary from Dumbarton at the start of the Castle to Crane Race, which will take them from Dumbarton Castle to the Finnieston Crane in Glasgow.

Most of the county is consumed by Loch Lomond, which contains numerous islands making up part of the county and a national park. Some of these islands include the Island I Vow, Tarbet Isle, Torrance, Aber Isle, and the much smaller ones, Loch Sloy, Geal Loch, and Lochan Beinn Damhain. The surrounding area is home to Ben Vrolich, the highest point in the county at 3,094 feet.

Dunbarton is known for its robust transport system; the West Highland Line railway runs through the county, connecting Glasgow to Oban and Fort William. The railway line's spectacularly scenic views as it passes through the Highlands makes it especially popular with tourists. Several ferries are also available to carry passengers back and forth across Loch Lomond, which is a great way to get from place to place while taking in beautiful natural landscape.

An aerial shot shows the green setting of Geilston Garden, a 200-year-old walled garden near the River Clyde.

## GEILSTON GARDEN

Situated along the dazzling banks of the River Clyde in northwest Cardross, these 200-year-old gardens owned by the National Trust for Scotland feature stone walls and a play area for children. The grounds are lined with vibrant rhododendrons, and the gardens even contain giant rhubarb and gunnera, which can grow leaves the size of an eagle's wingspan. This walled garden has a dominating 100-foot Wellingtonia tree towering in the center of its lawn, standing well above the surrounding plant life. The garden was first constructed in 1797, and is open to the public from April to October. The Geilston Burn meanders through the grounds of the garden, followed closely by a lush path lined with flowers, eventually making its way north to join the River Clyde. There is an antique cannon somewhere in the garden, which is believed to have been brought home by a previous owner of the estate as a trophy from the Battle of Corunna. The gardens regularly host special events, which can be viewed ahead of time online.

## OVERTOUN HOUSE

Overtoun House is a 19th-century country house originally constructed in 1862. The estate can be found in West Dunbartonshire, on a hill overlooking the River Clyde just north of the village of Milton. The Overtoun estate boasts lush gardens, Victorian-style architecture, thriving wildlife, and picturesque picnic areas overlooking Dumbarton and the nearby River Clyde. Plans for the Overtoun House were first made in 1859 when James White, a retired lawyer and co-owner of the J & J White Chemical Company, bought a plot of land with the intent of building a farm there. The house was designed by architect James Smith, although his early death meant the project was passed on to one of his partners. The house served many uses over the years, from a convalescent home during World War II to a maternity hospital in 1947. Today the house features the Centre for Hope and Healing, as well as a tearoom. Over the course of the summer, Overtoun House offers many guided walks and tours throughout the grounds.

A stone bridge spans a deep ravine to leads visitors to Overtoun House.

# DUNBARTONSHIRE

Dumbarton Castle nestled in the rocks over the Firth of Clyde.

## DUMBARTON CASTLE

Standing proud atop a volcanic rock outcropping on the banks of the Firth of Clyde, this impressive castle once housed royalty central to the ancient kingdom of Scotland. Upon its creation, the castle was known as Alt Clut, for "Rock of the Clyde," in reference to its location near the confluence of the River Leven and the River Clyde. Today, most of the earliest medieval structures of the castle are lost to time, either crumbled into ruins or replaced in many instances of remodeling and rebuilding over the centuries. The oldest still-existing parts are the 14th-century Portcullis Arch, the foundations of the Wallace Tower, and what may be the foundations of the White Tower. Most of the structures still standing today were built in the 18th century, including the Governor's House and fortifications, which demonstrates a great deal of skill displayed by military engineers of the time. This castle has the most extensive recorded history of any stronghold in Scotland. Several lists of its contents and furnishings exist, including inventories from 1510, 1571, 1580, 1644 and 1688, all recording the collections of weapons, furniture, and art stored in the castle's many rooms. On a visit here, be sure to take in the beautiful view from the twin summits of the White Tower Crag and the Beak—it will be clear just why this rocky outcrop was chosen as the fortress of the Britons centuries ago.

A cannon aims over the castle's ramparts to the Firth below.

## OTHER TOP SITES

- **BUBBLE SOCCER SCOTLAND**

Created in 2014, this engaging pastime involves a small indoor soccer field and inflatable, wearable plastic bubbles. Visitors suit up, don their cleats, and play a full-contact game from the safety of their own "personal bubbles," which generally leads to people bouncing off of each other and tumbling harmlessly across the field. A visit to Bubble Soccer Scotland is a fun way to let off some steam, get some exercise, and give any children traveling with you a break from taking in so many other historic, scholarly landmarks.

- **SCOTTISH MARITIME MUSEUM**

The most extensive collection of shipbuilding machinery and tools in the country is found at the Scottish Maritime Museum, which includes historic personal effects, artifacts, vessels, and art pertaining to life at sea. Located on the William Denny Shipyard site, the Dumbarton location features the world's first commercial ship-testing facility, the Denny Ship Model Experiment Tank.

- **DUMBARTON FOOTBALL STADIUM**

This 2,050-person-capacity stadium consists of a large grass soccer pitch and was opened in 2000 beneath the impressive Castle Rock. Due to the stadium's proximity to this natural geographic formation, many fans simply refer to the grounds as the "Rock Stadium." As the name implies, it is mostly used for football matches and is the home ground of Dumbarton Football Club. It was built on the part of the site formerly occupied by Denny's shipyard. The stadium is a 5-to-10-minutes' walk from Dumbarton railway station on the North Clyde

# EAST LOTHIAN

## TOP SITES IN EAST LOTHIAN

- Bass Rock
- National Museum of Flight
- Tantallon Castle
- John Muir Country Park
- The John Muir Way
- Belhaven Beach

Known as Scotland's golf coast, East Lothian sits perched on Scotland's rugged, southeast shoreline and is the current home of the Scottish Open. It is one of the 32 council areas of Scotland, a historic county, registration county, and a lieutenancy area. The county was formerly called Haddingtonshire. The historic county was incorporated for local government purposes in 1975 into the Lothian region as East Lothian District, with minor changes in its boundaries. There are 19 golf courses in East Lothian, including the oldest golf course in the world, Musselburgh Links.

A famous folktale suggests the origin of the flag of Scotland was conceived after the battle between the Angles and the Picts in East Lothian in the year 823. Initially, the area belonged to Ancient Britons under the kingdom of Bernicia before being claimed by the Scottish monarchy in the 10th century and was later named as a county of Scotland in the 12th century. This county was heavily involved in several medieval early modern conflicts, and many historically significant castles—such as Dunbar Castle, Tantallon Castle, and Dirleton Castle—were built during this period. In the 12th and 13th centuries, the palace of Haddington was one of the seats of the kings of Scotland. King William, the Lion of Scotland, used the palace from time to time, and it was the birthplace of Alexander II in 1198. East Lothian was also the site of conflict during the war of the Rough Wooing; many houses and villages were burned by the English in May 1544 after the sacking of Edinburgh.

This primarily rural county has 40 miles of coastline, including the breathtaking Firth of Forth. With exceptionally fertile

**Top:** An Avro Vulcan Bomber stands on display at the National Museum of Flight at the East Fortune Airfield.

The craggy cliffs of Bass Rock are home to thousands of northern gannets.

soil, agriculture has long been a primary source of economic revenue for the county. Other contributors to East Lothian's modern economy include cement, engineering, and brewing and distilling.

## BASS ROCK

This rock island, located just off of North Berwick, is home to the world's largest colony of northern gannets. Described by Sir David Attenborough as "one of the 12 wildlife wonders of the world," Bass Rock is a sanctuary for the gannets, hosting more than 150,000 of them during peak breeding season. Not only is it the closest bird sanctuary to the mainland, but it was also the first to be studied by ornithologists, who gave the gannet the scientific name *Morus bassanus* after the rock itself. From a distance, what at first appears to be layers of snow on the rock's surface is actually thousands of birds and their droppings—they can be so numerous that the rock itself becomes difficult to see. Bass Rock is an iconic tourist site believed to have formed from a plug of volcanic rock in the Firth of Forth. Today, it is uninhabited, except for its many feathered residents. With jagged rocks that are beaten by the waves in stormy weather, the ruins of an ancient chapel, and the remains of a castle, the site has a distinctly wild and forsaken atmosphere—a stark contrast against the charming lighthouse that was erected in 1902 on the location of the castle keep.

## NATIONAL MUSEUM OF FLIGHT

The National Museum of Flight was originally a World War II airfield, utilizing only the existing buildings of Royal Air Force Station East Fortune. RAF East Fortune is a registered ancient monument, so no permanent structures can be or have been added by the museum. The control towers, hangars, and stores were designed to be category B listed buildings by Historic Scotland. This designation, however, was removed in 2013 because they were already covered by stricter scheduling. The National Museum of Flight Houses

The John Muir Way is signposted throughout using a purple logo.

81

# EAST LOTHIAN

a world-class collection of aircraft and aviation-related artifacts; the collection was first started in 1909 with the acquisition of Percy Pilcher's Hawk glider, the first aircraft officially collected by any museum in the UK. One of the foremost aviation museums in the world, it helps preserve the stories behind historically significant aircraft and the talented pilots who flew them. The museum's multiple aircraft hangers feature military aviation, civil aviation, and an exhibit called "The Concorde Experience," which includes a guided tour around a Concorde aircraft and an in-depth explanation of the history, mechanics, and production of the supersonic passenger airliner.

## TANTALLON CASTLE

Tantallon Castle is a mid-14th-century fortress located not far from North Berwick and built on the edge of a cliff. This solid castle was a stronghold of the Red Douglas dynasty, the family that often clashed with the Crown. The castle was besieged by James IV and James V on several occasions and was eventually destroyed by Oliver Cromwell's troops in 1651. The remaining structure in this site holds the history of the great dynasty, and it is an incredible sight to see. Tantallon was built by William Douglas, 1st Earl of Douglas. It was passed to his illegitimate son, George Douglas, who later

**Opposite: Tantallon Castle is a semi-ruined cliff-top fortress dating to the mid-14th century, and it can boast of its historic connections to the Douglas dynasty, Oliver Cromwell, and Mary, Queen of Scots.**

became Earl of Angus. Tantallon Castle remained the property of Douglas and his family for much of its history. Tantallon Castle first saw combat in the First Bishops' War in 1639 and again during Oliver Cromwell's invasion of Scotland in 1651, before it was eventually sold to the Marquis of Douglas in 1699. As of today, the ruins of Tantallon Castle are in the care of Historic Environment Scotland.

## JOHN MUIR COUNTRY PARK

Named after Dunbar native John Muir, the famous naturalist and geologist who later emigrated to the United States, where he became an early advocate for the preservation of wilderness and became known as the "Father of the National Parks," the John Muir Country Park lies within UNESCO's Firth of Forth Ramsar Site. It is located near the village of West Barns, a part of the town of Dunbar, and covers 1,763 acres, stretching along 8 miles of coastline from Pfeffer Sands to Dunbar Castle. It is also a Site of Special Scientific Interest and a Special Protection Area.

The park has a mixture of mainly seminatural habitats, from woodland through grasslands and saltmarsh to coastal dunes and rocky and sandy shorelines. Approximately 400 plant species have been recorded here, including sea aster, sea rocket, biting stonecrop, and marram grass, as well as common wildflowers like birds-foot trefoil, meadow cranesbill, and viper's bugloss. It also abounds with birdlife, with a variety of wildfowl,

**Above: A ramble through the John Muir Country Park brings you through a saltmarsh known as Heckie's Hole, where hidden gems, such as an old World War II building, wait to be found. Below: On Dunbar High Street outside the Dunbar Museum stands a vibrant statue of John Muir as a young boy.**

# EAST LOTHIAN

A coastline path offers a peaceful view to North Berwick at the foot of North Berwick Law. This path along the coast is one of the alternatives offered to walkers on the John Muir Way.

## OTHER TOP SITES

- **JOHN MUIR ALPACAS HIKING TRAILS**

Located in the coastal town of Dunbar, this is an exciting tourist's ranch that offers daily hiking and trekking experiences, with beautiful views of lush bushes and verdant fields, as well as the chance to meet adorable animals. This site is an ideal place for picnics and outings with the whole family, and the alpaca enclosure is especially popular with children. John Muir Alpacas can be found near the John Muir Country Park and John Muir Way; the natural beauty of this region enhances an already memorable experience spent hiking along natural trails alongside these unique animals. For visitors with young children, the site also offers shorter, less taxing "mini treks" and picnic sessions.

- **NB DISTILLERY**

It is not just whisky distilleries in Scotland, and you can visit this distillery in North Berwick, which produces award-winning NB Gin, vodka, and rum. It offers a luxury visitor experience and the Cellar Door shop, where you can purchase bottles to take home.

waders, gulls, and terns, including whooper swan, common greenshank, Eurasian whimbrel, and little tern as residents and migrants. The woodlands and grasslands are home to common crossbill, green woodpecker, Eurasian jay, European stonechat, and Eurasian skylark. You can also often spot several species of butterflies.

## THE JOHN MUIR WAY

The John Muir Way originally existed as a trail that wound through East Lothian only, but starting in 2014, this older route was absorbed into a much longer one, running from Helensburgh in Argyll and Bute in the west to Dunbar in East Lothian in the east. In 2017 this new route was designated as one of Scotland's Great Trails by *NatureScot*. Between 240,000 and 300,000 people now walk the path every year—some even manage the entire coast-to-coast route across Scotland, which links Muir's birthplace with Helensburgh. It is suitable for walkers and cyclists, but cyclists should be aware that some of the rougher sections might not be suitable for road bikes.

In a trek starting at it western point, along with providing stunning views of Scotland's first national park, Loch Lomond and the Trossachs, the trail takes you through some wild and rugged terrain over windswept, high moorland with little shelter before crossing the West Highland Way near Dumgoyne hill and the Glengoyne Distillery. At Kirkintilloch, the trail picks up the Forth and Clyde Canal and heads through Strathkelvin to Falkirk. En route you can appreciate the ruins of Roman forts and the Antonine Wall and the ancient town of Linlithgow with its imposing palace of Mary, Queen of Scots. You then follow the seashore to the harbor town of Bo'ness, then coast along to Blackness Castle and the bridge town of South Queensferry. In the Edinburgh section, the trail becomes greener before again taking you past coastal birding and golf spots via Aberlady and North Berwick. At the trail's end in Dunbar, you can visit the museum dedicated to Muir.

## BELHAVEN BEACH

This broad shallow-water beach is one of the premier surfing sites in Scotland. Belhaven Beach is set in John Muir Park and equipped with charming box homes built to serve as overnight shelters for ramblers passing through. The beach is also home to the famous "bridge to nowhere," a small bridge leading from nowhere to nowhere. This sandy beach has a lovely view of the Forth Estuary and spans approximately a mile in length. Belhaven's vast sands are backed with a dune ridge, the perfect spot for building sandcastles, playing beach games, and having a family day out. Surfers and kite fliers make the most of crashing waves and high winds, and swimming is safe in calm weather, although jellyfish are often found here. There is no lifeguard cover at any time.

*Opposite: The peculiar "bridge to nowhere" creates a surreal, lonely image as it rises from the waters bounding Belhaven Beach.*

85

# EDINBURGH

## TOP SITES IN EDINBURGH

- Edinburgh Castle
- Princes Street Gardens
- Scottish National Gallery
- National Museum of Scotland
- Edinburgh Old Town and the Royal Mile
- Palace of Holyroodhouse and Holyrood Abbey
- Greyfriars Kirk and Greyfriars Bobby Fountain
- Edinburgh Zoo
- Royal Botanic Garden Edinburgh
- Scottish National Gallery of Modern Art
- Camera Obscura and World of Illusions
- Royal Yacht *Britannia*
- Calton Hill

Edinburgh is the capital city of Scotland and has held that title since the early 15th century. This modern council area is nestled in the southeast and is beloved by travelers for its rich and vibrant culture. The city has long been known for its high standard of education in a variety of different fields, and its universities have produced scholars in fields such as medicine, literature, philosophy, and the sciences. Edinburgh is also renowned for its deep heritage and cultural festivals, and it's a great place to explore World Heritage Sites, as well as a variety of attractions, such as museums, galleries, pubs, and more. It is notably home to the Palace of Holyroodhouse, the official British royal residence in Scotland. Considered one of the liveliest cities in Europe, it is the UK's second-most popular tourist destination, receiving millions of new visitors each year.

**Top:** Victoria Street is a picturesque ribbon winding through the Old Town with the northside arches filled in with shops. This quirky street is said to be the inspiration for Harry Potter's Diagon Alley.

The city lies on the southern shore of the Firth of Forth, and the bulk of the city's modern area covers seven large hills: Calton Hill, Corstorphine Hill, Craiglockhart Hill, Braid Hill, Blackford Hill, Arthur's Seat, and the Castle Rock. The council area of Edinburgh also includes many colorful, character-filled towns and villages, which retain much of their original attributes from before their absorption into the ever-growing city over the centuries. Tourists can take a long walk around the city to explore the many sites of its historic core, which is divided into "Old Town" to the south and "New Town" to the north.

Its spectacular geography, rustic buildings, and variety of medieval and classic architecture are just a few of the many reasons to visit this picturesque city. The lush, green hills, the blue-tinted sea, and red cliffs surrounding it also make for a city that people love to explore, and

The Dugald Stewart Monument looks out over the city from Calton Hill.

hikers, cyclists, and joggers are common sights. The general urban scenery is blended with amazing ancient structures and modern architecture and makes Edinburgh a one-of-a-kind destination.

## EDINBURGH CASTLE

Edinburgh Castle has been a major part of Scottish history for centuries. Although the castle was once a vital strategic location—so much so that it is often referred to as the "most besieged place in Great Britain"—it now stands as one of Scotland's most popular tourist attractions. The fascinating historic site the castle calls home, Castle Rock, has been occupied by humans since the Iron Age, if not earlier, and the natural geography of the area makes it clear why it was such a valuable military position to maintain; Castle rock stands 430 feet above sea level, looking out over sharp, glacier-cut cliffs, and it is only accessible from one direction, giving the castle a great defensive advantage. It has been involved in many historical conflicts, ranging from the Wars of Scottish Independence in the 14th century to the Jacobite rising of 1745. The castle houses many forms of Scottish regalia and is the site of the Scottish National War Memorial.

The castle was home to kings and queens for many centuries; above the door to the Royal Palace are the initials "MAH," which stands for Mary, Queen of Scots, and her second husband Henry Stewart, Lord Darnley. The iconic Stone of Destiny, used for centuries to inaugurate monarchs, is also on display in the Crown Room. The castle's forecourt serves as a parade ground that dates back to 1820 and offers fantastic views over the city toward the Pentland Hills. Right inside the entrance, a cobblestone lane leads you to the 16th-century Portcullis Gate. At the far end of Mills Mount Battery is the One O'Clock Gun: a magnificent WWII 25-pounder cannon that fires a loud "time signal" at one o'clock almost every day. This fortress has decorated the skyline for centuries, and now provides guided and audio guided tours in eight languages.

A costumed minstrel character plays medieval tunes to entertain visitors to the Great Hall of Edinburgh Castle.

# EDINBURGH

Top: The neoclassical Scottish National Gallery sits on Edinburgh's Mound. Middle: The Wojtek the Soldier Bear Memorial in Princes Street Gardens honors a much-beloved bear that served in the Polish military during World War II, as well as the Polish soldiers who ultimately found refuge in Scotland. Bottom: A frieze in the Great Hall of the National Portrait Gallery depicts famous Scots.

## PRINCES STREET GARDENS

The Princes Street Gardens are two of Edinburgh's most beautiful landmarks. The two gardens, East Princes Street Gardens and West, can be found along the southern side of Princes Street, near the National Gallery of Scotland and Edinburgh Castle. The valley that now houses these vibrant gardens was once occupied by the Nor' Loch, or North Loch, and a stretch of unnavigable marshland, until the area was drained in the early 19th century. The marshland surrounding the loch had initially been used as a natural defense in medieval times, protecting Edinburgh Castle from attack. The Mound, an artificial hill connecting Edinburgh's New and Old Town, divides the two sections, which together cover over 37 acres. First designed in the 1770s the gardens were only eventually inaugurated in 1820, when the loch was finally fully drained over the course of seven years. They are stunning all year round and serve as great locations for locals to meet, walk, and spend a day relaxing in the sun. A popular landmark is the Ross Fountain and Bandstand, found at the very center of West Princes Street Park and often host to concerts and fireworks displays. Every Christmas season, a section of the gardens is transformed into a winter wonderland, even including an artificial ice rink. The views from Princes Street look onto the expansive public gardens beneath the basalt cliffs where Edinburgh's Castle stands. In 1840, one of the most prominent features of the gardens, the Scott Monument, was constructed. This is a memorial to the beloved Scottish author Sir Walter Scott. The Scott Monument is the tallest monument dedicated to an author anywhere in the world.

## SCOTTISH NATIONAL GALLERY

Located right in the heart of Edinburgh, the Scottish National Gallery is home to one of the most extensive collections of art in the world. It is located on the Mound in central Edinburgh, an artificial hill that divides the East and West Gardens of Princes Street. The gallery is home to many masterpieces, including world-famous works by Titian, Constable, Monet, Van Gogh, and Gauguin. The gallery is a popular yet peaceful attraction that offers free admission to the permanent collection, although some of the rotating exhibitions require a ticket. This art gallery is part of the National Galleries of Scotland, which includes the Scottish National Portrait Gallery and the Scottish National Gallery of Modern Art. The building was originally designed in a Neoclassical style by architect William Henry Playfair and was first opened to the public in 1859. Making up one-third of Scotland's official national collection of fine art, it spans from Scottish to

**Opposite: Edinburgh Castle looms over the Ross Fountain in West Princes Street Gardens.**

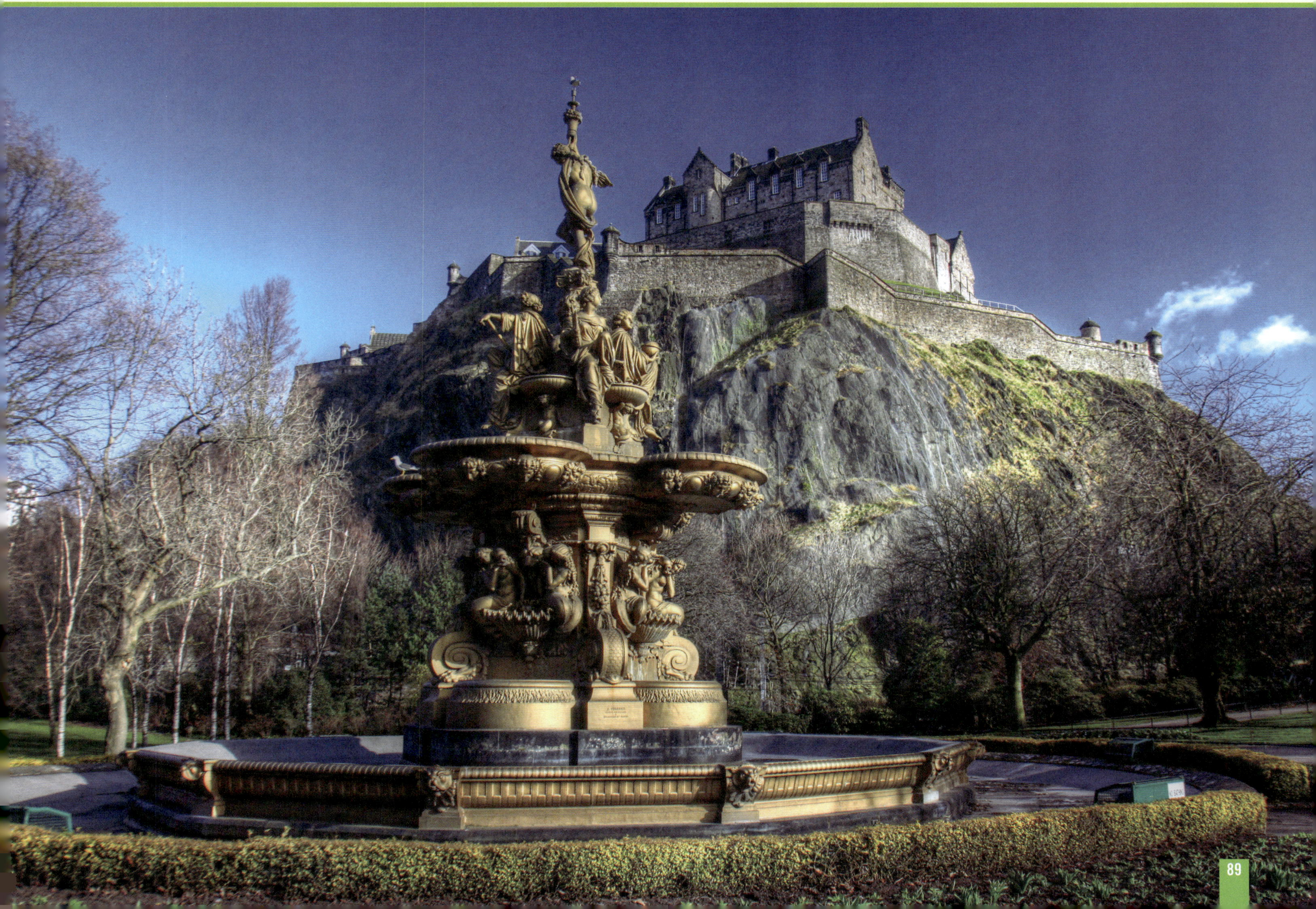

# EDINBURGH

international art and includes pieces from the early Renaissance up to the start of the 20th century. The building contains octagonal rooms that are lit by skylights and have been restored to their original Victorian décor, decorated with vibrant green carpets and red walls. The upstairs galleries house portraits and paintings, including Monet's *Poplars at the River Epte* and Van Gogh's colorful *Orchard In Blossom (Plum Trees)*. You can round off your visit with delicious cake and coffee and even sample great, local Scottish produce at the award-winning Scottish Cafe and Restaurant. You can also explore the gallery's gift shop, with its wide selection of books, prints, posters, jewelry, and toys.

## NATIONAL MUSEUM OF SCOTLAND

The National Museum of Scotland contains an extensive collection that is spread between two buildings. One building, previously called the Museum of Scotland dates to 1998; the other, the Royal Scottish Museum, dates back to 1861. The buildings connect, and the older houses collections that cover natural history, design and fashion, archaeology, science and technology, and works of art from all over the world. The modern building, known for a striking design that makes it one of the city's most iconic landmarks, has an equally expansive collection of exhibits and artifacts throughout its five floors. Audio guides are available for these stimulating tours. The museum incorporates the collections of the former National

**Top: The clean lines of the Museum of Scotland provide a modern contrast in the ancient city. Bottom: Edinburgh Castle stands guard over the streets of the city, including the narrow, lamp-lit Vennel. A tour through the Old Town will take you through many such alleyways.**

Museum of Antiquities of Scotland and is one of Scotland's most popular tourist attractions, bringing in millions of visitors every year. This highly informative, and culturally rich landmark is also free to the public. The most memorable and historically valuable exhibits remain year-round, but the museum also features a series of rotating exhibitions and events, meaning there is always something new for visitors to see each year. The museum is also extremely accessible, offering many ramps, elevators, and complimentary wheelchairs. Tours for deaf, visually impaired, and autistic visitors are also available. The Tower Restaurant can be found up on the roof and offers stunning views over the Old Town and Edinburgh Castle.

## EDINBURGH OLD TOWN AND THE ROYAL MILE

The Old Town is known for being Edinburgh's oldest neighborhood. It dates all the way back to medieval times and is filled with shops, pubs, and historical monuments. The architecture and culture of the Old Town has been carefully preserved over the centuries, and today the whole town is one of Edinburgh's many protected UNESCO World Heritage Sites. The Royal Mile, the main street of the Old Town, stretches down a slope that reaches all the way from Edinburgh Castle to Holyroodhouse Palace. The total length of the streets between these two iconic castles is almost exactly a mile, hence the name. The streets that make up the Royal Mile are Castlehill, the Lawnmarket, the High Street, the Canongate, and Abbey Strand. The Royal

**Opposite: The Royal Mile stretches from Edinburgh Castle to Holyroodhouse Palace.**

# EDINBURGH

Left: In the Old Town, you will find tiny stairway alleys, often just a few feet wide. Below: An archway allows a glimpse into the splendid grounds of Holyroodhouse Palace.

Mile is by far the busiest tourist street in the Old Town, but the businesses here face competition from the bustling Princes Street located in the New Town to the north. Distinctive features such as tall stone buildings and narrow alleyways are remnants of vast overcrowding in the town's past; Notable historic buildings here include St Giles' Cathedral, the General Assembly Hall of the Church of Scotland, and the National Museum of Scotland. St Giles' Cathedral—famous for its towering and beautiful architecture—dates back to the 15th century and today is home to the Thistle Chapel. Outside the cathedral doors, a heart made of paving stones is set into the cobbled street. This mosaic, known as the Heart of Midlothian, marks the former site of the Old Tolbooth, which served as a meeting place for parliament, the town council, and the General Assembly of the Reformed Kirk before it was demolished in 1817. It is tradition for passers-by to spit on the heart for luck. The overall layout of the Old Town is quite unusual, and one reason for this is because of the land that it is built on: the city sits on a "crag and tail" formation that tracks a path down the side of a long-extinct volcano, one ridge of which is marked out by the Royal Mile.

## PALACE OF HOLYROODHOUSE AND HOLYROOD ABBEY

When the Queen is in town, she stays at the Palace of Holyroodhouse. The stunning rooms of the palace are filled with portraits, antiques, and carefully preserved furniture, and the beautiful gardens outside are a delight. The estate serves as the official residence in Scotland of Her Majesty The Queen, but the palace is also open to the public throughout the year, allowing you to come explore. You can view 14 historic state apartments and the romantic ruins of the 12th-century Holyrood Abbey with a multimedia self-guided tour offered in 10 languages. The Queen's Gallery hosts a program of regularly changing exhibitions from the Royal Collection. Queen Victoria and Prince Albert were enthusiastic patrons of the art of watercolor painting in particular, which accounts for a good portion of the collection. The gallery features an exhibition that documents the lives of Victoria and Albert and includes many depictions of Victorian Edinburgh that cannot be seen anywhere else.

"This is a city of shifting light, of changing skies, of sudden vistas. A city so beautiful it breaks the heart again and again."

—ALEXANDER MCCALL SMITH

Opposite: A statue of John Knox, the founder of the Presbyterian Church of Scotland, stands in front of the stunningly ornate St Giles' Cathedral, a city landmark standing about midway along the Royal Mile.

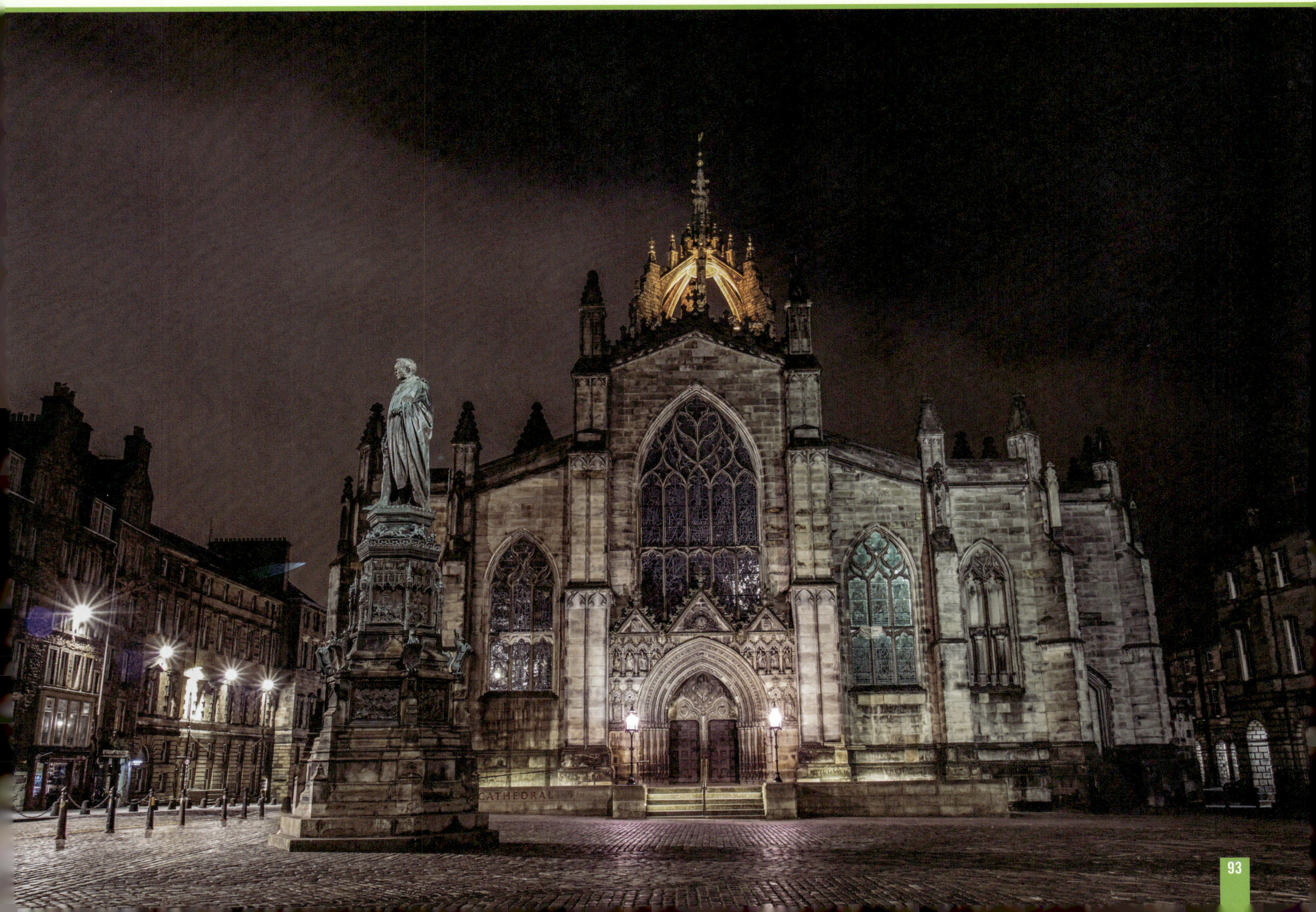
CATHEDRAL

# EDINBURGH

The palace was designed by Sir William Bruce in a classical-style three-story quadrangle layout and was built between the years 1671 and 1678. The 16th-century north-west tower has a matching southwest tower, and each has circular angle-turrets with a bell-cast roof. The abbey's choir and transepts were lost after the Protestant Reformation, though the nave survived as a parish church; James VII and II evicted the worshipers in 1687, however, and the remainder of the abbey fell to ruins. You can wander the abbey nave and gardens after a tour of the palace and take in the west front view of the rebuilt abbey church, one of the most impressive Gothic facades in Scotland.

## GREYFRIARS KIRK AND GREYFRIARS BOBBY FOUNTAIN

Greyfriars Bobby Fountain is a unique tourist attraction with a touching story. The fountain is a commemorative statue to a 19th-century Skye Terrier by the name of Bobby, who—after the death and burial of his owner, John Gray—guarded his master's grave for 14 years. Bobby died in 1872 and was buried in Greyfriars Kirkyard near the grave of John Gray. The story of Greyfriars Bobby is displayed on the board outside the kirkyard and is by far the most well-known and frequently visited grave inside. The statue of Bobby is located on the corner of Candlemaker Row and George IV Bridge and is visited by thousands of tourists every year. The granite memorial for Bobby is in front of the east gable of the Kirk, and John Gray's memorial headstone is nearby to the north and is made of red granite. Bobby captured the hearts of many, and locals were known to bring him food and other comforts during his 14-year vigil. The story is well known in Scotland and has gone on to inspire other legends; in more recent years, the story has also been adapted into books and films, one of which was released by Disney in 1961. The graveyard is also a place popular for Harry Potter fans, as author J.K. Rowling once suggested that the names on the gravestones there had originally inspired the names of some of her characters. The bronze statue of Bobby is now a major city tourist attraction, and his nose has been rubbed so much by visitors that it has turned from dark gray to a shiny bronze color. This location is also where the National Covenant was signed in 1638, when the Presbyterians of Edinburgh pledged to uphold their beliefs against the imposition of Episcopalism.

**Generations of admirers have rubbed the patina of Greyfriar Bobby's nose down to its original bright bronze.**

**Opposite: The atmospheric churchyard of Greyfriars Kirk is the burial site of many illustrious Scots.**

## THE WIZARDING WORLD OF EDINBURGH

In 1990, J.K. Rowling sat down to write, and seven years later she published *Harry Potter and the Philosopher's Stone*, the first book in series about a boy wizard that became a world-wide phenomenon. Rowling wrote most of the Harry Potter series in Edinburgh, and there are lots of opportunities for Potterheads to tour some of the sites associated with their favorite books. Much of Rowling's early writing was done in Edinburgh's cafes. The Elephant Café, which bills itself as the "Birthplace of Harry Potter" is where Rowling penned much of the early novels in the back room overlooking Edinburgh Castle. In a series with so much emphasis on death it is no surprise that Rowling seems to have taken inspiration for character names from tombstones in the Greyfriars Kirkyard, including a William McGonagall and a Thomas Riddell, Esq. Other points of interest are George Heriot's School, thought to be a partial inspiration for Hogwarts, and Victoria Street and Grassmarket with their resemblance to Diagon Alley. Those with deep pockets can even stay in the J.K. Rowling suite at the Balmoral Hotel, where Rowling finished the last books in the series after she could no longer work unnoticed in the city's cafes. As well as the desk she wrote on, the room is filled with Potteresque touches, such as an owl doorknocker and a statuette of a stag.

# EDINBURGH

**Tian Tian the giant panda is a star of the Edinburgh Zoo.**

## EDINBURGH ZOO

First opened in 1913 and one of the world's leading conservation zoos, the Edinburgh Zoo is known for its captive breeding program that has successfully helped save multiple endangered species from near extinction. The zoo spans an impressive 82 acres of parkland and sits 2.5 miles west of the city center, and among its over 1,000 rare and endangered species are Siberian tigers, red pandas, chimpanzees, sun bears, Indian rhinos, and pygmy hippos. It is also known for being the only zoo in Britain with a collection of Queensland koalas and giant pandas. Its main attractions are two giant pandas, named Tian Tian and Yang Guang, as well as the penguin parade that takes place every day when the zoo allows its penguins to go out for a stroll through the grounds. Guests can explore the Budongo Trail that houses chimpanzees, where a theatre, interactive displays, and games teach visitors about the lifestyle of great apes. Penguins' Rock is the habitat of many of the zoo's penguins. Wallabies and pelicans can be viewed in the walk-through habitats or at daily animal-handling sessions. Edinburgh Zoo was the first zoo in the world to display and breed penguins; the first of the collection were three king penguins, which arrived in 1913. The Giraffe House contains a bachelor herd of five male Nubian giraffes, and you can watch a Sumatran tiger walk right over your head in Tiger Tracks, which is an amazing glass viewing tunnel straight through the tiger enclosure.

The zoo's site faces south on the slopes of Corstorphine Hill, which provides wonderful views of the city. In addition to all of the amazing wildlife to discover, you can enjoy educational events, food and drinks, play areas, and a gift shop. The zoo also contains gardens that feature one of the most diverse tree collections in the Lothians. Edinburgh Zoo is involved in many scientific pursuits outside of conservation and is a vital source for research into animal behavior and physiology.

## ROYAL BOTANIC GARDEN EDINBURGH

The Royal Botanic Garden of Edinburgh offers its many visitors a much-needed moment of peace and tranquility. The grounds of the garden are littered with a beautiful array of thriving flora throughout its stunning 72 acres, conveniently located in the very center of Edinburgh. First founded in 1670, the garden is known today as one of the finest botanic gardens in the world. It serves as both a beloved tourist destination and an irreplaceable scientific center for the study of plants, biodiversity, and conservation, and it now occupies four sites across Scotland, each with its own unique collection. The Edinburgh site, which is the original and main garden and the headquarters of the RBGE, is the second oldest botanic garden in the UK. The gardens are part of multiple conservation projects in the UK and worldwide. In addition to their scientific activities, the garden remains an iconic landmark for both tourists and locals. Locally known as "The Botanics," the garden is the perfect place to go for a walk or spend a day out with the family. Throughout the year the garden hosts many exciting events that include live performances, guided tours, and interesting exhibitions. Some of the most notable collections located at the botanic garden in Edinburgh include Alpine Plants, Peat Walls, the Chinese Hillside, the Cryptogamic Garden, the Rock Garden, and The Queen Mother's Memorial Garden. The Royal Botanic Garden is open to the public and to visitors of all ages and offers fantastic views of the capital's skyline.

**Opposite: Opened in 1858, the Temperate Palm House at the Royal Botanic Garden is a masterpiece of Victorian engineering.**

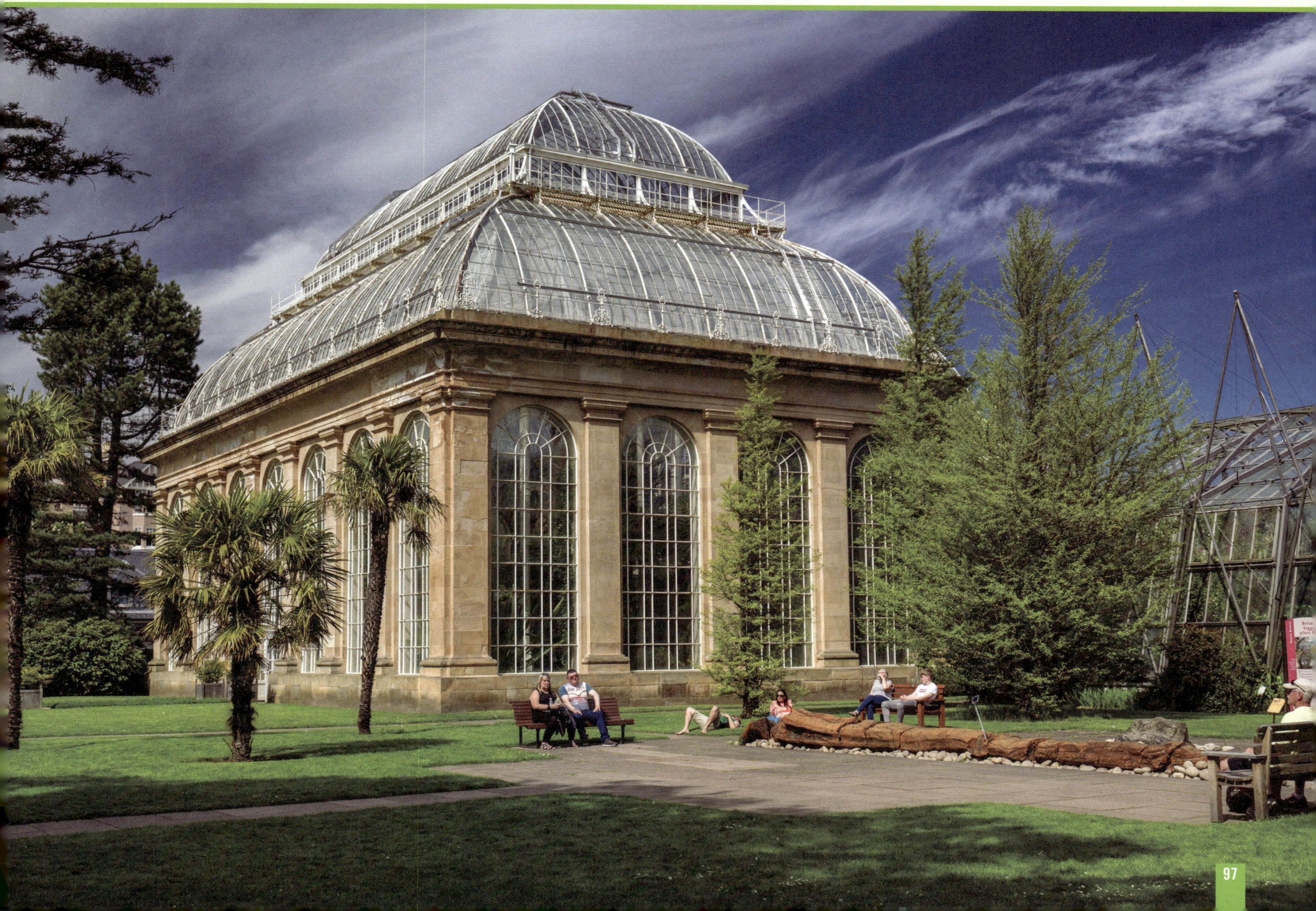

# EDINBURGH

*Above: The Scottish National Gallery of Modern Art features Charles Jencks's* Landform Ueda, *which comprises a stepped, serpentine-shaped mound complemented by crescent-shaped pools of water.*
*Below: The Outlook Tower tops the Camera Obscura building.*

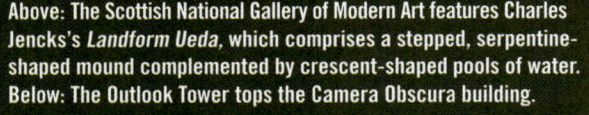

## SCOTTISH NATIONAL GALLERY OF MODERN ART

Edinburgh's Scottish National Gallery of Modern Art consists of two impressive neoclassical buildings that are surrounded by lovely, well-landscaped grounds. They showcase a stunning collection of paintings, including works by the post-Impressionist Scottish Colorists. The main collection, which is known as Modern One, primarily features 20th-century art from various European movements represented by Matisse, Picasso, Kirchner, and others. American and English artists are also represented, though the majority of the works belong to Scottish painters. The significant collection of more than 6,000 paintings, sculptures, installations, video work, prints, and drawings is regularly augmented by new exhibits. The gallery also offers an excellent cafe, and the surrounding park features sculptures by major artists, as well as a "landform artwork" by Charles Jencks. A footpath and stairs at the back of the gallery lead down to the Water of Leith Walkway, a 4-mile stroll along the river that leads to Leith.

Across the road from the main building, the Modern Two collection can be found in what was known as the Dean Orphan Hospital until it was repurposed in 1999. Modern Two features changing world-class exhibitions, as well permanent artwork; the gallery is notably home to a world-famous collection of surrealist works, including pieces by Salvador Dalí, René Magritte, and Giacometti.

## CAMERA OBSCURA AND WORLD OF ILLUSIONS

Edinburgh's popular camera obscura is a 19th-century device that has been in constant use since 1853 and is located in the Outlook Tower on the Royal Mile. It uses lenses and mirrors to create a live image of the city, which is then projected onto a large screen. The intriguing exhibition includes an accompanying commentary that is both entertaining and informative, lending the whole experience a quirky charm. Outlook Tower was built in 1852; it was known as "Short's Observatory" until it was repurposed into a museum in 1892. Guests of all ages can experience over 100 illusions throughout the multiple floors, including many interactive exhibits such as the vortex tunnel, mirror maze, and shrinking room. Although the project is primarily a tourist attraction, it also serves as a learning center about optical illusions, holograms, and the origins of photography, offering several informative displays and presentations. Stairs lead up through the many various displays, and the rooftop views offer a 360-degree panorama of Edinburgh. The tower also provides free, high-power telescopes to give you a close-up view of the city and beyond. Some other notable exhibits include the Bewilderworld exhibit, the Magic Gallery, and the Light Fantastic. The museum also houses a gift shop offering some particularly unique games, toys, and souvenirs.

**Opposite: Modern Art Two is housed in the former Dean Orphan Hospital.**

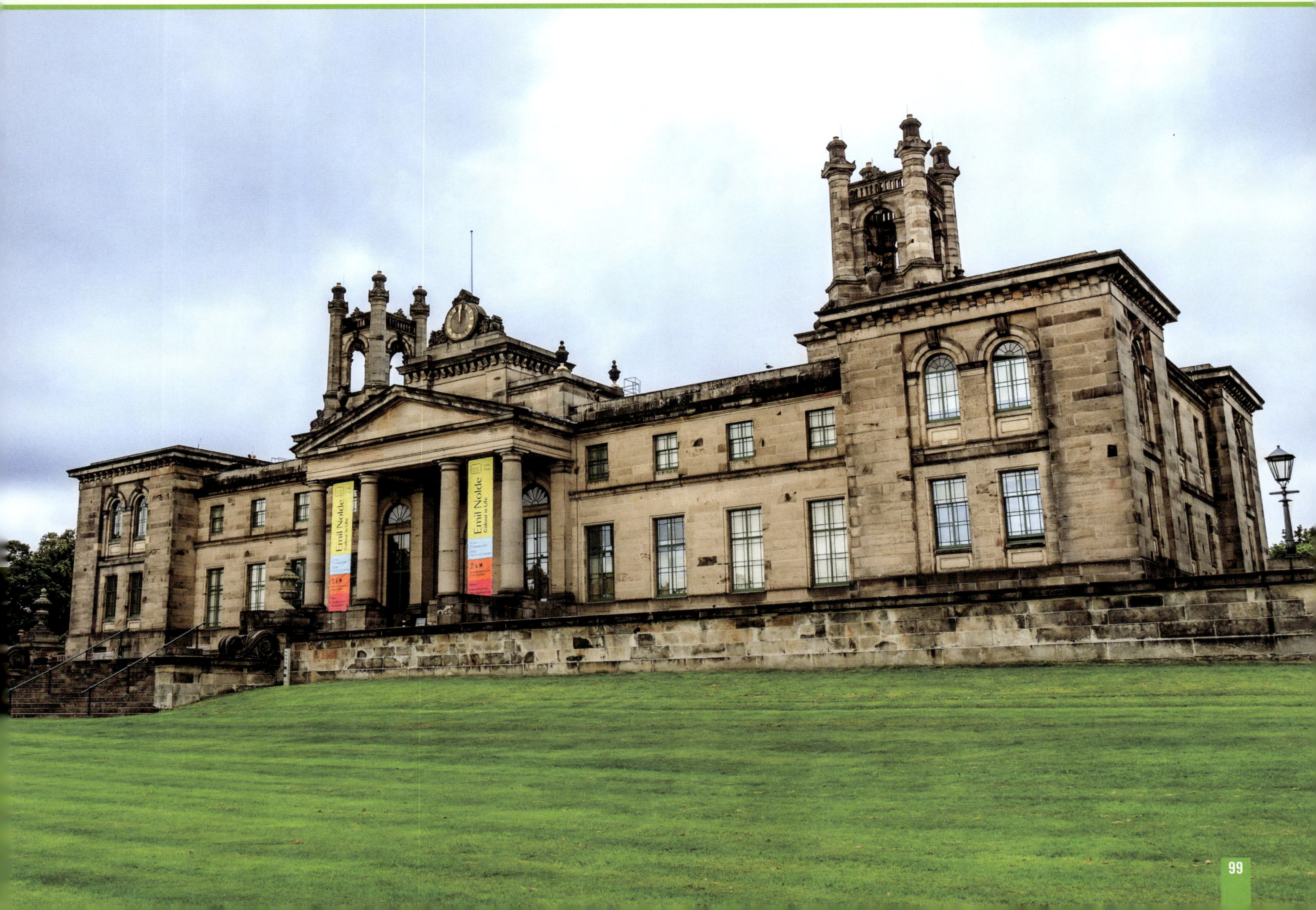
Emil Nolde
Colour is Life
Emil Nolde
Colour is Life

# EDINBURGH

Above: Standing beside a life belt life ring quayside at the Royal Yacht *Britannia* is the bronze metal figure of Royal Navy sailor yachtsman Ellis Norrie Norrell. Opposite: Once the luxurious ocean-going holiday home of the Queen and the Royal Family, the *Britannia* is now retired from service and is permanently berthed at Ocean Terminal.

## ROYAL YACHT *BRITANNIA*

The Royal Yacht *Britannia* was built in 1952 at the John Brown & Co. Ltd shipyard in Dunbartonshire. The *Britannia* was the first Royal Yacht to be built with complete ocean-traveling capacity, because its original purpose was to be the floating holiday home of the Royal Family for any foreign travel. Its secondary purpose was to entertain guests from all around the world. John Brown was already a famous shipyard before the *Britannia* was constructed, as the company was previously hired to build famous ships such as RMS *Queen Elizabeth* and RMS *Queen Mary*. When the Royal Yacht was completed, the ship's name was a closely guarded secret that was only revealed when the Queen herself smashed a bottle of wine on the hull and announced to the expectant crowds, "I name this ship Britannia . . . I wish success to her and all who sail in her." It was decommissioned in 1997 and now permanently sits in front of Ocean Terminal as a floating museum. The ship offers a self-guided tour including an audio guide that is offered in 30 languages. The exhibits within the ship showcase the everyday lives of the royals, and the entire interior has been preserved as a monument to 1950s luxury. When the Queen traveled, her 45 members of the royal household and five tons of luggage traveled with her, and even her Rolls-Royce was carefully squeezed into a specially built garage on the deck of this ship. The ship's staff was robust, consisting of an admiral, 20 officers, and 220 other crewmates. The five decks are all accessible to the public and allow for the exploration of the Royal Deck Tea Room that offers waterfront views, the crew's quarters, the engine room, and more. Visitors can learn about the history of royal yachts, view informational displays and historical photographs, and relax as waiters serve tea, coffee, and scones, all of which are made on board. The gift shop in Ocean Terminal offers souvenirs, toys, and nautical-themed novelties.

## CALTON HILL

Located east of New Town, Calton Hill is marked as a UNESCO World Heritage Site. This location provides some of the city's best panoramic views, particularly in the early morning for the spectacular

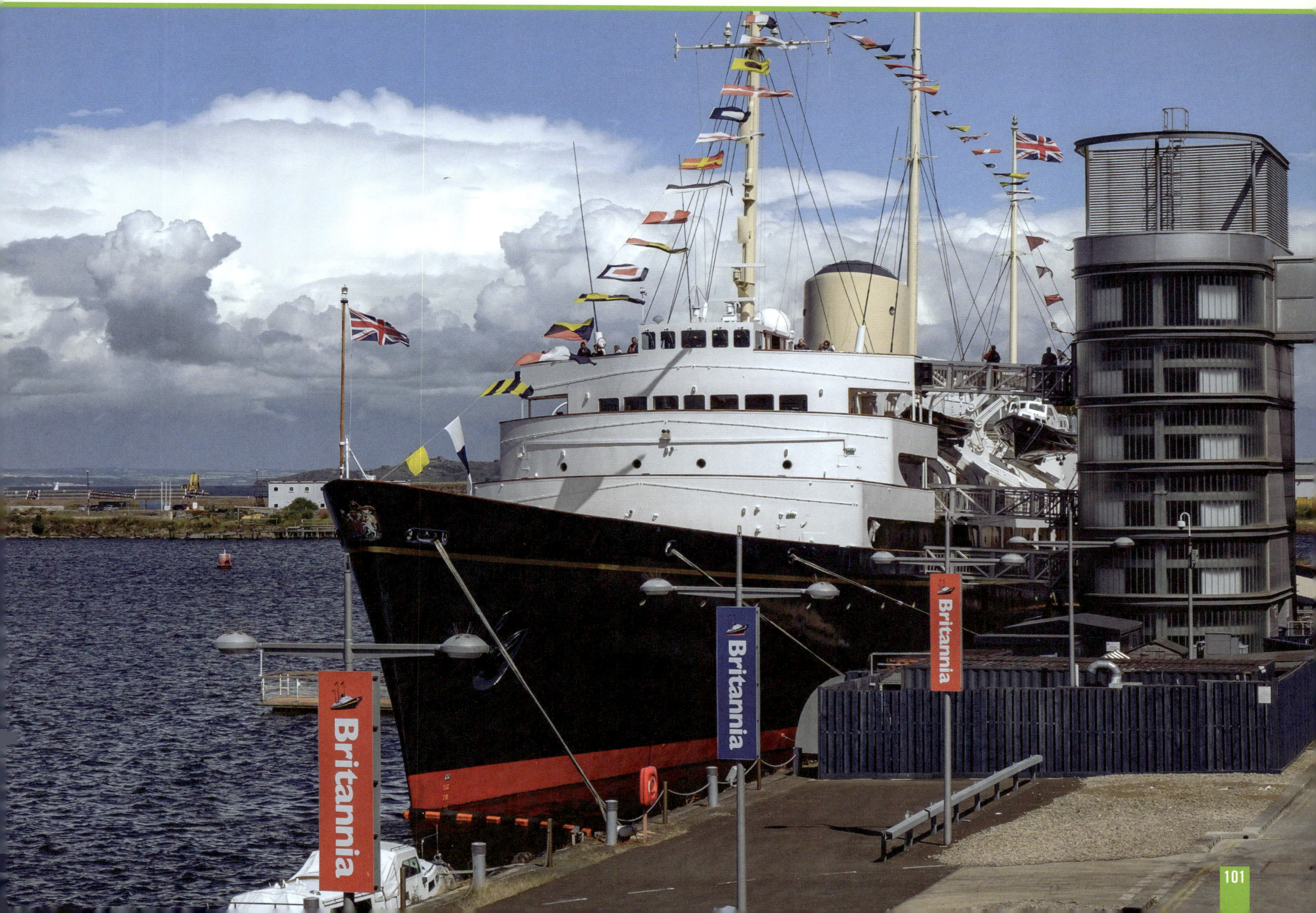
Britannia
Britannia
Britannia

# EDINBURGH

sunrises over the city. Calton Hill is also famous for its collection of historic monuments, especially the National Monument, inspired by the Parthenon in Athens. This monument, intended to commemorate the Scottish servicemen who died in the Napoleonic Wars, is actually an unfinished structure—when only half the money needed for its construction was collected, work on it stopped in 1829 with only the 12 columns you see today finished.

The Nelson Monument, shaped like an up-turned telescope, was erected in 1816 to commemorate the death of Admiral Lord Nelson at the Battle of Trafalgar in 1805. In 1852 a time ball was added to the top to enable ships moored in the Firth of Forth to set their time-pieces accurately; it still drops at one o'clock six days a week.

The oft-photographed Dugald Stewart Monument, a memorial to the Scottish philosopher, Dugald Stewart (1753–1828), was designed by Scottish architect William Henry Playfair and completed in September 1831. Its vantage point on the hill makes it a favorite viewing spot. Other monuments on Calton Hill include the Old Royal High School, Robert Burns Monument, and the Political Martyrs' Monument. The City Observatory, a Greek temple–styled building constructed in 1818, and also designed by Playfair, is located here as well.

**A brilliant view from the National Monument on Calton Hill takes in some of Edinburgh's most famous landmarks, such as Edinburgh Castle in the distance, the Clock Tower of the Balmoral Hotel, and the spire of St Giles' Cathedral.**

**The Nelson Monument and National Monument stand side by side on the volcanic rock of Calton Hill high above the city.**

## OTHER TOP SITES

- **THE MUSEUM OF CHILDHOOD**

The first in the world to be dedicated to the history of childhood, this specialty museum displays toys, games, clothes, books, and dolls, dating from the 1800s to the present day.

- **DYNAMIC EARTH: EDINBURGH'S SCIENCE CENTRE**

Taking you from the Big Bang to the modern day, this science center is Scotland's largest interactive visitor attraction.

- **THE REAL MARY KING'S CLOSE**

Located under buildings on the Royal Mile, the Real Mary King's Close and its warren of streets, homes, and passageways allow you to immerse yourself in the 17th-century city to discover the stories of the people who lived, worked, and died here.

- **JOHN KNOX HOUSE**

It is up for debate whether the firebrand preacher ever lived here, but a visit to this picturesque house—one of the oldest in the city—is worth your time. It tells a compelling tale of the Reformation and shows how people lived 400 years ago. It is now incorporated into the next-door Scottish Storytelling Centre. The Centre runs story tours of the surrounding Netherbow area and also hosts two annual festivals.

# FALKIRK

## TOP SITES IN FALKIRK

- Antonine Wall
- Falkirk Wheel
- Callendar House
- The Kelpies and the Helix

Since 1996, Falkirk has been one of 32 unitary authority council areas of Scotland, formed from the exact boundaries of Falkirk District, one of three parts of the Central region created in 1975, which was abolished at that time. The majority of the council area was part of the historic county of Stirlingshire, and a small part was part of the former county of West Lothian. Falkirk shares borders with North Lanarkshire, Stirling, and West Lothian, and, across the Firth of Forth to the northeast, Clackmannanshire and Fife. The largest town is Falkirk; other settlements surround Falkirk within 6 miles of its center and include Bo'ness, Bonnybridge, Denny, Grangemouth, Larbert, Polmont, Shieldhill and Stenhousemuir. Falkirk's location at the junction of the Forth and Clyde and Union Canals proved key to its growth as a center of heavy industry during the Industrial Revolution. Attractions in and around Falkirk include the Falkirk Wheel, the Helix, the Kelpies, Callendar House and Park, and remnants of the Antonine Wall.

## ANTONINE WALL

Once spanning close to 40 miles, the Romans built the Antonine Wall around 142 CE at the northwest frontier of their empire. At the time it was the most awe-inspiring engineering project the people of Scotland had ever seen, stretching right across the country, from Clyde to Forth. The Romans were ruthless in their building, cutting through native settlements. It was constructed mostly out of layers of turf—unlike the stone-built Hadrian's Wall to the south—and the rampart reached nearly 10 feet. The wall was also backed by a deep ditch, nearly 16 feet deep in places. Along the wall, 17 forts, augmented by smaller "fortlets," housed the 6,000 to 7,000 men needed to guard the border. The

Top: The ditch along the Antonine Wall is still visible at Roughcastle.

The sun sets over the marvelous Falkirk Wheel, the world's only rotating boat lift.

military way built to the south of the wall completed the defensive plan, enabling troops to move swiftly, bearing supplies, commands, and news. Remnants of the wall still survive, many of them within Falkirk, such as those at Polmont Wood, Kinneil Fortlet in Kinneil Estate, Callendar Park, Tamfourhill in Camelon, and Seabegs Wood. The Rough Castle site is one of the best-preserved Roman forts. The sites are great for a few hours of roaming.

## FALKIRK WHEEL

The world's first and only rotating boat lift, the Falkirk Wheel was built to connect the Forth and Clyde Canal and the Union Canal. This impressive feat of engineering stands 115 feet tall and requires only the power of eight domestic kettles to sail boats through the air and transfer them between the two canals. Located in Tamfourhill, it opened in 2002 as part of the Millennium Link project and replaced a series of lock gates built in the 19th century, allowing coast-to-coast navigation across central Scotland for the first time in over 40 years.

As well as being a mechanical marvel, the Falkirk Wheel is a work of art that had quickly risen to icon status, attracting over 500,000 visitors a year. A visit to the site provides a fun family day out with plenty of attractions for kids, such as the Childrens Activity Zone and Mini Canal and Water Play Park. Woodland walks take you past parts of the Antonine Wall and Roughcastle Roman Fort. You can also stop at the free visitor center and have a hot drink while watching the Wheel turn. A boat trip allows you to experience first-hand the wonder of the Wheel, and you might even spot a Kelpie in the distance.

## CALLENDAR HOUSE

Set within the grounds of Callendar Park in Falkirk town, Callendar House traces its roots to a 14th-century tower house. During the 19th century, it was redesigned and extended in the style of a French Renaissance château fused with elements of Scottish Baronial architecture to create the striking mansion you see today. Lying on the line of the 2nd-century Antonine Wall, the site was once

The Pineapple is an elaborate two-story summerhouse in Dunmore Park that has been ranked "the most bizarre building in Scotland."

# FALKIRK

a seat of the Callendar family, who were Thanes of Callendar. For six centuries, as it changed hands several times, it lasted through wars, rebellions, and the Industrial Revolution. Callendar House has played host to many great historical figures, including Mary, Queen of Scots, Cromwell, and Bonnie Prince Charlie. Now under the care of the Falkirk Community Trust, the house is open to visitors as the district's principal art, history, and historic house museum. Two magnificent reception rooms, the Pink Room (the drawing room) and the Green Room (the morning room) are part of a tour of the site, as well as a fully working Georgian period kitchen. Here costumed interpreters bring history to life, giving you the chance to sample authentic Georgian food, listen to stories about life below stairs, and watch the kitchen staff go about their daily tasks. The grounds contain a pitch-and-putt course, crazy golf, a children's adventure playground, a boating lake, and the Antonine Wall. There is also a contemporary art space, the Park Gallery, which has been relocated into Callendar House itself. You can also enjoy woodland walks through the 500-acre estate, which is home to the Forbes family mausoleum, a large, domed, circular Grecian-Doric building.

## THE KELPIES AND THE HELIX

The colossal Kelpies dominate the skyline between Falkirk and Grangemouth. They are the centerpiece of the Helix, a project that set out to

*Callendar House blends elements of Renaissance and Scottish Baronial styles in a sprawling building set in verdant gardens and woodland.*

transform underused land between Falkirk and Grangemouth into a thriving urban green space. It now covers some 860 acres and has 17 miles of cycleways and footpaths to provide access around the development. The central area is known as Helix Park, and the site includes the Plaza Cafe, the lagoon, woodland and wetland areas, miles of pathways, and the Adventure Zone play area, but the jewels in the Helix project are the Kelpies. The world's largest equine sculptures, each stands about 100 feet high and weigh over 300 tons. Andy Scott, who also created the "Heavy Horse" sculpture at the side of the M8 motorway between Glasgow and Edinburgh, was the sculptor responsible for these masterpieces. The Kelpies are a monument to Scotland's horse-powered heritage, and it is said that Scott took his inspiration from Carnera, the UK's largest Clydesdale horse, who hauled wagons of the soft drink Irn-Bru over the cobbled streets of Falkirk and the surrounding area during the 1930s.

A guided tour allows you to examine the Kelpies' complex and impressive internal structure. The Visitor Centre is open daily and contains a cafe, a gift shop, and toilet facilities.

## OTHER TOP SITES

- **THE PINEAPPLE AT DUNMORE PARK**

A bit out of the way, but well worth a look for a photo op is one of the most recognizable follies in Scotland. The bizarre pineapple top dates back to the days when international travel was purely a pastime of the wealthy, and they would signal their return home by placing a pineapple on top of their gateposts. John Murray, 4th Earl of Dunmore, went a bit further and built this fruity-domed folly to let everyone know that he had a bigger pineapple than everyone else. The house at Dunmore Park is not open to the public, but you can tour trails around the gardens.

**Opposite:** Lit up for the evening, the colossal Kelpies are an awe-inspiring sight.

# FIFE

## TOP SITES IN FIFE

- University of St Andrews
- The Cathedral of St Andrew
- The Swilcan Bridge
- Pittencrieff Park
- Dunfermline Abbey and Palace
- St Andrews Castle
- Devilla Forest

Located on Scotland's eastern coastline between the Firth of Tay and the Firth of Forth, Fife is home to the third-densest population per county in Scotland and contains one of the oldest-surviving education establishments in the world, the University of St Andrews, which was founded in 1410. Once believed to have been a sub-kingdom for a Pictish king, Fife has the nickname the "Kingdom of Fife," though this is now thought to have associations with the Earl of Fife in 1678. The Kingdom of Fife is also known throughout the world as the "Home of Golf." It boasts more than 40 courses, from the famed fairways of St Andrews and several traditional seaside links to beautifully landscaped parkland and heathland courses suitable for golfers of all levels. Despite its small size—barely 50 miles at its widest point—Fife encompasses several different regions, with a marked difference between the semi-industrial south and the rural north. Southern Fife is dominated by Dunfermline, a former capital of Scotland, and the "Lang Toun" of Kirkcaldy, Fife's largest settlement. The Forth Road and Rail Bridges are the most memorable sights on this stretch of coastline.

Once a booming coal industry site in the 19th century, Fife now attracts hundreds of thousands of tourists throughout the year and hosts a slew of different festivals annually. Outside of the revenue brought in by Fife's many world-famous golf courses, another large part of the economy stems from university students.

### UNIVERSITY OF ST ANDREWS

The oldest of the four ancient universities of Scotland and, following Oxford and Cambridge universities, the third-oldest university in the

*Top: A gated archway leads into a quad of the University of St Andrews, one of Scotland's most storied institutions of higher learning.*

*The Swilcan Bridge spans the Swilcan Burn between the 1st and 18th fairways on the Old Course of St Andrews Links.*

English-speaking world, St Andrews was founded in 1413 by a small group of Augustinian clergy. Through the centuries its stellar reputation grew, and along with the universities of Glasgow, Edinburgh, and Aberdeen, St Andrews was a leading light of the 18th-century Scottish Enlightenment. Its noteworthy alumni are too numerous to list in entirety, but among the best-known names are leader of the Protestant Reformation John Knox, journalist and politician during the French Revolution Jean-Paul Marat, and pioneer of the smallpox vaccine Edward Jenner. In recent times, the university became known as the place the future king met his future queen—Prince William, Duke of Cambridge, and Catherine, Duchess of Cambridge, graduated together in 2005 with degrees in Geography and History of Art respectively. A guided walking tour through the picturesque town of St Andrews will bring you past many of the university buildings and places linked to the venerable institution, including colleges, libraries, chapels, and student halls.

## THE CATHEDRAL OF ST ANDREW

Featuring medieval sculptures, prehistoric relics and even a magnificent, intricately carved Pictish sarcophagus, the Cathedral of St Andrew is one of the cornerstones of Scotland's Catholic history. Formerly Scotland's largest cathedral and the seat of power of the medieval Church, the cathedral was intrinsically linked to Scotland's tumultuous history. St Rule's Tower, located a little way from the cathedral, was part of the first church of the Augustinian canons at St Andrews built in the early 12th century, and its ruins are breathtaking. The cathedral's outer walls in particular are exceptionally well preserved, but even in a state of collapse, the remains show how impressive the building once was. The cathedral now houses an outstanding collection of early- and later-medieval sculptures and other relics found on-site.

## THE SWILCAN BRIDGE

The Swilcan Bridge is a small, robust stone bridge that was built over 700 years ago to serve the

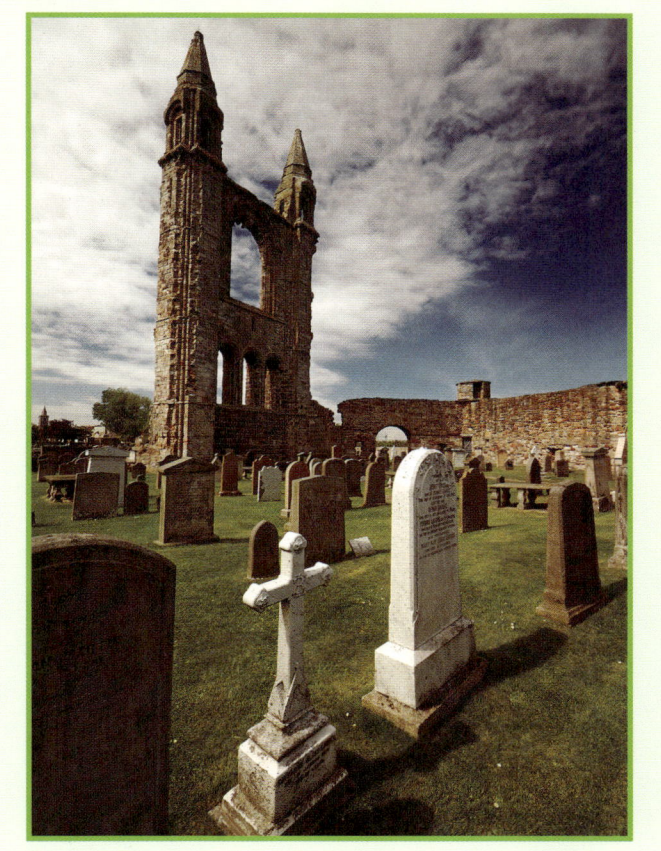

*The Eastern Cemetery shares the extensive grounds of the ruined Cathedral of St Andrew and St Rule's Tower.*

# FIFE

shepherds who regularly needed to move their flocks across the Swilcan Burn. Today, the bridge is situated in the St Andrews Links golf course; this historic stone arch is a favorite tourist spot year-round and has provided an iconic setting for many golf games, spanning the burn between the 1st and 18th fairways. This iconic little bridge has become such a core part of the St Andrews Links course that it has made its way into the rituals and ceremonies surrounding the games that take place there; many champions have their pictures taken paying homage to the bridge in some manner, and a life-size replica of the bridge can be found in the World Golf Hall of Fame Museum in Florida.

## PITTENCRIEFF PARK

Pittencrieff Park, or the Glen, as it is locally known, covers 76 acres and offers greenhouses, woodland walks, beautiful gardens, and recreational facilities. It is an ideal site for family outings; kids will have a hard time getting bored in the park's expansive playground. The park is of substantial historical and cultural significance to Dunfermline, West Fife, and beyond; Pittencrieff was originally owned by Colonel James Maitland Hunt but was purchased in 1902 by the famous philanthropist Andrew Carnegie, who donated it to Dunfermline, his birthplace. Pittencrieff Park plays host to many events throughout the year, including the Bruce Festival and the annual fireworks display that people of all ages enjoy. The Glen Pavilion within the park is a lovely Art Deco—style building that is a popular venue for weddings, meetings, conferences, and corporate events. The park grounds also house the well-curated Pittencrieff House Museum and an impressive statute of Andrew Carnegie.

## DUNFERMLINE ABBEY AND PALACE

Now one of Scotland's foremost medieval interiors and most important royal sites, Dunfermline Abbey was founded as a priory in about 1080, the time of Malcolm III and his queen, Margaret, who had it sited at the place she had married Malcolm. In the 12th century, their son, David I, raised the status of the little priory to abbey, richly endowing it and bringing stonemasons from Durham Cathedral to build a new church on a grand scale.

The magnificent nave survives to this day, and the Romanesque pillars are similar to those of Durham Cathedral, so it's likely that the same masons carved them. In 1250, St Margaret's remains were moved to an elaborate shrine at the east end of the church, the first of many illustrious entombments. After Edward I badly damaged Dunfermline Abbey in 1303, Robert I, better known as Robert the Bruce, financed its rebuilding. The most impressive of the new buildings was the monks' refectory, a soaring structure with an elaborate facade, which took full advantage of the sloping site, and proclaimed to the world the

*A small bridge spans the River Tower burn in public Pittencrieff Park.*

**Opposite:** The Abbey Church, the centerpiece of Dunfermline, has "King Robert the Bruce" cut into the masonry of the four faces of the tower to commemorate the most famous of the monarchs buried here.

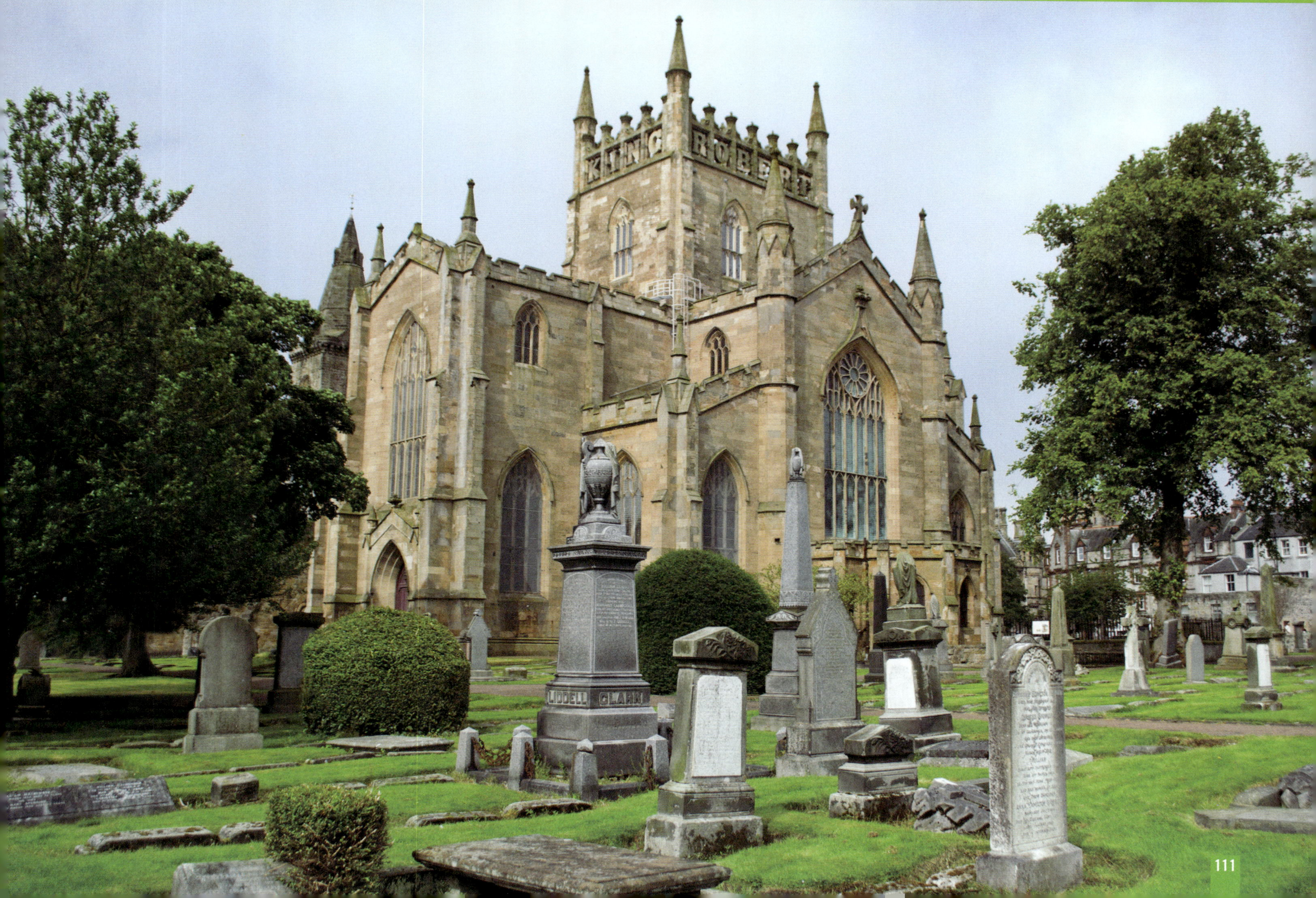
KING ROBERT
LIDDELL CLARK

# FIFE

*Abandoned at the very end of the 16th century, St Andrews Castle rapidly fell into ruin, and in 1801 the Great Hall collapsed and most of it plunged into the sea below its rocky promontory.*

power of Scotland. Upon his death in 1329, Robert was buried in the medieval choir, now beneath the Abbey church of 1821.

Medieval abbeys typically had several grades of accommodation, and it's likely that the guest house here was a royal residence right from the start. After the Reformation of 1560, James VI's queen, Anna of Denmark, created an imposing palace with the monastic guest house at its heart. Charles I was born here in 1600—the last monarch to be born in Scotland. Royal interest in Dunfermline waned, however, when James and Anna left for London in 1603, and the palace fell into disrepair. The site is still magnificent, though, and a visit here is sure to impress—the abbey's great nave is surely the most visually stunning example of Romanesque architecture in Scotland. You can also view the monks' refectory, a towering structure that speaks volumes about Robert I's confidence in his kingdom.

## ST ANDREWS CASTLE

Built in the 13th century, St Andrews Castle once sprawled atop a rocky promontory overlooking a small beach called Castle Sands and the adjoining North Sea. The ruins of the castle of the Archbishop of St Andrew hide an underground 16th-century siege mine, a counter-mine, and an infamous bottle dungeon, a prison cut out of solid rock. It is located in the coastal Royal Burgh of St Andrews and was the residence of the archbishop at the time it was built. When Cardinal Beaton was murdered in 1546, his body was believed to have been hidden in the bottle dungeon beneath the castle. John Knox and George Wishart were also suspected of having been imprisoned in this dark, airless space. In the time since the castle was built, it has suffered from sieges, storm damage, and bombardments by French ships, and little is left standing today. Indeed, you can see most of the remains from the perimeter wall. Although most of St Andrews Castle has gone, a visit is still enjoyable, as the visitor center provides a small but informative exhibition that summarizes the history of the town. The exhibition explains how the city came to be named Saint Andrews after it became home to an ancient sarcophagus, which was believed to contain relics of the saint. The Saint Andrews Sarcophagus can still be seen in the remains of St Andrews Cathedral.

## DEVILLA FOREST

Devilla Forest, which covers parts of Fife and Clackmannanshire, is beloved by locals and travelers alike for its enchanting wildlife, thriving flora, and long, looping circular walking paths that are perfect for hiking, jogging, or cycling. Among the many routes to choose from is the Red Squirrel Trail, Devilla's only waymarked route. This short trail guides you through verdant woodland to the picturesque Bordie Loch. Along the way you will find information panels, picnic tables at the loch, and animal carvings. Many visitors also hope to spot the elusive red squirrels scurrying through the Scots pine, and there also signs pointing out likely sites. Devilla Forest Circular Walk is a 7-mile-long trail that loops back on itself, located near Clackmannan. The trail is easy enough to walk at your own pace, and lesser-used paths that cut through the forest let you get even closer to nature as you go. While preparing to visit this forest, remember to pack hiking boots or at least comfortable walking shoes, especially when visiting during the rainy season, as the trails can become muddy and uneven. Many ancient artifacts have been discovered in this forest—a lucky visitor might stumble across a prehistoric coffin, a standing stone circle, or a Roman urn.

One of the many walks through Fife's share of Devilla Forest takes you past the deep blue waters of Bordie Loch.

## OTHER TOP SITES

- **THE R&A WORLD GOLF MUSEUM**

Golf aficionados can take a day off the links to explore this museum devoted to their favorite game just yards away from the 1st tee of the iconic Old Course at St Andrews Links.

- **EDEN MILL DISTILLERY AND BREWING**

Scotland's first single-site brewery and distillery officially started operation in 2012, but the location of Eden Mill has a history of beer brewing that dates back to 1810. Visitors can take a guided tour to observe the hands-on process used in the distillery, as well as learning about the history of Eden Mill and the surrounding region. Eden Mill leans heavily on its heritage as a beer brewer when it comes to defining the style of its single-malt Scotch whisky by choosing malts inherent to beer in its mash: pale malt, chocolate malt, and crystal malt.

- **ST ANDREWS BOTANIC GARDEN**

This garden features inspirational plant displays that cover rock and scree hillsides, ponds, woodland, and herbaceous borders. Botanical and geographic garden displays and huge glasshouses hold alpines, desert plants, and tropical exotics. From April to September it also hosts a fully immersive Tropical Butterfly Experience and Pollinator Challenge.

# GLASGOW

## TOP SITES IN GLASGOW

- Glasgow Science Center
- Glasgow Necropolis
- Kelvingrove Art Gallery and Museum
- Glasgow Cathedral
- Riverside Museum and Tall Ship
- Gallery of Modern Art
- George Square and the Merchant City
- Pollok House and Pollok Country Park
- University of Glasgow

Glasgow (*Glaschu* in Scottish Gaelic, meaning "Green Glen") is the largest and most populated city in Scotland, the 4th-most-populated in the UK, and the 27th-most-populated in Europe. It is one of Scotland's 32 council areas and located within the historic county of Lanarkshire. When compared to its earliest origins, Glasgow has exploded in all aspects of urban life over the centuries. The first known signs of human life in the area are the ruins of a small prehistoric village, although Glasgow only truly began to develop as a city in the 6th century, when Saint Kentigern (also known as Saint Mungo) established a church where the famous Glasgow Cathedral stands today. Glasgow established itself over the years as a religious site, until it was finally recognized as a city around the end of the 11th century. Glasgow continued to expand steadily, both in population and industry, until the University of Glasgow was founded in the 15th century, which pushed the city into the spotlight as a vital center for academic pursuits. Over the next few centuries, Glasgow's now-famous university and its advantageous position on the river Clyde allowed it to explode into an international hub of trade, culture, and commerce; what was once a small settlement built around a single church eventually became a giant of global industry. By the 19th century, Glasgow was one of Europe's leading cities in everything from shipbuilding to publishing to cigarette-making; it was known as the "Second City of the Empire" for much of the 19th century. Outside of industry, Glasgow also saw huge growth in the arts and in civil engineering, and

**Top: The Glasgow Riverside Museum, with its distinctive wave-like lines, is the permanent home of the tall ship *Glenlee*.**

A view across the River Clyde shows the modern skyline of the Clydeside area, which includes the Glasgow Science Centre and IMAX Theatre.

the city developed museums, parks, galleries, water-treatment facilities, and the Glasgow Subway.

Today, Glasgow still boasts the largest economy in all of Scotland; the city is as famous for its architecture, music, and high-profile arts scene as it is for its still-vital contributions to global industry.

## GLASGOW SCIENCE CENTER

Glasgow Science Center is an extremely popular tourist attraction and learning center located on the south bank of the River Clyde in the Clyde Waterfront Regeneration area. The center's doors first opened in 2001, during a ceremony presided over by Queen Elizabeth II, and it is currently registered as a charity. The GSC is made up of three main buildings: the Science Mall, Glasgow Tower, and a stand-alone IMAX theater.

Of the three buildings, the largest by far is the Science Mall. The outer structure takes the shape of a curving titanium and glass crescent, lending the building an appropriately futuristic look. The first floor is home to the Science Show Theatre, used for videos, presentations, and educational events for a large audience, and the Glasgow Science Center Planetarium, which uses a Zeiss optical-mechanical projector to cast images of the night sky onto the 50-foot-diameter dome overhead. Visitors can also find many interactive exhibits demonstrating core scientific principles on this floor, as well as a child-friendly exhibit called the Big Explorer.

The second floor gives visitors a chance to learn about possible careers in STEM fields; the My World of Work interactive exhibit helps teach children—and older guests too—about the many possible ways to find a career path in science.

The third floor features an interactive exhibit called Bodyworks, where guests are given in-depth information about the functions of human biology. This floor features 115 interactive displays and exhibits that help teach visitors important information about how they can improve their own health and well-being.

Capturing the contrasts between old and new within the city itself, a contemporary sign for the Merchant City, the historic trading center of Glasgow, forms a contrast with the ancient Tolbooth Steeple.

# GLASGOW

> "Glasgow's a bit like Nashville, Tennessee: it doesn't care much for the living, but it really looks after the dead."
>
> —BILLY CONNOLLY

## GLASGOW NECROPOLIS

As tourist attractions go, the Glasgow Necropolis is unique. This landmark is an expansive Victorian cemetery located east of Glasgow Cathedral, first established in 1832. The name *necropolis*—meaning "city of the dead"—is certainly fitting, as over 50,000 people have been buried within its grounds. Many of the graves are unnamed, and many are without a stone entirely; some others were marked with giant, ornately carved monuments, of which some 3,500 are still standing. A large statue of Scottish theologian John Knox, predating the Necropolis itself, can be found at the top of the hill. The Necropolis is famous for the architectural beauty of some of its more prominent tombs. The cemetery is accessed by a bridge known as the "bridge of sighs," which is preceded by a series of three memorials dedicated to stillborn children, victims of the Korean War, and Glaswegian receivers of the Victoria Cross. The cemetery itself is cut through with a series of meandering paths and walkways, allowing visitors to explore without any particular sense of direction until eventually convening at the John Knox statue.

## KELVINGROVE ART GALLERY AND MUSEUM

The Kelvingrove Art Gallery and Museum is one of Scotland's most popular centers of art, history, and culture all gathered in one massive building. The museum's exhibits feature everything from taxidermy to Renaissance art to ancient Egyptian relics, and the 22 galleries contained within its walls feature both permanent and rotating installations. The museum features one of Europe's most impressive collections of medieval armor and weaponry, and the art on display includes pieces from some of the greats: works by Rembrandt, Monet, and Van Gogh can all be found here.

The gallery was designed by architects Sir John W. Simpson and E.J. Milner Allen; the building

Opposite: Headstones, tombs, and monuments to the dead spill over the low hills of the Glasgow Necropolis. Right: Haunting statues are scattered throughout the Necropolis.

Above: The Kelvingrove is a stunning red sandstone building in the Spanish Baroque style. Below: The rather creepy Floating Heads by Sophie Cave was one of Kelvingrove's temporary installations.

117

# GLASGOW

*Also known as High Kirk or St Mungo's, Glasgow Cathedral has a stunning interior, including the original choir with its soaring lines.*

follows a Spanish Baroque style and is built out of the same Locharbriggs red sandstone as many other historic Glaswegian buildings. Kelvingrove's construction began in 1888, and it was first opened in 1901. It was originally known as the Palace of Fine Arts and was used to house the Glasgow International Exhibition of 1901. One of the cornerstones of the Glasgow International Exhibition was an ornate concert pipe organ located in the concert hall of the building; the organ was purchased after the exhibition ended and remains in the concert hall to this day.

## GLASGOW CATHEDRAL

Glasgow Cathedral, a parish Church of Scotland, is the oldest building in the City of Glasgow—and the oldest building in all of mainland Scotland. This cathedral and St Magnus Cathedral in Orkney remain Scotland's only medieval cathedrals to survive the Reformation and remain virtually intact. Glasgow Cathedral served as the seat of the Archbishop of Glasgow and was mother church to both the Archdiocese of Glasgow and the Province of Glasgow until the Scottish Reformation of the 16th century.

The original structure, dedicated to Saint Mungo (the patron saint of Glasgow), was built in 1136 on high ground above the Molendinar Burn's western bank. It is believed Saint Mungo buried the body of Fergus, a holy man, in the 6th century at a site in Cathures (now known as Glasgow), and that he later built a monastery at that burial site. Upon his death in 614, he was interred in his church on the monastery grounds, above which the first iteration of the Glasgow Cathedral was eventually built. Although little remains of this first cathedral, fragments of the building have since been discovered beneath the present-day structure. The cathedral that stands today was first constructed in 1197, though it underwent major repairs and renovations in the 13th century. St Mungo's shrine, located in the Lower Church, was an important pilgrims' sanctuary during the medieval period.

The cathedral's chapter house was the venue for the University of Glasgow's first classes when the university was founded in 1451. It was internally partitioned after the Reformation to serve three separate congregations—the Barony, Inner High, and Outer High. In 1835 both the Barony and Outer High congregations moved to another location in the city. The migration of the Barony and Outer High assemblies allowed the cathedral to be almost fully restored to its original design.

The Glasgow Cathedral building remained the property of the crown from 1587 to 1857, when it was transferred to the state. It is currently in the care of the Historic Environment Scotland. Its present-day congregation are members of the Church of Scotland's Presbytery of Glasgow.

## RIVERSIDE MUSEUM AND TALL SHIP

Located in Pointhouse Quay, the Riverside Museum houses the Glasgow Museum of Transport. Designed by renowned architect Dame Zaha Hadid to mimic the lines of a wave and completed over the span of four years, the Riverside Museum houses over 3,000 items relating to the city of Glasgow's centuries-old history of transportation technology. The collection reflects the city's global contribution to major world industries, including engineering, shipbuilding, and train manufacturing.

*Opposite: Gothic Glasgow Cathedral is one of the few that withstood the destruction of ecclesiastical sites during the Reformation.*

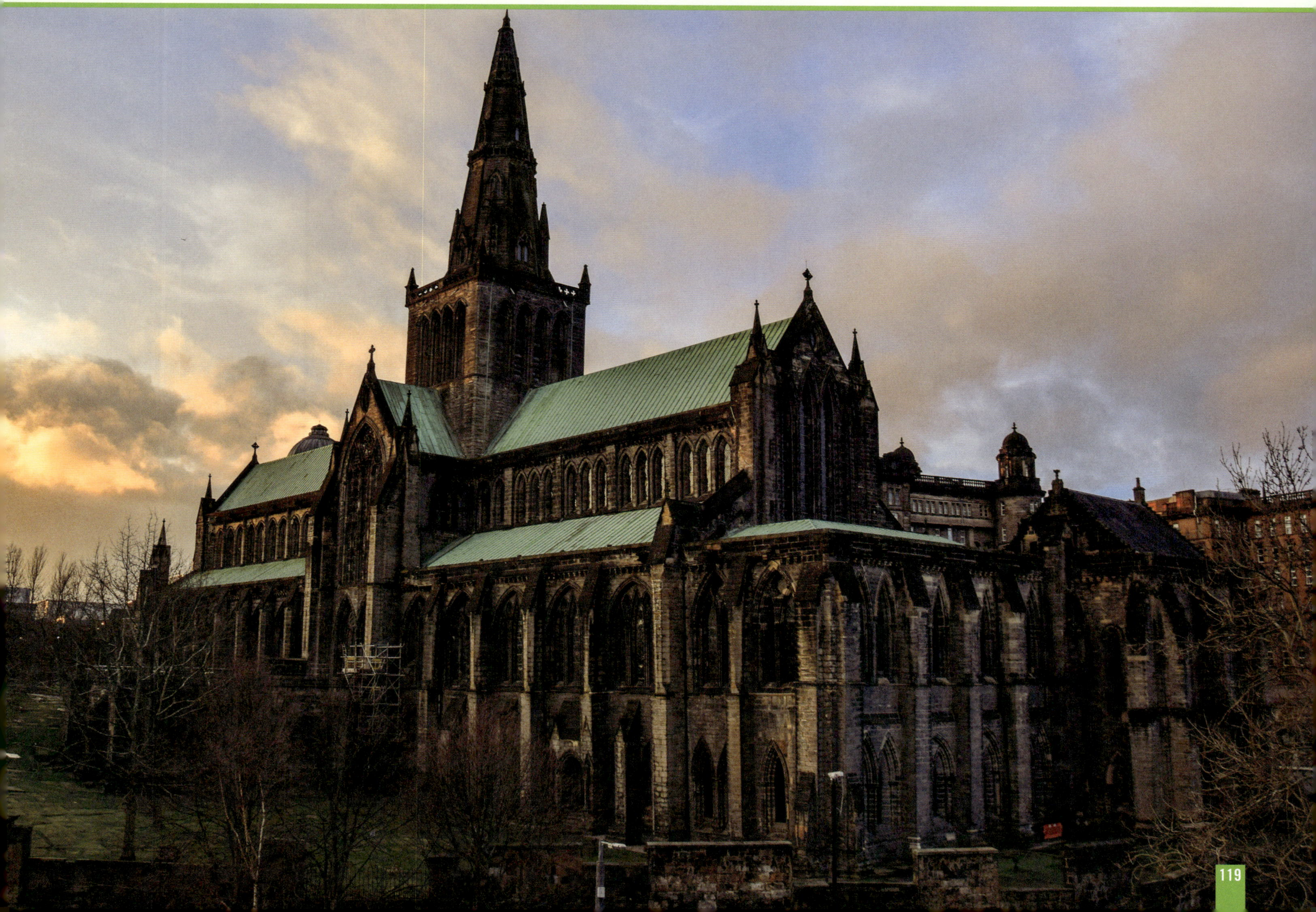

# GLASGOW

One of the museum's unique displays is the *Glenlee,* a cargo ship built at Port Glasgow in 1896. The *Glenlee* was renamed multiple times over the years; in 1922, she operated in the Spanish Navy under the name of *Galatea* as a sail training ship, serving for over 47 years. Eventually, the ship was completely de-rigged down to a hulk and was towed to Seville to be repurposed as a floating museum. In Seville, the *Glenlee* deteriorated so badly that it was decided she was to be scrapped; this was prevented by her discovery by British naval architect Dr Sir John Brown in 1990, who rescued her from her fate in the scrap yard. Repaired to seaworthiness, and returned to Glasgow, she has been a Riverside Museum ship since 1993 under her original name. Famously known as Glasgow Harbor's "Tall Ship," *Glenlee* is home to a unique collection of artifacts and information, offering educational programs, special events, and unique exhibitions detailing little-known aspects of naval history.

## GALLERY OF MODERN ART

The Gallery of Modern Art, commonly referred to as GoMA, is home to Glasgow's foremost collection of modern and contemporary art. Although GoMA was opened in 1996, the building itself was built in the late 18th century for tobacco magnate and slave trader William Cunninghame. The building changed hands many times over the years, before it

**Opposite: The Gallery of Modern Art, Scotland's most visited art gallery, is the main gallery of contemporary art in Glasgow.**

was eventually restored, updated, and expanded for its use as a distinguished art gallery. Aside from the world-famous collection of modern art that has drawn in millions of visitors over the years, the gallery also offers workshops, master classes, a dedicated studio, a "learning library" in the basement, and free Internet access for visitors. The gallery's cafe also serves freshly made food and refreshments.

## GEORGE SQUARE AND THE MERCHANT CITY

The famous George Square is located in the heart of Glasgow and is one of the city's most important municipal plazas. It is one of six squares that make up the city's center; the others are St Andrew's Square, Cathedral Square, Royal Exchange Square, St Enoch Square, and Blythswood Square.

The original plans for George Square, named for King George III, were drawn up in 1781, but the square wasn't actually built for another 20 years. It is surrounded on all sides by a number of historically and architecturally significant buildings, notably including the grandiose Municipal Chambers to the east, built in 1883 and headquarters of Glasgow City Council. The west side of the square is home to the Merchants' House, a faithful and historically accurate recreation of a local merchant's home constructed and maintained by the Glasgow Corporation.

The square is also home to a collection of famous monuments to Scottish heroes, such as those

## THE DUKE'S HAT

Outside GoMA in front of the Queen Street entrance is another notable landmark: a large equestrian statue of Arthur Wellesley, 1st Duke of Wellington, sculpted by Carlo Marochetti in 1844 and perpetually adorned with a bright orange traffic cone for a hat. The tradition of placing a traffic cone on the statue's head began as a practical joke, but after decades of government officials removing the cone and locals immediately replacing it, the cone hat has since become a core Glaswegian tradition, representing the sense of light-hearted rebellion associated with Glasgow's culture.

# GLASGOW

George Square is one of the city's prominent green spaces and is surrounded by several landmark buildings, such as the Municipal Chambers.

dedicated to James Watt, Robert Burns, Sir Walter Scott, and Sir Robert Peel. It is also the ground for political events and protests. Perhaps the most well-known is the Battle of George Square in 1919, when skilled engineers protesting for a 40-hour working week were met with a violent police response and a military deployment of more than 10,000 soldiers.

The Merchant City is an area near George Square. The "city" is bustling and lively, packed with restaurants, apartments, bars, and stores of all kinds. Although many of the businesses in the Merchant City are modern, much of the architecture of the area dates as far back as medieval times. The Glasgow Gallery of Modern Art can be found here, as well as the Scottish Youth Theatre. Many annual festivals are held in the Merchant City.

## GLASGOW GREEN AND THE PEOPLE'S PALACE

The oldest park in the city, Glasgow Green can be found in the East End on the River Clyde's northern bank and spans an area of 136 acres. The park was founded in 1450 by Bishop William Turnbull, who developed the rough swamplands of the original grounds into a public park that was open to all the people of Glasgow. The park has been in use for hundreds of years, so it has been home to some notable historic events: for instance, Glasgow Green is believed to be the place where James Watt was first inspired to create the Watt steam engine, which was instrumental in the onset of the Industrial Revolution. The park has also hosted several important protests, demonstrations, and political movements over the centuries, and it also served as the meeting place for the women's suffrage movement in Glasgow for over a century.

The Green is home to a number of well-known landmarks and monuments, including Nelson's Monument (a 143-foot-tall obelisk erected in 1806 in memory of Admiral Horatio Nelson), St Andrew's Suspension Bridge, the Glasgow Humane Society's officer's house and boatyard, the Templeton Carpet Factory, the McLennan Arch, and the People's Palace and Winter Gardens.

The People's Palace, a combined museum and greenhouse, is of particular significance among the landmarks that populate Glasgow Green. The building was first opened in 1898, at a time when the East End of Glasgow was direly overpopulated, dangerous, and perceived to be lacking in cultural value. The People's Palace was conceived as a way to give the people of the East End access to fine art, sculpture, and exhibits of local history. The attached greenhouse, thoroughly restored and refurnished, is now home to a thriving collection of plants, flowers, and trees. The People's Palace is also home to the Doulton Fountain, the world's largest terracotta fountain, which sits directly in front of the museum.

Opposite: The People's Palace and Winter Garden sits in one of Europe's largest urban parks.

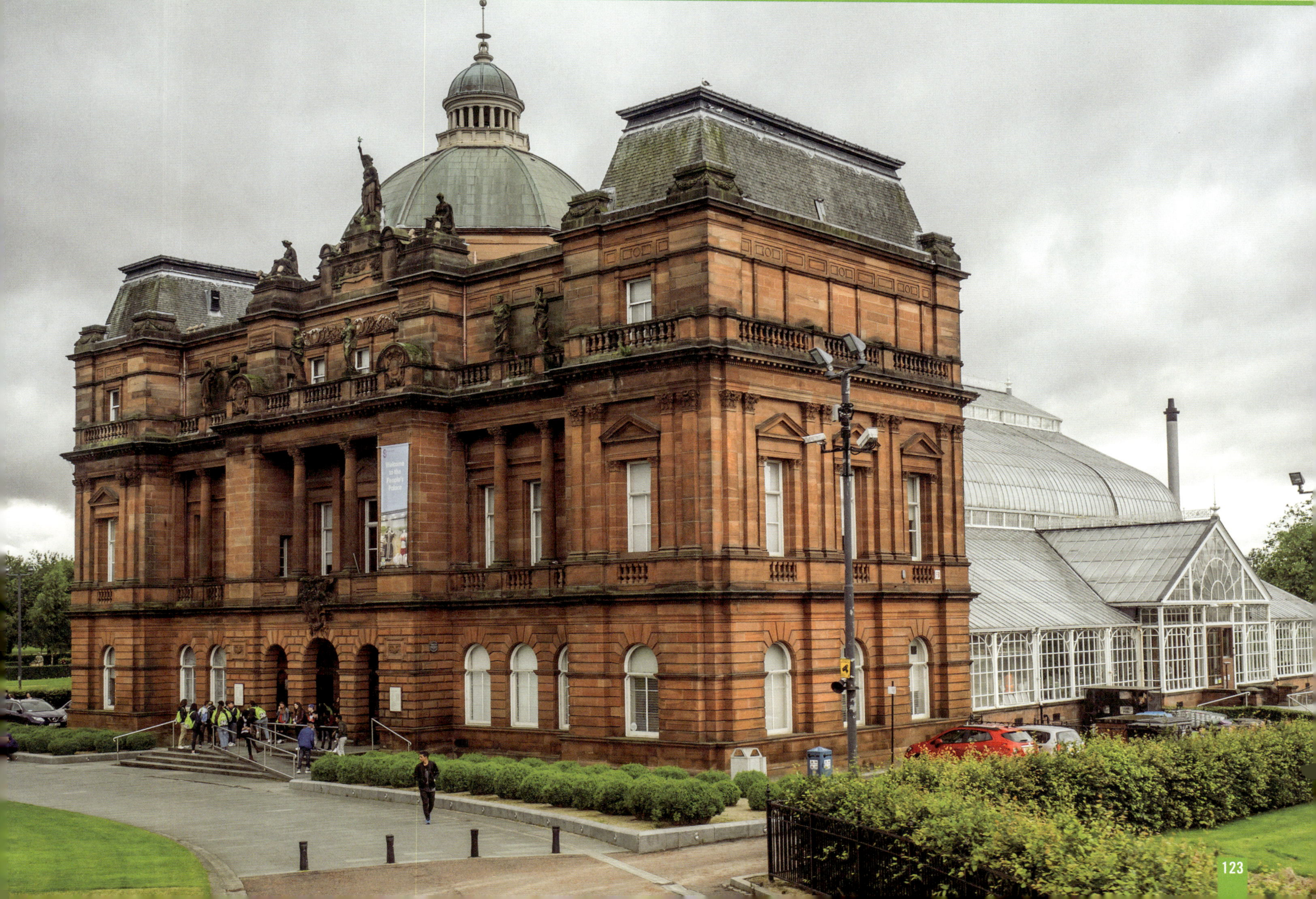

# GLASGOW

## POLLOK HOUSE AND POLLOK COUNTRY PARK

Located in Pollok Country Park, Pollok House is the Stirling Maxwell family's ancestral home and one of Scotland's best-loved tourist attractions. Built in 1752, the house is believed to have been designed by William Adam, but underwent a modernized interior redesign in 1899. Its initial structure was extended in the early 20th century and given to the City of Glasgow by Dame Anne Maxwell Macdonald in 1966, after the property had been a part of her family's estates for close to 700 years. It is now being managed by the National Trust for Scotland.

Pollok House boasts several exhibits, including an extensive private Spanish painting collection featuring works by Murillo, El Greco, and Goya, as well as masterpieces by Rubens and William Blake. Other notable pieces include antique furniture, glassware, porcelain, and silverware. Also open to touring is the house's servants' quarters.

Pollok House also offers a sprawling garden with a vast collection of rhododendron species and the 250-year-old Pollok Park Beech. The grounds also contain a series of offices, a sawmill, horse stables dating far back as the 18th century, and a stone arch bridge entrance dating back to 1757. Pollok Country Park is the largest in Glasgow and houses the Burrel Collection, a building designed and built to hold shipping magnate William Burrel's extensive antique and art collections, which he donated to the City of Glasgow upon his death. Other unique tour features of the Pollok Estate include the award-winning fold of Highland cattle and its two allotment gardens, one situated at Pollokshaws and the other near the Haggs Castle Golf Club.

## UNIVERSITY OF GLASGOW

Founded in 1451, the University of Glasgow is the fourth-oldest university in the English-speaking world. This university is in the top 1 percent of universities worldwide and has alumni that range from prime ministers to engineers to Olympic gold medalists. As with most early universities, its founding had ecclesiastical connections: its history began with a papal bull. It first classes were conducted in the Chapter House of Glasgow Cathedral before moving to nearby Rottenrow, in a building known as the "Auld Pedagogy." From its founding until about 1870, the university held classes in various locations around the city. A replacement campus was designed by Sir George Gilbert Scott in the West End in Gilmorehill. Its Main Building is the second-largest Gothic-Revival building in the UK. Remnants of the earlier Scottish Renaissance High Street building were transferred to the Gilmorehill campus, including the Lion and Unicorn Staircase, which is now attached to the Main Building. Completed in 1929, the University Chapel was constructed as a memorial to the 755 sons of the university who had lost their lives in World War I.

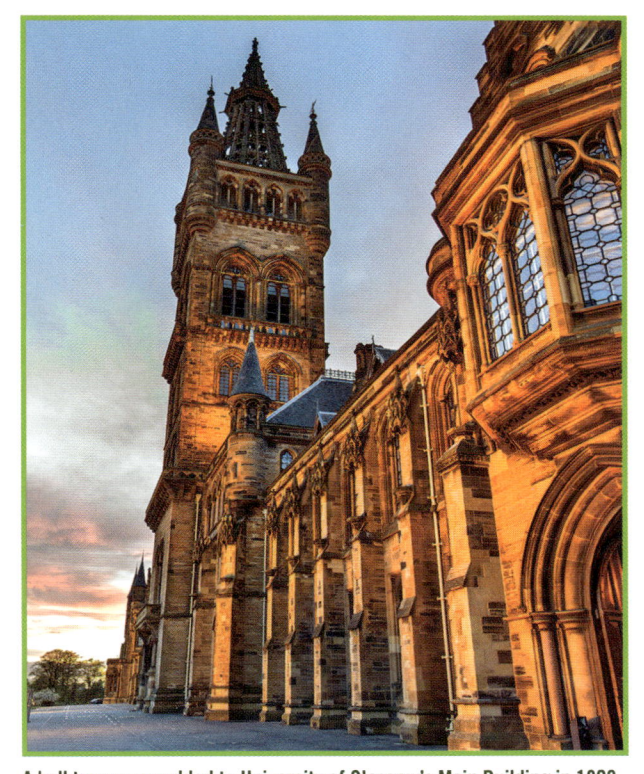

A bell tower was added to University of Glasgow's Main Building in 1893.

### OTHER TOP SITES

- **GLASGOW SCHOOL OF ART**
This is one of the foremost art schools in all of Scotland. Established in 1845, the prestigious university has produced dozens of world-famous artists, filmmakers, writers, and musicians.

- **NATIONAL PIPING CENTRE AND THE BAGPIPE MUSEUM**
The National Piping Centre is dedicated to supporting the practice and preserving the history of Scotland's iconic instrument, the bagpipe. The National Piping Centre is also home to the Bagpipe Shop, which acts as a combination gift store and professional music shop where visitors can buy everything from sheet music to accessories to genuine sets of bagpipes.

Opposite: The gate piers of Pollok House feature a set of heraldic lions designed by Huw Lorimer in 1950.

# HIGHLAND

## TOP SITES IN HIGHLAND

- Ben Nevis
- Isle of Skye
- Glen Coe
- Loch Ness and Urquhart Castle
- Cairngorms National Park
- Castle Sinclair Girnigoe
- Keiss Castle
- Duncansby Head
- Stoer Lighthouse
- Grey Cairns of Camster
- The Castle and Gardens of Mey
- Dunrobin Castle and Gardens
- Bealach Na Bà
- Dornoch Beach
- Sango Bay and Smoo Cave
- Cape Wrath
- Inverewe Garden
- Chanonry Point
- Dulsie Bridge
- Cawdor Castle
- Nairn Beach
- Fort George
- North Coast 500
- Inverness Botanic Gardens
- Eilean Donan
- Inverness Castle

Renowned for stunning, dramatic beauty, the Highlands have long drawn travelers to explore its diverse terrain. In traditional Scottish geography, the "Highlands" refers to the region northwest of the Highland Boundary Fault, which crosses mainland Scotland in a near straight line from Helensburgh in Argyll and Bute to Stonehaven in Aberdeenshire, but the area is still somewhat flexible. The Highland Council area excludes a large area of the southern and eastern Highlands and the Western Isles but includes the historic county of Caithness, which unlike the rest of the area, is generally rather flat. Caithness shares a land boundary with the historic county of Sutherland to the west and is otherwise bounded by the sea. Making up a large chunk of Scotland's northernmost peninsula, Sutherland is home to some of the most spectacular natural scenery in the whole of Europe, primarily where its western mountains meet the sea. The county stretches from the Atlantic in the west, up to the Pentland Firth, and across to the North Sea in the east. Like some other parts of the Highlands, Sutherland once experienced the Highland Clearances, a mass eviction of tenants from 18th- and 19th-century landowners to make way for large sheep farms. More than 1,000 families were evicted and resettled in coastal areas, but many chose to leave the fishing industry to settle in Canada, the United States, or Australia. Sutherland is also home to Britain's highest waterfall with a sheer drop of more than 650 feet.

Ross-shire and Cromartyshire is also part of Highland and is a large, northern region that also includes the Isle of Lewis in the Western Isles. With ample lakes, bays, and

**Top: Majestic Ben Nevis reaches into the clouds.**

The harbor at Portree, Skye's largest settlement, is lined with colorful buildings set against the island's rugged landscape.

lochs, Ross and Cromarty also features a mountainous Highland region to the west and a flatter agrarian landscape to the east, which is notably more populous.

The town of Nairn, a former fishing port and market town, is in the area that was once the historic county of Nairnshire. Nairnshire is about 22 miles long and 15 miles in breadth; it takes up an area of about 128,000 acres, which is part of the reason why Nairn's wide sandy beaches were used extensively for training preparation for the Normandy landings during World War II. Its primary industries, in addition to hospitality, include whisky distilling, tourism, and granite quarrying. Nairn is home to the Nairn International Jazz Festival, which occurs every August. Nairn also hosts the largest Highland Games festival in northern Scotland and the only synchronized swimming club in Scotland's rugged north.

Inverness is regarded as the capital of the Highlands. Once a primary stronghold of the Picts, Inverness's strong strategic potential led to a tumultuous history of battles, raids, and coups. The Gaelic king upon whom Shakespeare based his play *Macbeth* held a castle within Inverness in the 11th century. Each September, Inverness hosts the Northern Meeting for bagpipe enthusiasts and is known for the Inverness Cape, a garment intended to shield outdoor pipers from Scotland's perpetual rain.

## BEN NEVIS

Ben Nevis is called the "mountain with its head in the clouds" for good reason—it is the tallest mountain in the UK. The ancient giant was once a massive active volcano that exploded and collapsed inward on itself millions of years ago. If you reach its mist-shrouded summit, you will find evidence of an explosion in the form of light-colored granite.

The distinctive Highland cow is a common sight on Skye.

# HIGHLAND

*The towering "Old Man" is a large pinnacle in the Storr, a ridge of ancient rock on Skye's Trotternish peninsula. The Five Sisters of Kintail mountain range is also visible in the distance.*

Part of the Grampian Mountain range, it stands as king of them all, located in the northwest Highlands, near the town of Fort William. One of Scotland's top attractions, it has long drawn travelers from far and wide, whether they are serious trekkers, avid amblers, or just aficionados of stunning landscapes. Be aware, though, if you take up the challenge of walking Ben Nevis, be sure to get detailed maps, difficulty levels, and walking advice. You'll need a good amount of hill-walking experience, fitness, and navigation skills using a map and compass before attempting any Scottish mountains, especially in winter. Ben Nevis is also at the top of the Munro list, a list of Scottish mountains named after Sir Hugh T. Munro, who surveyed and cataloged them in 1891. Experienced walkers make it a challenge to complete the list, or at least "bag a Munro."

## ISLE OF SKYE

Beloved for its breathtaking scenery, Skye, the largest and northernmost of the major islands in the Inner Hebrides, is one Scotland's top tourist destinations. Picturesque Portree in the north is the largest town on Skye and is the best base for touring the island. Skye is a series of peninsulas that radiate from a mountainous hub dominated by the Cuillin hills. It is a world-class destination for walkers and climbers. The Black Cuillin include 12 Munros and provides some of the most dramatic and challenging mountain terrain in Scotland. For the truly experienced and adventurous, Sgùrr a' Ghreadaidh presents the longest rock climbs in Britain and the Inaccessible Pinnacle requires technical climbing skills to reach the summit. Sgùrr Alasdair, the tallest mountain on any Scottish island, makes for a demanding but scenic walk. The Red Hills to the east have weathered into more rounded hills, and Glamaig, the highest point of these hills, is one of only two Corbetts on Skye. Like the Munros, the Corbetts is a list of mountains that form a challenge to hill walkers. As with much of the Hebrides, the island lacks the biodiversity of the mainland, but there are still many interesting creatures for wildlife watchers to appreciate, including the white-tailed sea eagle, otters, seals, whales, dolphins, and red deer.

## GLEN COE

The otherworldly beauty of a landscape carved by icy glaciers and volcanic explosions make Glen Coe one of the most stunning places on earth. A stark contrast between its high mountain pass and the lightly wooded lower glen draws in walkers and climbers by the score. Notable climbing venues include Buachaille Etive Mòr and various routes on the Three Sisters. For adventurous, experienced hillwalkers, the Aonach Eagach offers one of the finest mainland scrambles in Scotland and boasts

## WIZARDING WORLD OF THE HIGHLANDS

Scotland, and the Highlands in particular, formed the backdrop of many scenes in the Harry Potter films. To name a few, Rannoch Moor is the place where Death Eaters board the train in *Deathly Hallows: Part 1*. A journey on the West Highland Line to Fort William will give you a view of this stunning moor. The West Highland Line will also take you over the renowned Glenfinnan Viaduct (above), a part of the Hogwarts Express route, and its image is now an iconic part of the film franchise. In *Goblet of Fire*, Harry faces down a Hungarian Horntail against the backdrop of the stunning Steall Waterfall. Glen Coe forms the backdrop of several scenes—but most will remember it for the satisfying moment when Hermione punches Draco Malfoy. Loch Eilt was used as a location in both *Prisoner of Azkaban* and *Deathly Hallows: Part 1*. Its small island of Eilean na Moine is the site of Dumbledore's final place.

*Opposite: An ancient supervolcano formed the breathtakingly beautiful landscape of Glen Coe.*

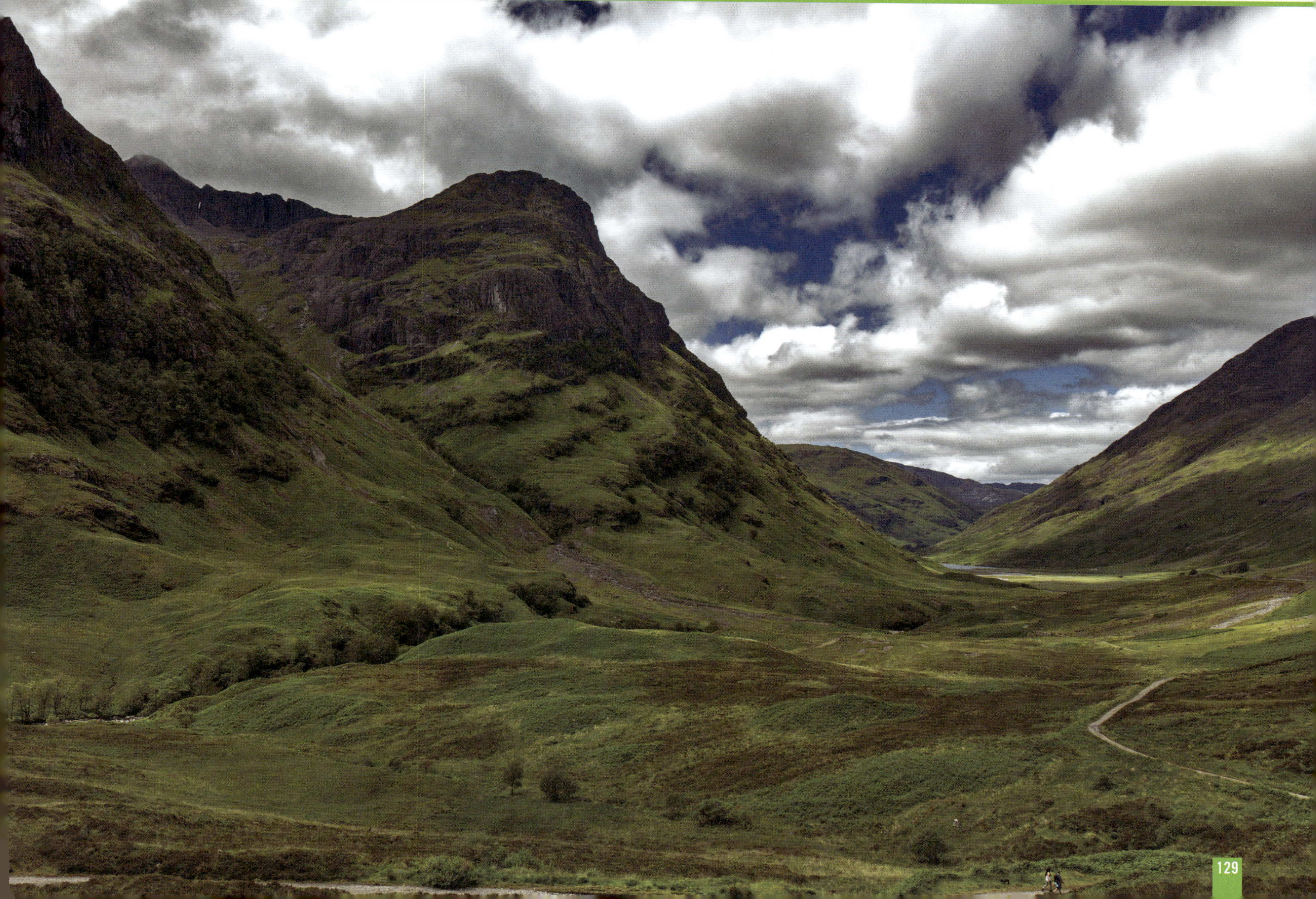

# HIGHLAND

Opposite: Castle Urquhart looks over the deep waters of Loch Ness.
Right: The Loch Ness Centre & Exhibition both explains the real history of the loch and explores the tales of its legendary monster.

two of Scotland's trickiest Munro summits, Sgorr nam Fiannaidh and Meall Dearg. Wild camping is permitted in certain areas of the Glen, but strict rules must be followed in order to protect the environment. The contrasting landscape also gives the area diverse flora and fauna; habitats within Glen Coe include birch woodland, moorland, and peatbogs, with alpine and subalpine plants in the upper parts of the glen.

## LOCH NESS AND URQUHART CASTLE

What would a visit to the Highlands be without a stop at its most famous lake? This large, deep, freshwater loch has been the source of myth and legend since sightings of the mysterious monster within in depths was first brought to the world's attention in 1933. That this great loch contains more water than all the lakes in England and Wales combined surely adds to its strange allure, but it is only the second-largest Scottish loch by surface area after Loch Lomond. It expanse is broken by just one island, Cherry Island, at the southwestern end of the loch, near Fort Augustus. For those drawn here for mystical monsters, the Loch Ness Centre & Exhibition features a hi-tech multimedia presentation that leads you through seven themed areas and 500 million years of history, natural mystery, and legend to reveal the unique environment of Loch Ness and the famous Nessie legend. The monster, however, is not the only thing to appreciate about the area. It offers excellent opportunities to explore the stunning loch region on land or water, or you can simply recharge here, soaking up the spectacular scenery.

Among the most spectacular bits of scenery on Loch Ness are the ruins of Urquhart Castle, the greatest castle in the Highlands. Once a mighty medieval stronghold, it overlooks the loch from a rocky promontory that dominates the surrounding area. A visit here allows you to hear tales of its 1,000 years of dramatic history. The site, where St Columba is said to have worked miracles in the 6th century, has witnessed some of the most dramatic chapters in Scottish history—it is where acts of chivalry and defiance provided inspiration during the Wars of Independence and where the MacDonald Lords of the Isles struggled with the Crown for power. While enjoying stunning views over

## THE LEGEND OF NESSIE

The Loch Ness Monster, affectionately known as "Nessie," has been no secret to locals since the 6th century when St Columba had the first encounter, but she shot to world renown after the *Inverness Courier* published a vivid account of an alleged sighting in 1933. With public interest piqued, others sought out their own encounters with the creature described as a "monster fish," "sea serpent," or "dragon," and when the "surgeon's photograph" of 1934 depicting a large, long-necked creature with one or more humps protruding from the water made news, interest truly skyrocketed. We now know that famous photo was a hoax, but interest in Nessie has never really waned, and much of the area's tourism pays her at least some modicum of homage.

# HIGHLAND

*The ruins of a small 14th-century castle sit on an island in Loch an Eilein, one of the numerous lakes in Cairngorms National Park.*

*Opposite: Its dramatic coastline setting is one of the many reasons tourists flock to the ruins of the once-mighty Castle Sinclair Girnigoe.*

the loch, you can get a glimpse of medieval life, climbing to the top of Grant Tower—which watches over the iconic loch—peering into a miserable prison cell said to have held the legendary Gaelic bard Domhnall Donn, and imagining the splendid banquets staged in the Great Hall. Urquhart's distinctly Highland heritage is also told through an impressive collection of artifacts left by its residents, historic replicas, including a full-sized, working trebuchet siege engine, and a short film. You can also just chill out and take in the views as you enjoy refreshments in the cafe.

## CAIRNGORMS NATIONAL PARK

The vast 1,748-square-mile Cairngorms National Park spreads out over the council areas of Highland, Aberdeenshire, Moray, Angus, and Perth and Kinross. The second of Scotland's national parks, it is also its largest, covering the Cairngorms range of mountains and surrounding hills. The spectacular Cairngorms provide a unique alpine semi-tundra moorland habitat, in which many rare plants, birds, and animals thrive, including the only herd of reindeer in the British Isles. Nine of Scotland's national nature reserves are located within the park, too, and most all of them fall within some category of special conservation. In such a large space, expect a great deal of diversity—from picturesque villages to scenic lochs, mountain, rivers, and forests, there is so much to see and do. Hillwalkers especially love the park, and walking, cycling, mountain biking, climbing, and canoing are also popular. For winter sports, three of Scotland's five ski resorts are found here. The Highland Wildlife Park also lies within the national park, and the Frank Bruce Sculpture Trail is located near Feshiebridge. Whisky connoisseurs won't be disappointed either: Dalwhinnie, Glenlivet, Tomintoul, Royal Lochnagar, Balmenach, and the Speyside all have distilleries within the park. The park's stunning landscape has also made it a favorite of filmmakers who want to capture the essence of the Highlands, with *Monarch of the Glen, The Crown, Mrs Brown,* and *Outlander* among the many shows and movies filmed here.

## CASTLE SINCLAIR GIRNIGOE

The imposing ruins of this once-mighty castle are tucked into the rocky cliffs of Caithness, at the southeastern part of Sinclair Bay, near Noss Head. Originally thought to be two distinct fortresses, Castle Sinclair Girnigoe is a complex of ruined stone structures built and modified over a 200-year period by the powerful Sinclair earls of Caithness. What was once called Girnigoe Castle dates back as early as 1470, though pieces of its structure were gradually added over time. Positioned overlooking the North Sea, the ruins are silhouetted as a crumbling, mossy tumble of ancient stone blocks perched at the very edge of a low cliff. Some features can still be made out in the ruins, such as a few windows, structural pillars, and stairways,

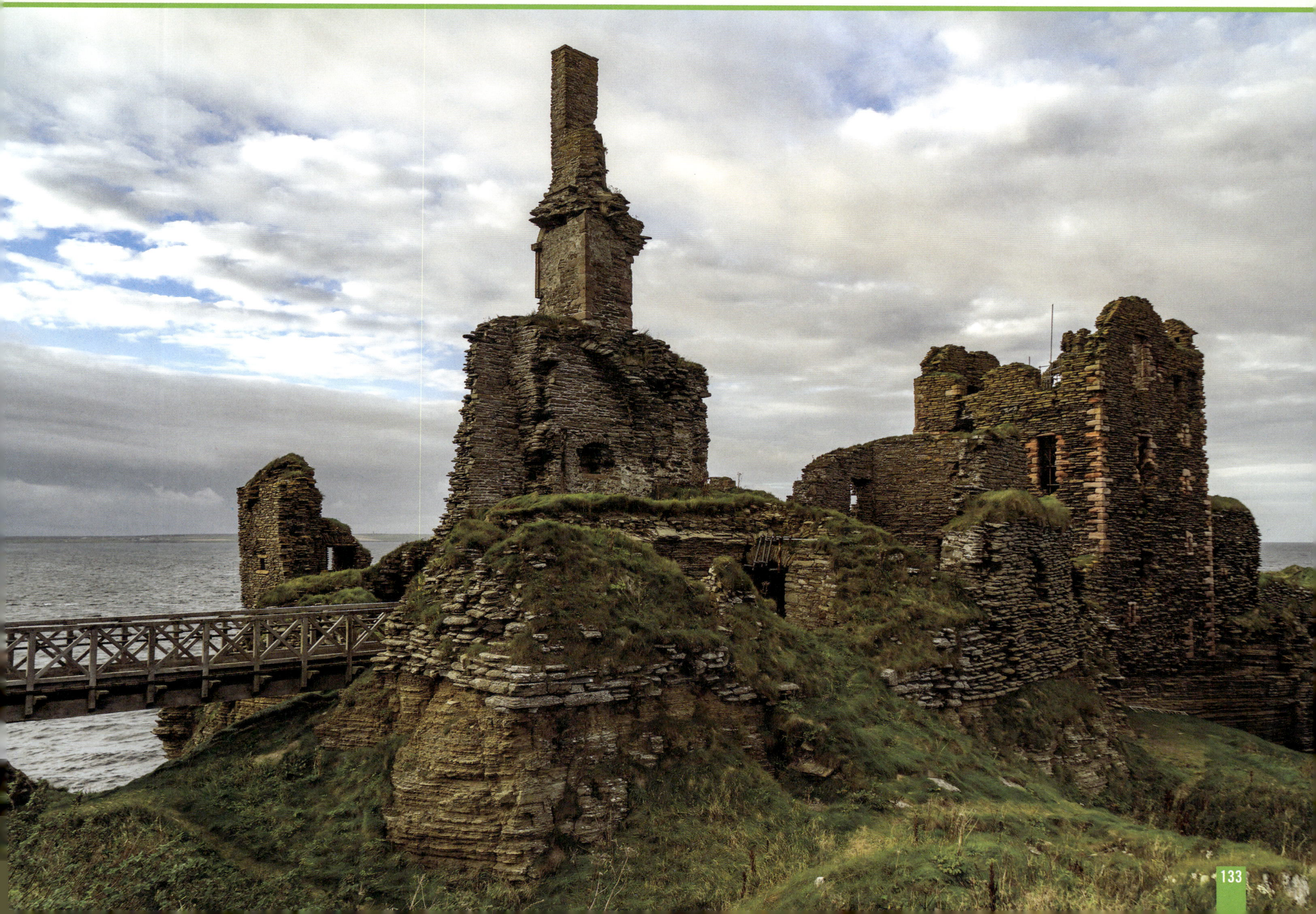

# HIGHLAND

but over the years the bulk of the castle has been reduced to rubble. The only surviving structures recognizable today are a great tower gate dating back to the 14th century, the shell of a large hall and defensive wall from the 15th century, and a tower house constructed in the 16th century.

## KEISS CASTLE

Perched precariously on the very northern tip of mainland Scotland, close to John o' Groats, the dramatic ruins of Keiss Castle overlook Sinclair Bay. Built in the late 16th to early 17th century for George Sinclair, 5th Earl of Caithness, it was one of three fortifications that controlled this territory, along with Ackergill and Girnigoe castles. When the Earl defied James VI I of England, the King dispatched his forces to raid Caithness, and all three castles surrendered without a fight. By the 18th century the castle had already fallen into disrepair. Today, due to the decaying nature of the ruins and its hazardous proximity to the sheer cliff edge, it's not possible to visit here. Still, the spectacular castle is worth a look—and maybe a few photos—from a distance.

## DUNCANSBY HEAD

Home to a lighthouse dating back to 1924, Duncansby Head offers breathtaking views of sheer oceanside cliffs, a natural arch carved by the sea, and the distinct Stacks of Duncansby. Duncansby Head Lighthouse is located in the highlands of Caithness; in fact, the lighthouse is the farthest northeast point on the island of Great Britain. Duncansby Head offers much more than just the striking views from the northern side of the area, however; a short walk over the highest point leads to the southern side of the cliffs, where an entirely different landscape opens up on the horizon. Occasionally, the northern lights can be seen from the southern side. Although the lighthouse itself is not open to the public, the surrounding area provides more than enough fascinating, beautiful scenery to spend the day exploring.

## STOER LIGHTHOUSE

This completely automatic lighthouse is located near Lochinver in Sutherland, the second-biggest fishing port in Scotland. Its stands at the edge of the Stoer Peninsula and marks the northern entrance to the Minch, a strait separating the northwest Highlands and the northern Inner Hebrides from Lewis and Harris in the Outer Hebrides. Being halfway between the village of Drumbeg and Lochinver, Stoer Lighthouse gives you the opportunity to access both the picturesque village set on beautiful lochs and the small local port where you can find many eateries, pubs, and shops. Visitors flock here year-round to fish, climb at the famous Old Man of Stoer, explore amazing waterfalls, swim, snorkel, and cycle. The lighthouse itself dates back to the 1870s, although it has been regularly refurbished and maintained over the years.

Above: Duncansby Head is the most northeasterly part of the Scottish mainland, including even the famous John o' Groats.
Below: Stoer Lighthouse stands at the edge of the dramatic cliffs on the coastline of the Stoer Peninsula.

**Opposite: The ruins of Keiss Castle look ready to tumble into the sea.**

# HIGHLAND

## GREY CAIRNS OF CAMSTER

Camster's Grey Cairns in Caithness are two of Scotland's best-protected Neolithic chambered cairns. There are two developments on the site: one round cairn with a breadth of 60 feet and another, longer cairn spanning 230 feet across. Both cairns were built roughly 5,000 years ago, during the Neolithic period, making them some of the oldest structures in Scotland. The cairns are proof of the complexity of Neolithic architecture; the burial chambers within can be accessed through narrow passages from the outside, and the structures supporting these passages have lasted for thousands of years. The cairns were excavated and restored in the late 20th century by Historic Environment Scotland and are now open to the public.

## THE CASTLE AND GARDENS OF MEY

Originally built in the 1500s, the Castle of Mey went through many hands before eventually being bought by the Queen Mother in 1952. She chose to restore the castle's physical form, but also changed its name back to Mey—at the time, it was known as Barrogill Castle. In the Castle and Gardens of Mey, you may choose to have a delicious snack in the tearoom, browse the gift shop, visit the on-site animal center, or simply stroll through the expansive grounds and lush gardens. While wandering, you can admire the magnificent scenery across the Pentland Firth to Hoy, the nearest of the Orkney islands. On a clear, sunny day, it's even possible to see the Old Man of Hoy—a natural rock formation—on the horizon. The gardens, castle, and animal center are all child-friendly, providing unique insights into the history of the estate to interest visitors of all ages.

## DUNROBIN CASTLE AND GARDENS

Dunrobin Castle is currently the most northerly of Scotland's ancient castles, and its gigantic structure and numerous rooms speak to the sense of wealth and luxury the estate was designed to convey. Between 1835 and 1850, Sir Charles Barry, the architect behind London's Houses of Parliament, remodeled the existing castle on the site for the 2nd Duke of Sutherland in the distinctive Scottish Baronial style with influences from French châteaux. This impressive stately home is set in impeccably manicured grounds and is sure to leave an impression, especially if you have a chance to tour the interior with its astounding 189 rooms. The unique historic aspects of Dunrobin Castle and Gardens, combined with the sheer architectural and natural beauty of the castle and surrounding estate, makes it a must-see site for anyone visiting Sutherland.

## BEALACH NA BÀ

The Applecross landmass in the Highlands of Scotland is home to Bealach na Bà, a twisting and precarious mountain road. The name is Scottish Gaelic for "pass of the cattle," as it was historically

**Top:** The Grey Cairns of Camster were constructed about 5,000 years ago. **Bottom:** Walkways lined with brilliantly colored blooms in the Gardens of Mey lead up to the castle that was once a holiday home for Queen Elizabeth, the Queen Mother.

**Opposite:** The extravagant expanse of the fairytale Dunrobin Castle is surrounded by formal gardens.

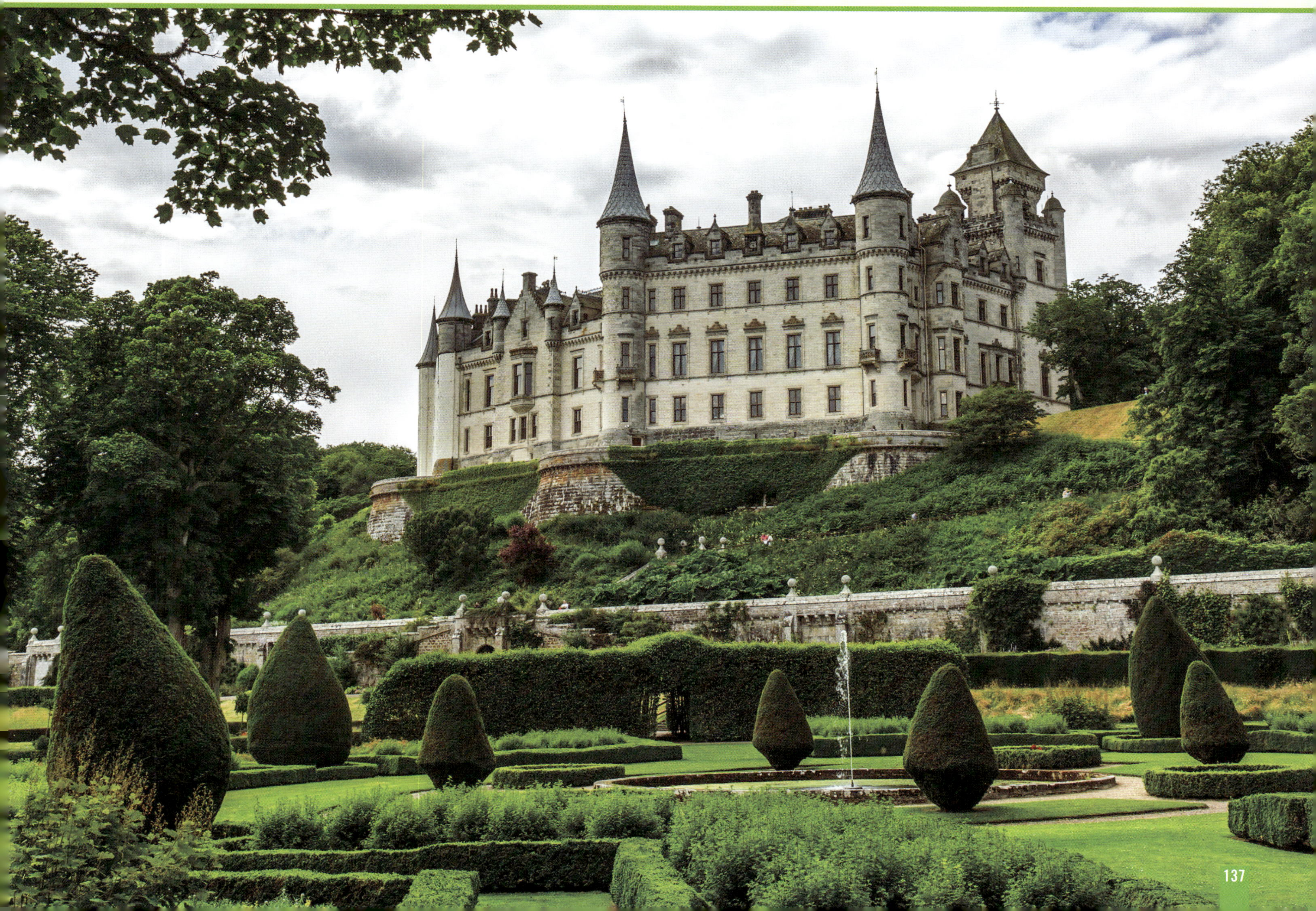

# HIGHLAND

used as a drovers' road. This winding, single-lane road is Scotland's third-most elevated, ascending more than 2,000 feet above ocean level. Described as one of the longest and toughest stretches, it is nonetheless one of the world's most beautiful scenic drives, offering breathtaking views over the hills and valleys below. The road's many sudden bends and steep inclines, as well as very limited passing opportunities, can make this a somewhat harrowing trip for inexperienced drivers. This road reaches the steepest gradient of ascension of any road in the UK, reaching a gradient of 20 percent at its sharpest incline.

## DORNOCH BEACH

Only a mile from the center of Sutherland's seaside town of Dornoch, Dornoch Beach stretches along the serene Dornoch Firth. Popular with dog walkers all year round, it is a Blue Flag beach ideal for families, with gentle shallows, sheltering dunes, and miles of golden sands. The beach runs south from the rocks at Dornoch Point, where there is a shelter on a windy day, to the mouth of the Dornoch Firth. The beach has also been named a Site of Special Scientific Interest, as many unique species of birds, plants, and other wildlife have settled along the shore. This fine beach has been given the seaside award status as a clean bathing beach and is open to the public all year round.

**Opposite: The treacherous Bealach na Bà road twists its way through the breathtaking, craggy Highlands landscape, stretching for miles with the Isle of Skye on the distant horizon.**

**Tumbled boulders and extraordinary sea stacks are part of the amazing scenery of the Sango Bay shores.**

## SANGO BAY AND SMOO CAVE

Sango Bay is one of the most stunning seashores in Highland, with its sharp bluffs, rocks, and rolling sand dunes. This beach is ideal for caravaning, and many campgrounds are available just a short walk's distance from the beach, and the views from the cliffs overlooking the beach are awe-inspiring. Surfing is also popular here, and you can rent surfboards from nearby vendors. The bay is regularly visited by geologists, as the rocks here are a part of an unusual formation called the Moine Thrust Belt.

Farther east is the dramatic and spectacular Smoo Cave, a combined sea cave and freshwater cave set into the limestone cliffs near Durness. The daring might fancy a trip into one of the area's most popular tourist sites. The entrance to the cave is in a steeply walled inlet 50 feet high and 130 feet wide and accessible only through a circular walkway, which appears quite steep and rough-surfaced in some areas and may be difficult to traverse. Once inside the cave, you arrive at a covered wooden pathway and bridge leading to a magnificent waterfall.

# HIGHLAND

## CAPE WRATH

Designated as both a Special Protection Area for Birds and a Site of Special Scientific Interest, Cape Wrath, at the tip of northwest Scotland, is a must-visit location for anyone interested in natural beauty or ocean birds. It features spectacular views, dramatic, sheer cliffs, and the Cape Wrath Lighthouse, which has been in use since 1828. On a clear day, the islands of Orkney can be seen to the northeast, while the Western Isles are visible to the southwest. The cape is cut off from the rest of the mainland by the Kyle of Durness and contains over 100 square miles of untamed moorland known as the Parph. Some parts of the Cape are also used as military training grounds by the Ministry of Defense. The cape was once populated by crofting families and shepherds, but it is essentially unpopulated today. Much of the land that was historically used for herding still serves that purpose today.

Located near Cape Wrath, Balnakeil Beach features large, white dunes and a vast expanse of pristine sand. The west-facing bay of the beach is known in particular for its unparalleled sunsets. The sand dunes that line the beach are home to a wide array of thriving wildlife; many interesting species of seabirds can be regularly spotted flying over the water or nesting in the dunes.

*Top: Windswept dunes line the pristine Balnakeil Beach not far from Cape Wrath. Middle: A mother bottlenose dolphin and her calf breach the waters off Chanonry Point. Bottom: Inverewe Gardens is home to an extensive collection of exotic plants.*

*Opposite: The Cape Wrath Lighthouse stands at the edge of cliffs in the vast and rugged wilderness of this remote corner of the Highlands.*

## INVEREWE GARDEN

The Inverewe Garden is well-known for the extraordinary and varied plants in its collection. It was established in 1862 by Ozgood Mackenzie to cultivate as many exotic plants in one place as possible. When Mackenzie died in 1922, having spent much of his life caring for and curating his collection, the garden passed to his daughter, Mairi Sawyer. Sawyer later donated the garden to the National Trust for Scotland. The garden itself covers over 50 acres of land and is home to over 2,500 species of exotic plants, and the surrounding grounds cover another 2,000 acres that are reserved for conservation and recreation activities. The garden is open year-round, and you are welcome to explore the grounds and learn about all the unique and vibrant plant life maintained there to this day.

## CHANONRY POINT

Chanonry Point is perhaps best known as one of Scotland's best places to go dolphin watching. Chanonry Point can be found on the Black Isle, roughly located between Fortrose and Rosemarkie. The Point offers stunning views across the Moray Firth to Fort George, and pods of dolphins can regularly be seen cresting the nearby waters. The chances of seeing dolphins from Chanonry Point

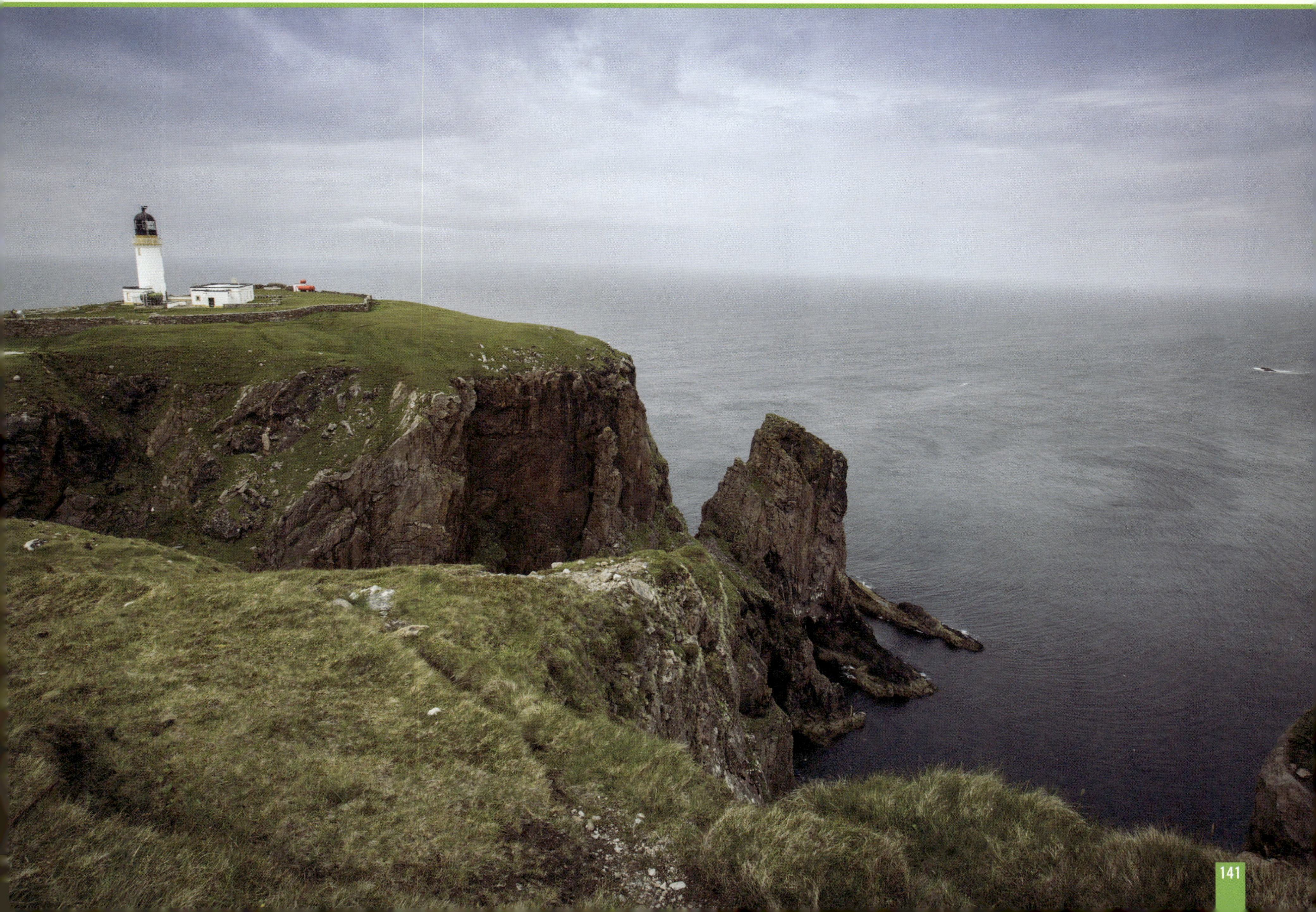

# HIGHLAND

are highest when the tide is just coming in, but many have reported seeing bottlenose dolphins in particular all throughout the year. With luck, you might also spot more elusive wildlife, such as porpoises, grey seals, and European otters. The very tip of the Point is also home to a historic lighthouse, designed in 1846 and running entirely autonomously since 1984. For travelers and campers, caravan grounds can also be found toward the northern end of the Point.

## DULSIE BRIDGE

This striking and picturesque stone bridge crosses a deep, twisting gorge carved by the River Findhorn and carries the once vitally important military road that linked Braemar to Fort George on the Moray Firth. The bridge is an integral part of the area's history, and its construction dates back to the 18th century. It is made of Ardclach granite stone, which gives the bridge both a sense of visual beauty and the physical resilience required to last several hundred years without collapsing. It is also a well-known tombstoning bridge jumping spot, as it stands about 60 feet above the summer water level. The smooth gray stone of the bridge and the dark water shining underneath give the whole scene an otherworldly, magical atmosphere; this landmark is especially beautiful during the spring and summer months. To fully appreciate the scale of the bridge, climb down to the edge of the river by following a rough path from the northern side of the bridge.

**The Dulsie Bridge spans a dramatic gorge of the River Findhorn.**

> "[Macbeth] is historically set in a place depicted by Shakespeare as brutal and violent, incredibly superstitious, and that's something that I do believe is Scottish."
>
> —JAMES MCAVOY

## CAWDOR CASTLE

This castle is perhaps best known for its common association with Shakespeare's *Macbeth* and is widely thought to be the most romantic castle in the Scottish Highlands. Built around a 15th-century tower house, Cawdor Castle is located in the borough of Cawdor on the east bank of the steep valley of Allt Dearg and is approximately 10 miles from Inverness and 5 miles from Nairn. The ancient castle housed first the Cawdor family and then passed to the Campbells in the 16th century and has been left unchanged for more than 600 years. This castle is listed as category A, and the land is included in Scotland's Inventory of Gardens and Designed Landscapes, the national listing of significant gardens. It is packed with beautiful furniture, fine portraits, intriguing artifacts, and eye-catching tapestries for visitors to admire. The castle is currently home to the Dowager Countess Cawdor, stepmother of Colin Cawdor, 7th Earl Cawdor.

**The bright gardens of Cawdor Castle create a cheerful setting that seems to repudiate the famous castle's links to the grim *Macbeth*.**

# HIGHLAND

**A cannon aims out over the walls of Fort George.**

## NAIRN BEACH
Nairn is a beautiful coastal town offshore of Scotland. You can find everything you might expect from a relaxing seaside resort here; there are two championship golf courses, a play park, a tennis court, and several charming tea houses. Hot chocolate and fish-and-chip stands are also widely available. A marina on the seashore leads onto another on the River Nairn, allowing boats to access the sea. Next to the marina can be found a collection of bars and restaurants. A bridge spans the river from the marina, leading to a vast stretch of pristine beach bordered by a vacation community. Tourists and locals alike flock to this beach every summer to surf, swim, sunbathe, and enjoy the beautiful waves and sunny weather. The climate in this region is mild most of the year round, making it a perfect summertime destination.

## FORT GEORGE
This 18th-century fortress sprawls over a level spit of land at Ardersier, which forms a promontory jutting into the Moray Firth. The site proved advantageous, as it could control the sea approach to Inverness to the northeast and had its own harbor below the walls, so that supplies could reach the fort in the event of a siege. The artillery fortification here were built in the aftermath of the 1746 defeat at the Battle of Culloden, after a nearby fort had been blown up in 1746 to prevent the Hanoverians from using it as a base. This star-shaped fortress was constructed to control the Scottish Highlands and designed to evade capture, showing admirable military engineering. It was a success, because it has never been attacked and has remained in continuous use as a garrison. It remains virtually unaltered and is open to visitors, while still serving as an army barracks. For a fascinating insight into 18th-century military life, you can explore the garrison buildings, bristling with cannons, bayoneted muskets, ammunition pouches, spikes, and heavy swords. The former Lieutenant Governors' House is home to the Highlanders' Museum, and you can also visit the regimental chapel.

**Left: The bronze *Nairn Fishwife* standing in Nairn Harbour represents the fishwives of Nairn who were important to the thriving 19th-century fishing industry. Opposite: Kylesku Bridge crosses the Loch a' Chàirn Bhàin on the North Coast 500.**

## NORTH COAST 500
This 516-mile-long road trip gives travelers stunning views of the Highlands, ranging from white sand beaches and fairytale castles to historical ruins and monumental mountains. This scenic route around the north coast of Scotland starts and ends at Inverness Castle, forming a large loop. The road, also known as the NC500, connects many features in the northern Highlands of Scotland in one touring route. The NC500 can be a controversial subject, however, as the increase in traffic has also led to some instances of harmful and dangerous driving, as well as damage to the roads and increased concerns about environmental impact.

## INVERNESS BOTANIC GARDENS
Take a break from the hustle and bustle of city life in these serene gardens. Like a green emerald in the city center, the gardens are adorned with a cascading waterfall, impressive glasshouses, and an exotic array of beautiful plants that can survive in even the harshest environments. The gardens are open to the public all year round, and whatever

CAOLAS CUMHANN

# HIGHLAND

the weather or the season, there is something for everyone—horticulturists will be inspired by the rare and beautiful specimens, families with children may explore the many hidden corners of the gardens, or you can simply take a stroll or sit and enjoy the peaceful surroundings.

## EILEAN DONAN

One of the most beautiful castles in all of Scotland, Eilean Donan stands surrounded by majestic scenery on an island at the point where three great sea lochs meet. Recognized world over as one of the country's most iconic images, this castle earns its reputation as one of the most visited and important attractions in the Highlands. Its site at the confluence of Loch Duich, Loch Long, and Loch Alsh was first inhabited as early as the 6th century, but it was not until the middle of the 13th that the first fortified castle was built here to stand guard over the lands of Kintail. Through the site's history, at least four different versions of the castle were built and re-built. After it was partially destroyed in a Jacobite uprising in 1719, Eilean Donan lay in ruins for nearly 200 years until Lieutenant Colonel John MacRae-Gilstrap bought the island in 1911 and set out to restore the castle to its former glory. His 20 years of toil and labor were rewarded when the castle was re-opened in 1932. To this day the Macrae family acts as Constables of Eilean Donan. A visit to this site lets you explore nearly every part of the castle: you can climb the steps to the Keep

**The stately Inverness Castle stands on a hill beside the River Ness.**

Door or discover the Billeting Room, which displays a fascinating collection of Macrae family and local history artifacts, along with excellent examples of Chippendale and Sheraton furniture, cannonballs fired during the bombardment of 1719, tea sets of Liverpool china, dueling pistols, and dirks. In the Banqueting Hall gaze upward to appreciate the timber ceiling beams of Douglas fir that were a gift from the Macraes of Canada.

## INVERNESS CASTLE

On a cliff overlooking the River Ness stands the red sandstone Inverness Castle on a site where a succession of castles has stood since 1057. The castellated building we see today is the work of several architects and was built in 1836. The castle's north tower is open to the public as a viewing point of the surrounding area, and you can tour the site's lovely grounds.

> # OTHER TOP SITES
>
> **· RIVER NESS**
> This river is a great nature watching site brimming with seals and seabirds, and its shores feature many of Inverness's attractions, including Whin Park and Inverness Castle. Several bridges cross the river, and you may also want to walk across to the beautiful Ness Islands, which are famous for nature walks.
>
> **· INVERNESS MUSEUM AND ART GALLERY**
> The Inverness Museum and Art Gallery includes a collection of fine arts from local artists and crafters, unique artifacts that mark the distinct history and culture of the city, and art collections that celebrate Highland life and Scottish heritage.
>
> **· PULTENEY DISTILLERY**
> Located in Wick, Caithness, this distillery dates back to 1826 and features unusually shaped pot stills designed to cultivate a more fragrant character in their malt whisky. The distillery offers tours, whisky tastings, and educational events.
>
> **· NAIRN MUSEUM**
> Since 1858, the Nairn Museum has been an excellent source of unusual objects, including art installations from the old Fishertown Museum, one of which narrates the tale of Nairn's sailors and their close-knit community, where whole families supported the fishermen at sea.
>
> **· GLENMORANGIE DISTILLERY**
> The distillery was officially founded in 1843 at the Morangie Farm, although that plot of land had already been home to previous breweries and distilleries since the 1700s. Today, this distillery is the producer of one of Scotland's most popular single-malts and has been consistently for the last several decades.
>
> **· TOMATIN DISTILLERY**
> This long-running distillery was officially established in 1897, though it is believed that whiskey has been distilled in the site as far back as the 16th century.
>
> **· STEALL WATERFALL**
> Cascading over the mountainside of Glen Nevis near Fort William is Steall Waterfall, also known as An Steall Bàn. Its single drop of 390 feet makes it is Scotland's second-highest waterfall, after Eas a' Chual Aluinn, also in Highland and the highest in the entire UK.

**Opposite:** The magnificent Eilean Donan stands on a small tidal island in the Western Highlands.

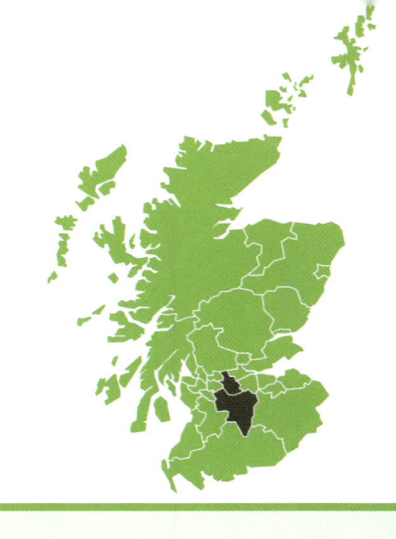

# LANARK

## TOP SITES IN LANARK

- New Lanark World Heritage
- Falls of Clyde
- Craignethan Castle
- Strathclyde Country Park
- Bothwell Castle
- Chatelherault Country Park

Located in the central lowlands of Scotland in the valley of the River Clyde, Lanark is now divided into the council areas of North Lanarkshire and South Lanarkshire. The traditional county of Lanarkshire is bounded to the north by the counties of Stirlingshire and Dunbartonshire. Historically, Lanarkshire was always divided into two administrative areas, but in the mid-18th century, it was divided again into three wards: the upper, middle, and lower wards, with their administrative centers at Lanark, Hamilton, and Glasgow, respectively, and it remained this way until 1889.

Lanark in South Lanarkshire, was historically the county town of Lanarkshire. In previous times, it had more expansive town limits, including neighboring Renfrewshire, until 1402. There are other significant settlements, such as Coatbridge, East Kilbride, Motherwell, Airdrie, Blantyre, Cambuslang, Rutherglen, Wishaw, Bellshill, Strathaven, and Carluke The county was once the site of a coal mining boom that lasted more than 100 years and brought about the creation of 13 recorded mining communities.

Today, Lanark council area ranks second only to Glasgow City in population. The region's current industry relies primarily on commercial business, but there are many traces of its storied history. Its castles include Bedlay Castle, Bothwell Castle, Calderwood Castle, Craignethan Castle, and scores more. Lanarkshire boasts two out of the six UNESCO World Heritage Sites in Scotland: New Lanark and parts of the Antonine Wall. Lanarkshire is also home to the Hamilton Mausoleum, where the unique acoustics can create an amazing 15-second echo—the longest such sound in the world.

**Top:** The ruins of the medieval Craignethan Castle stand in a beautiful setting above the River Nethen in South Lanarkshire.

Capturing a moment in time, the UNESCO World Heritage site of New Lanark is a restored 18th-century mill village.

## NEW LANARK WORLD HERITAGE

Founded in the 18th century and sited on the River Clyde less than an hour from Glasgow and Edinburgh, this remarkable mill village was transformed into a UNESCO World Heritage site that welcomes over 300,000 visitors per year and acts as a gateway to the Falls of Clyde. It is one of six UNESCO World Heritage sites in Scotland and an Anchor Point of the European Route of Industrial Heritage. Featuring historic buildings, beautiful landscapes, and more than 200 years of rich history and culture, New Lanark is a deeply valuable portion of North Lanarkshire. It offers stunning woodland walks, wildlife reserves, textile milling sightseeing, and a range of relaxation spots to make any visit worthwhile. Although the village was slow to provide essentials, such as electricity and indoor plumbing for the first half of the 20th century, much of New Lanark has now been updated to fit the modern era. An estimated 130 people live in New Lanark, and of all the residential buildings, only Mantilla Row has not yet been restored.

## FALLS OF CLYDE

This spectacular waterfall reserve in North Lanarkshire is home to four waterfalls, a 3.4-mile circular trail, over 100 bird species, and several scenic woodland walks. The four waterfalls known collectively as the Falls of Clyde include the upper falls of Bonnington Linn, Corra Linn, Dundaff Linn and the lowest Stonebyress Linn. Cora Linn is considered the largest waterfall in Great Britain. This site, formerly the Corehouse Nature Reserve, as part of the Clyde Valley Woodlands National Nature Reserve, is mixed woodland, including semi-natural native oakwoods and some areas of conifer plantation. This provides a conducive habitat for badgers, roe deer, and many species of birds. The site is well known for its resident breeding pair of peregrine falcons, protected during the breeding season by Operation Peregrine—a movement to provide security for the birds and aid the public in their birdwatching endeavors. Within the reserve, the Clyde River is a suitable habitat for otters and kingfishers, as well as the protected brook lamprey.

Lovely Corra Linn, one of the Falls of Clyde, is Great Britain's largest.

# LANARK

*The artificial Strathclyde Loch divides the Strathclyde Country Park from M&D's Scotland's Theme Park.*

inspire you as well, and hikers can take advantage of the scenic landscape of the woodland nature trail that descends from the castle.

## STRATHCLYDE COUNTRY PARK

Covering 400 hectares on the outskirts of Motherwell, this extensive country park is filled with woodland beauty and remnants of ancient history, such as the ruins of a Roman fort. It surrounds the Strathclyde Loch and affords views across the River Clyde. M&D's Scotland's Theme Park borders the park for a different kind of fun day out.

The Falls of Clyde Visitor Centre is operated by the Scottish Wildlife Trust, and it features exhibits about the waterfalls, the woodland and the area animals, as well as a unique bat display.

## CRAIGNETHAN CASTLE

Standing above the River Nethan just 2 miles west of the village of Crossford, are the ruins of Craignethan Castle. Built by the Hamilton family in the 16th century, it survives as an excellent early example of a sophisticated artillery fortification. The castle is filled with rich history and was the inspiration for Sir Walter Scott's novel *Old Mortality*. It also inspired artist J.M.W. Turner to create many sketches and drawings of the atmospheric castle. A visit to the castle can

*The former 18th-century hunting lodge of Hamilton Palace, now Chatelherault Country Park, features a parterre garden.*

## OTHER TOP SITES

- **NATIONAL MUSEUM OF RURAL LIFE**
You can experience a slice of Scotland's unique rural history at this museum in East Kilbride. It features Scotland's largest collection of farming machinery, and a short walk or tractor-trailer ride from the museum takes you to a working farm, home to Ayrshire, Aberdeen Angus, and Highland cattle, Tamworth pigs, sheep, hens and Clydesdale horses.

- **BLACK LOCH**
One of North Lanarkshire's most popular lochs, it a great place for fly fishing for trout. You can also just enjoy the stunning views across the water.

- **ST KENTIGERN'S CHURCH**
Believed to have been founded by St Kentigern himself shortly before 603 CE, it is also rumored to have once been attended by William Wallace. Although the church is now in ruins, St Kentigern's churchyard remains active; the scattering of grey tombstones adjacent to the dilapidated, roofless church building give this site an eerie atmosphere that is certainly worth a visit.

**Even in a ruined state, the remnants of grandiose Bothwell Castle are an impressive sight on extensive grounds overlooking the River Clyde.**

## BOTHWELL CASTLE

Built on a grand scale in the late 1200s, Bothwell Castle frequently passed back and forth between English and Scottish hands during the hotly fought Wars of Independence. Standing in a dramatic location by a winding curve in the River Clyde in South Lanarkshire, the castle was never completed to its original plan, stopped by such catastrophes as Edward I's great siege of 1301. It is still nonetheless one of Scotland's most impressive medieval strongholds still standing today. On a tour here you can see the unparalleled 13th-century donjon and the 14th-century chapel, an impressive remnant of the days of the Black Douglases. While there, be sure to stroll the woodland adjacent to the castle for wonderful views of over the river.

## CHATELHERAULT COUNTRY PARK

The lovely countryside of South Lanarkshire is at its best in Chatelherault Country Park. Open since 1548, it features several historical buildings, including a magnificent and well-preserved 18th-century hunting lodge and summer house. A stroll in the surrounding park offers beautiful views through ancient woodland known for its stately oaks. You can also cross the River Avon, which cuts through the park, on the landmark Dukes Bridge.

# MIDLOTHIAN

## TOP SITES IN MIDLOTHIAN

- Newbattle Abbey
- Penicuik House and Cafe
- Rosslyn Chapel
- Arniston House
- National Mining Museum of Scotland

Nestled in the southeast of Scotland's lowlands, Midlothian was once populated by ancient Britons following on the heels of the Roman occupation of Britain. Dominated by the city of Edinburgh, Midlothian once relied on industries like mining, agriculture, and fishing to support its economy—though today, due to border changes, it is landlocked and no longer relies on the ocean for its revenue. In one of its historic mining communities lies the National Mining Museum of Scotland, situated in charming Newtongrange. This attraction features a 1,625-foot shaft and a winding tower powered by the largest steam engine in Scotland. Dotting the countryside are former mining villages among its green, rolling hills, gradually climbing upward to the north from the Moorfoot Hills in the south.

**Top: Arniston House has been home to the same family for 400 years.**

Today, it is connected by the Borders Railway, which travels from Edinburgh south to Tweedbank, which is situated in the Scottish Borders. Significant remains of prehistoric forts are found on several hilltops in the historic county of Midlothian. Likewise Roman settlements have been identified at Inveresk and Cramond, which lay along what was probably the main Roman road leading northward from England. Along with the rest of the Lothian region, Midlothian was subsequently held by the Angles of Northumbria, but in the 11th century King Malcolm II of Scotland conquered the area. Later in the 15th century, Edinburgh became the capital of Scotland, and Midlothian's history from that time is essentially that of Edinburgh, and until the 20th century the county was known as Edinburghshire. Midlothian has the remains of many ecclesiastical buildings,

Once a stately home, Newbattle Abbey is now an adult college.

including the great Cistercian abbey at Newbattle and a church of the Knights Templar. There are numerous castles and country mansions built after 1400 that still survive, particularly near Edinburgh.

## NEWBATTLE ABBEY

Newbattle Abbey was formerly the grounds for a medieval Cistercian monastery near the village of Newbattle, but it is now a small adult residential college set on 125 acres of land not a long distance from Edinburgh. Newbattle Abbey was a filiation of Melrose Abbey and was situated according to Cistercian usages in a beautiful valley along the River South Esk. This hidden historical treasure also serves as a special event venue and regularly hosts workshops teaching survival skills like woodworking, weaving, foraging, and even beekeeping. Visit this unique ground to learn a valuable skill, research the local area's fascinating history, and admire the architectural finesse visible in the abbey's construction. The town of Newbattle has a robust transport system with roads, railways, and trains connecting the abbey to other counties and cities.

## PENICUIK HOUSE AND CAFE

The Penicuik House and Cafe is located 10 miles south of Edinburgh, situated on a lovingly maintained 1,000-acre stretch of land. Penicuik House is considered one of Scotland's finest examples of a Neo-Palladian mansion. This estate house was home to John Clerk's family and his descendants from 1646 until it was destroyed by a fire in 1899. Although the building was restored to an extent in 2014, it remains roofless and uninhabited. The estate surrounding the ruined house is preserved, now serving as a diversified rural business that includes farming operations, forestry, and recreation, with a special focus on promoting the conservation of similar sites. Old Penicuik House and New Penicuik House (the former stable block in which the Clerk family lived even before the fire) are both designated Category A listed buildings and are protected by Historic Environment Scotland.

The roofless Penicuik House still possesses a formidable character.

# MIDLOTHIAN

## ROSSLYN CHAPEL

The Rosslyn Chapel, formerly known as the Collegiate Chapel of St Matthew, is a 15th-century chapel located in the village of Roslin. This historic church is located just about 7 miles from Edinburgh city and was founded in 1446, but it took about 40 years to build. The chapel is distinguished by its ornate masonry and the mysterious symbols carved into the stone of the building itself. The chapel, however, has been associated with various myths and theories, some of which are yet to be confirmed or proven. Having featured in the bestselling novel *The Da Vinci Code*, Rosslyn Chapel has drawn attention from all parts of the world. Rosslyn Chapel is the third Sinclair place of worship at Roslin, the first being in Roslin Castle and the second in what is now Roslin Cemetery.

Also of interest is nearby Roslin Castle (also spelled Rosslyn). The ruined castle stands precipitously on a rocky promontory above a loop of the River North Esk. It has remained at least partially habitable ever since it was rebuilt in 1544. It was renovated in the 1980s and now serves as a holiday accommodation.

## ARNISTON HOUSE

This magnificent Palladian-style mansion house is set in acres of beautiful parkland just 11 miles from Edinburgh. Home to the Dundas family for over 400 years, you can take a guided tour of its interior, including the Portrait Room, which displays an impressive collection of paintings by Sir Henry Raeburn and Romney, the John Adam's Dining Room and Drawing Room, the atmospheric Oak Room—the oldest room in the house—and the original William Adam Library, which houses an extensive collection of ceramics. You are also encouraged to walk tranquil grounds in a lovely setting among ancient beech, lime and oak trees. The Sunken Garden gives a great view of the house's glorious south facade.

## NATIONAL MINING MUSEUM OF SCOTLAND

This 5-star tourist attraction is one of the few pristine examples of a Victorian colliery in Europe. It was, however, established in 1984 to preserve the physical remains at the surface of the sunken Lady Victoria Colliery at Newtongrange, a former mining village. Located about 8 miles from Edinburgh, the museum tells about Scotland's coal mining and exhibits the stories of the miners and their families. It also incorporates the collections of the former National Museum of Antiquities of Scotland. Also being the national collections center for Scottish archaeological finds and medieval objects, the museum contains artifacts from around the world, encompassing geology, archaeology, natural history, science, technology, art, and world cultures. About 16 new galleries were opened in 2011, including 8,000 objects, 80 percent of which were not formerly on display. The museum's library and visitor center are especially notable places to visit when taking a tour of this site.

*Above: A coal cutter stands on display at the National Mining Museum. Below: The partially ruined Roslin Castle sits just a few hundred feet from the famous Rosslyn Chapel.*

## OTHER TOP SITES

### • DALHOUSIE FALCONRY

This small family game business is set on the grounds of the 700-year-old Dalhousie Castle Hotel, and the falconry game is suitable for all ages. With about 45 birds of prey available, visitors are invited to spend a full two hours trying their hand at falcon prey hunting. The falconry is set within the grounds of the estate, and boasts of an impressive selection of birds. The Dalhousie Castle Falconry gives visitors a rare opportunity to have hands-on interactions with hawks, owls, falcons, and eagles under the expert supervision of trained falconers, an experience difficult to find anywhere else.

*Opposite: The mysterious decorations of Rosslyn Chapel have provoked much speculation.*

# MORAY

## TOP SITES IN MORAY

- Elgin Cathedral
- Brodie Castle
- Duffus Castle
- Glenfiddich Distillery
- Pluscarden Abbey

With a name derived from the Scottish Gaelic word *moireibh*, meaning "sea settlement," Moray is one of Scotland's local government council areas and lies on the scenic northeast of Scotland with a coastline on the Moray Firth. Moray has a varied landscape, extending from the high mountains of the Cairngorms in the south to the Moray Firth in the north, its width broadening on the way down. The River Spey flows through much of the area. In the middle Ages, Moray was significantly larger than today, covering much of what is now Aberdeenshire and nearby Highland, but it was gradually reduced in size after many transfers of power and leadership. The lively market town of Elgin is its capital, a town that grew up in the 13th century around the River Lossie. Here you will find much of the original medieval streets as they were centuries ago, and the busy main street opens out onto an old cobbled marketplace, and there are wynds and pends to explore. With its High Street pedestrianized is a great walking destination.

Natives here are called Moravians, and they can be proud that Moray has been voted as one of the top five rural regions in Scotland for quality of life. It is also known for its highly efficient council that is responsible for educating more than 13,000 students; Moray is home to the University of the Highlands and Islands-affiliated Moray College, as well as the famous Gordonstoun Independent boarding school. There is much to see in Moray: there are numerous distilleries to visit, as well as castles and cathedrals. One of the biggest events every year is the renowned Highland Games held at Gordon Castle in the village of Fochabers.

**Top: A participant in the 28-pound for distance competition takes his turn at the Gordon Castle Highland Games.**

*The medieval ruins of Elgin Cathedral stand tall on the banks of the River Lossie.*

## ELGIN CATHEDRAL

Also known as the "Lantern of the North," Elgin Cathedral is one of the most beautiful medieval buildings in Scotland. The cathedral was built around the 13th century, and although it is a ruin today, what is left of the architectural structure and the nearby grounds shows that it must have once been an impressive monument. A large wall, built to massive proportions, surrounds the cathedral; it was built to protect it, but only a small section has survived the ravages of time and the fires of 1270 and 1390. What still remains has been preserved through years of excavation and renovation. One of the major features of this site is the effigy of Bishop Archibald, as well as an impressive collection of medieval stones carved with intricate images of plants and animals.

## BRODIE CASTLE

This 16th-century castle with its Z-plan tower was the official home of the Brodie clan for over 400 years, and it is located at the west of Forres. The castle has an impregnable guard chamber and features one of Scotland's finest collections of furniture, ceramics, and artwork. In the collection are several works created by 17th-century Dutch masters, as well as a number of works attributed to notable 20th-century Scottish colorists. The building sits on a 71-hectare estate, and adding to the beauty of the setting are an adventure playground, wildlife reserve, walled garden, and a Pictish monument. The castle also has a very well-preserved 16th-century keep with five-story towers on opposing corners. The interior is also expertly preserved, right down to the original furniture.

## DUFFUS CASTLE

Standing in open countryside 1.5 miles southeast of Duffus, is Duffus Castle, a superbly preserved example of a motte-and-bailey. The first structure on the site was a wooden motte-and-bailey protected by a wooden palisade built some time before 1150 by Hugh de Freskyn, who wanted a stronghold on the lands he had recently been

*Springtime daffodils dot the field in front of Brodie Castle.*

# MORAY

Surrounded by gardens, the Glenfiddich Whisky Distillery makes for a picturesque sight in Dufftown, known as the "malt whisky capital."

## WHISKIES OF MORAY

Moray has more than its fair share of distilleries, including the world-famous Glenfiddich Distillery. Aberlour Distillery offers an interesting twist on the classic whisky tasting experience by giving you a chance to try a blind taste test. Located on the banks of the River Lossie in Elgin, the Glen Moray Distillery was established in 1897. It is a Speyside distillery that produces single-malt scotch whisky. A tour of this legendary distillery is worth the trip; it has been featured in the Scotland Malt whisky trail, a tourism initiative featuring seven working Speyside distilleries, including Glen Moray, Dallas Dhu Distillery, which is now a museum, and the Speyside Cooperage. In Rothes, you will find the very attractive Glen Grant Distillery (above). Other Moray distilleries include the extremely pretty Strathisla Distillery and the distilleries of Balvenie, Cragganmore, Cardhu, Glenfarclas, and Benromach.

granted from David I. The king actually stayed in this first iteration of the castle while arranging for the building of nearby Kinloss Abbey. The castle changed hands more than once, and at some point in the 1300s the wooden castle was rebuilt in stone. By the turn of the 18th century, it was in the possession of James Sutherland, 2nd Lord Duffus; in 1705, at his death, the family abandoned it. Today you can visit the ruins—large parts of the tower and curtain walls remain, as does the stone bridge over the ditch on that side.

### GLENFIDDICH DISTILLERY

*Glenfiddich* in Scottish Gaelic means "valley of the deer," which is why the Glenfiddich logo is a stag. This world-famous distillery was established in the glen of the River Fiddich in 1886 by William Grant, and today it accounts for an incredible 35 percent of all single malt sales throughout the world. The story behind this establishment by W. Grant and Sons is fascinating, and learning about the history of this prestigious distillery is reason enough to visit. With its reputation as the world's bestselling single-malt whisky, Glenfiddich Distillery lives up to its name. Visitors can relax in the whisky lounge on-site, partake in a whisky tasting, and follow along on the Spirit of Innovation Tour, learning how the world's most beloved whiskies are created.

### PLUSCARDEN ABBEY

Some 6 miles southwest of Elgin stands Pluscarden Abbey tucked into the tranquil, sheltered valley of the Black Burn. Pluscarden's story in one of abandonment after the Reformation in 1560, followed by a 20th-century restoration into a working church. Founded by Alexander II in 1230, by 1345, Pluscarden came under the control of the Bishop of Moray from his seat in Elgin Cathedral. A falling out with Alexander Stewart, the younger son of Robert II known as the "Wolf of Badenoch," resulted in Alexander and an armed band of Highlanders burning down Elgin Cathedral, much of the towns of Elgin and Forres, and Pluscarden Priory. Although initially repaired, by 1454 it was again in a state of disrepair. By 1897 the nave of the priory church had been removed and the transepts and choir were roofless. That year, however, John Crichton-Stuart, 3rd Marquess of Bute, began restoring the priory. The first mass was held in the roofless church in 1948, and in 1954 the tower was re-roofed. Since then restoration of Pluscarden Abbey has continued. You can visit today to view the splendid transepts and crossing and chapels in part of the choir, although much of the rest of the abbey is reserved for the use of the monks and guests on retreat.

Above: Duffus Castle is an excellent example of the motte-and-bailey style of fortress. Left: From roofless ruins to a welcoming sanctuary, Pluscarden Abbey has undergone a cycle of neglect and restoration.

## OTHER TOP SITES

- **DUFFTOWN WHISKY MUSEUM**

In a region with so many distilleries, it is natural that a museum devoted to the beverage exists. This specialty museum provides a unique opportunity to discover the secrets of whisky making in days gone by. It also gives a fascinating insight into the lives and times of whisky smugglers. Many of the exhibits were provided by local distillers and HM Custom and Excise.

# ORKNEY

## TOP SITES IN ORKNEY

- Old Man Of Hoy
- Ring of Brodgar
- Skara Brae
- Standing Stones of Stenness
- Scapa Flow
- The Italian Chapel
- St Magnus Cathedral
- Marwick Head

Located off the northernmost tip of Scotland, Orkney is an archipelago in the Northern Isles of Scotland. It is now one of the 32 council areas of Scotland. Orkney is also referred to as the Orkney Islands; out of roughly 70 islands, 20 are inhabited. Of these 20, Mainland is Orkney's largest and is home to Kirkwall, the region's main settlement and administrative center. In addition to Mainland, most of the remaining islands are divided into two groups: the North Isles and the South Isles.

Originally inhabited by Mesolithic, then Neolithic tribes and later the Picts, evidence of these early natives can be seen at the Heart of Neolithic Orkney, a UNESCO World Heritage Site on Mainland, This group of 5,000-year-old sites consists of the ancient settlement of Skara Brae, the chambered cairn and passage grave Maeshowe, and two ceremonial stone circles. Orkney was eventually annexed in 875 CE by Norway and settled by the Norse. In 1492 it was absorbed into the Kingdom of Scotland.

The climate is cool temperate and relatively mild, with soil that is extremely fertile. Most of the land is farmed, and agriculture is one of Orkney's primary sources of revenue. Significant wind and marine energy resources are also of growing importance. In fact, the amount of electricity generated annually by the Orkney from renewable energy sources exceeds its demand.

Orkney can be extraordinary, and it was named the best place to live in Scotland in 2013 and 2014 and was named the best place to live in the UK as a whole in 2019. Folks hailing from Orkney are referred to as Orcadians, and they speak a unique dialect of the Scots language.

**Top: The sun sets between the Standing Stones of Stenness.**

Boats dock in the harbor of Kirkwall, the ancient capital of Orkney.

## OLD MAN OF HOY

The coastline of Scotland it dotted with a peculiar kind of sea stack rock formation, often called an "old man" for the silhouette. The Old Man of Hoy, one of the UK's tallest sea stacks, is surely one of the most memorable. Standing 450 feet and surrounded by the high and dramatic sea cliffs at St John's Head off the island of Hoy, it is a destination for hardcore climbers. This red sandstone stack was first scaled in 1966, and since then many have made the ascent, including eight-year-old Edward Mills, who became the youngest to reach the top, when he made the climb to help raise money for the charity Climbers Against Cancer in 2018. The Old Man can be appreciated by non-climbers, too, just for the sheer beauty of this spectacular landmark.

## RING OF BRODGAR

This iconic symbol of Orkney's rich prehistoric past, the Ring of Brodgar is found in the West Mainland parish of Stenness standing on an eastward-sloping plateau on the Ness of Brodgar—a thin strip of land separating the Harray and Stenness lochs. The concentration of monuments in the area surrounding the Ness of Brodgar hints at the importance the area had for the ceremonies of the Neolithic people of Orkney, and, accordingly, the Ring is a UNESCO Heart of Neolithic Orkney World Heritage Site. The site has never been fully excavated or scientifically dated, so the monument's actual age remains uncertain. The best estimates assume it was erected between 2500 and 2000 BCE, making it the last of the great Neolithic monuments built on the Ness. The stone ring was built in a true circle, about 340 feet wide, covering an area of 90,790 square feet, and is the third-largest stone circle in the British Isles. Today, only 27 of the estimated 60 stones remain. According to legend, it was a religious shrine and possibly a place of ritual, while others believe the ring was built for the astronomical observation of the equinox and solstice. Whatever its original purpose, the Ring, set in a natural amphitheater of hills surrounded by a ditch, still exudes an aura of magic.

The Old Man of Hoy is one of Scotland's most famous sea stacks.

# ORKNEY

Opposite: The Ring of Brodgar is one of the most-photographed attractions in Orkney, particularly at sunset.

Nearby, you can also view another Heart of Neolithic Orkney site, Maeshowe. This design masterpiece is praised as one of Western Europe's finest burial chambers. Concealed within the grassy mound is an enormous 5,000-year-old cairn that displays superlative masonry and craftsmanship. Massive standing stones are also found within the main chamber, where you will see graffiti left by 12th-century Viking tomb raiders. Other Neolithic sites nearby include the solitary Comet Stone and the Barnhouse settlement, an excavated group of house dwellings dating from 3300 to 2600 BCE.

## SKARA BRAE

One of the top destinations in all of Scotland, Skara Brae is part of the Heart of Neolithic Orkney World Heritage Site. First uncovered by a storm in 1850, Skara Brae was a thriving village about 5,000 years ago. Once the site was discovered, it was excavated, renovated, and made available to the public. It is now the best-preserved Neolithic settlement in Western Europe. Skara Brae, which was primarily a fishing and farming village, is situated on the Bay of Skaill on the west coast of Mainland, where the environment is harsh and the weather can be brutal, resulting in a barren landscape practically devoid of trees. Because wood is scarce, people who lived there during the Neolithic period had to construct their houses out of granite slabs within depressions in the earth. A visit here takes you through a replica Neolithic house to see how its full interior might have looked—including "fitted" furniture, such as stone "dressers" and box beds—and allow you to imagine life for the farmers, hunters, and fisherfolk who lived in the village. From here, you can follow a path that overlooks nine surviving Neolithic houses, all but one of which can be viewed from the path. The site also allows you to take in the stunning variety of local bird life and wildflowers. There is also an on-site visitors center, which displays artifacts found in the village, such as gaming dice, tools, and jewelry.

The stone-built Neolithic settlement of Skara Brae looks out over the Bay of Skaill.

## STANDING STONES OF STENNESS

Another key Heart of Neolithic Orkney site is the impressive Standing Stones of Stenness, which is connected to the nearby Ring of Brodgar World Heritage site by a short bridge. Situated at the beginning of the Ness of Brodgar, these magnificent

# ORKNEY

megaliths measure nearly 20 feet tall and once stood as a ring of 12 that circled a large lone hearth. It is postulated that they were erected about 5,000 years ago as an ancient and possibly sacred ceremonial ground and might be the earliest henge monument in the British Isles. As with all of these ancient monuments, the real purpose of these stones is shrouded in mystery.

## SCAPA FLOW

With its waters sheltered by the islands of Mainland, Graemsay, Burray, South Ronaldsay, and Hoy, Scapa Flow has played an important role in travel, trade, and conflict throughout the centuries. Vikings anchored their longships here more than 1,000 years ago, and its position made it the perfect spot for the UK's chief naval base during World War I and II. Since the scuttling of the German fleet after World War I, its wrecks and their marine habitats form an internationally acclaimed wreck-diving site and an area of great natural, archaeological, and cultural interest. Military history buffs will know it, however, as the target of one of the first bombing attacks on Britain during World War II and site of the sinking of HMS *Royal Oak* by a German U-boat just three days earlier. In defense after these attacks, the so-called Churchill Barriers were created. The Churchill Barriers span a total of 1.5 miles running from Ronaldsay in the south and then passing through Burray, Lamb Holm, and Glimpse Holm. The A961 roadway currently runs along with the dams, linking Kirkwall with Barwick on South Ronaldsay Island. The bases of the barriers were made from gabions enclosing 250,000 tons of broken rock carried from remote quarries to Orkney. A project of this size takes a great amount of labor force, which was provided by 1,300 Italian prisoners of war who were captured and taken to Orkney in early 1942.

## THE ITALIAN CHAPEL

One of the most beloved tourist sites in Orkney is the delightful Italian Chapel on the uninhabited island of Lamb Holm. Built by the Italian prisoners of war shipped to Orkney during WWII to construct the Churchill Barriers, the chapel is a symbol of hope and faith, even in a time of war. It began life when the camp priest agreed that two Nissen huts could be joined to form a chapel. Among the prisoners in the camp was artist Domenico Chiocchetti, and he, along with a blacksmith and a cement worker, transformed the utilitarian huts into a work of art. Chiocchetti based the altar painting on an image of the Madonna and Child by Nicolo Barabino that was on a pray card he always kept with him.

## ST MAGNUS CATHEDRAL

This towering cathedral is a landmark in the skyline of Kirkwall. It was founded by the Viking Earl of Roegenwald in 1137 in honor of his uncle Saint Magnus. From the outside of the "Northern

*Top: A boat intentionally sunk to protect the natural harbor of Scapa Flow was part of the World War II defensive line known as the Churchill Barriers. Bottom: Richly colored paintings decorate the Italian Chapel, which was built by Italian prisoners of war during the construction of the Churchill Barriers on the east side of Scapa Flow.*

*Opposite: Weathered headstones fill the churchyard of St Magnus Cathedral.*

165

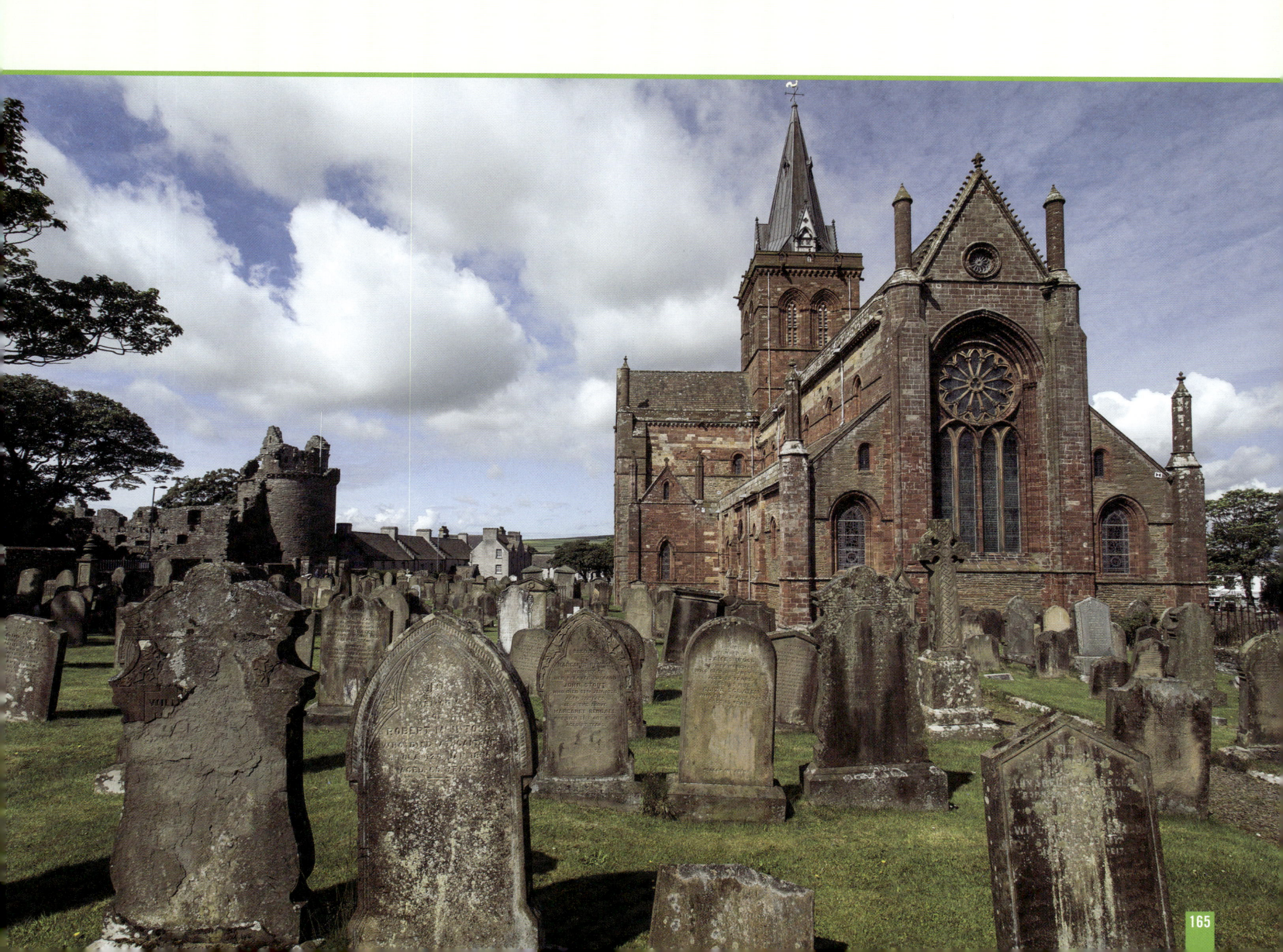

# ORKNEY

Light," as the cathedral is known, you can admire the building's beautiful sandstone construction. Centuries of weathering have given the edifice's facade a charm rarely found in other cathedrals. St Magnus is the most northerly cathedral in the United Kingdom and an exceptional example of Romanesque architecture. Inside, there are signs of the Viking Age Stone Manson, a medieval dungeon, and a bell from the HMS *Royal Oak,* which was sunk by the Germans during World War II. The cathedral also contains memorials to prominent Orcadians, including explorers William Balfour Baikie and Dr. John Rae, writers like Eric Linklater, George Mackay Brown, and Edwin Muir, artists like Stanley Crusitier, and psychiatrist Sir Thomas Clouston. The cathedral still hosts weekly services, weddings, and funerals.

## MARWICK HEAD

One of the finest coastal locations in Orkney, with stunning scenery and soaring cliffs, Marwick in West Mainland is destination not to be missed. This huge headland is part of a spectacular stretch of coastline, snaking down as far as Stromness, and brings together nature, wildlife, history, and breathtaking sea views. On a clear day you'll be able to see the Old Man of Hoy in the distance. As the site of RSPB Scotland Marwick Head nature reserve, which is the largest cliff-nesting seabird colony on the Orkney mainland, this is a birder's haven. Up to 25,000 seabirds come here to nest

**A fulmar hovers at a sea cliff at Marwick Head.**

during the summer, including puffins, fulmars, kittiwakes, and razorbills, and lucky bird-watchers might get a glimpse of Arctic skuas and red-throated divers.

For history buffs, there is the Kitchener Memorial, built in 1926 to commemorate World War I Minister for War, Lord Kitchener. Kitchener, along with 736 other died aboard HMS *Hampshire* in 1916 when the ship hit a mine just a few miles offshore from Marwick Head. A newer memorial wall is also there, built to fully commemorate the crew of HMS *Hampshire,* as well as those who lost their lives on board the *Laurel Crown* while mine-sweeping in the Marwick Head area the same year.

# OTHER TOP SITES

- **KNAP OF HOWAR**

If you can't get enough of Orkney's Neolithic heritage, you can travel north to the island of Papa Westray to view the Knap of Howar, the oldest standing stone buildings in all of northwest Europe. The site features remains of two well-preserved houses that still contain their original stone cupboards and stalls.

- **EDAY ISLAND**

A visit to this island allows you to visit the Setter's Stone and the monoliths of Vinquoy, Braeside, and Huntersquoy, as well as the 17th-century Carrick House. The island is also notable as the home to many seabirds.

- **ORKNEY MUSEUM**

Opened as a museum in 1968, the Orkney Museum is located in Kirkwall on Mainland. Starting with ancient periods, the museum chronicles the narrative of the Orkney Islands through the ages, from each stage of civilization to another, right through to the present day. There are displays on Neolithic Orkney, Pictish times, Viking times, and the Middle Ages. The Class I Stone of Picts Knowe of Burian, the finds of a Viking boat grave in Scar (Sanday) with a scar plate made of whalebone, and a wooden box containing the bones of Saint Magnus are among the highlights of its collection. This collection is of international relevance, and the museum hosts a constantly changing temporary exhibition program. The Orkney Museum used to be known as the Tankerness House and was the home of the Baikie family.

- **HIGHLAND PARK DISTILLERY**

With headquarters in Kirkwall, Highland Park is Scotland's most northerly whisky distillery and in fact one of the world's most northerly distilleries. It was founded by Magnus Eunson, a butcher and church official who had a very different personality and side job at night. In 1798, he was caught illegally drinking whisky on-site, and then in 1826, almost 30 years later, this distillery received an official license to distill whisky.

- **SANDS OF WRIGHT**

This hidden gem on South Ronaldsay is a gorgeous stretch of golden sand that is perfect for a scenic stroll. The area is rich in several varieties of seaweed and in the spring and summer blossoms with wildflowers.

**Opposite: The Kitchener Memorial stands atop the stark cliffs at Marwick Head.**

# PERTH AND KINROSS

## TOP SITES IN PERTH AND KINROSS

- Black Watch Castle and Museum
- Kinnoull Hill Park
- Scone Palace
- Lochleven Castle
- RSPB Loch Leven Nature Reserve
- Elcho Castle
- Blair Athol Distillery
- Birks of Aberfeldy
- Falls of Bruar
- Blair Castle and Hercules Garden

Geographically split by the Highland Boundary Fault into a more mountainous northern part and a flatter southern part, the council area of Perth and Kinross combines Scotland's smallest historic county, Kinross-shire, with Perth. Nestled in central Scotland, the old boundary of Kinross-shire boasts the massive Loch Leven, which holds two islands within its waters as well as a spectacular nature reserve. On one of the islands rests a castle where Mary, Queen of Scots, was once held prisoner in 1567 after the end of her remarkable reign. This part of Perth and Kinross has rich, fertile agricultural land, which has played a significant role in its industry. Though historically it was a relatively impoverished region, it became more prosperous with the advent of more advanced farming practices in the 19th century. Today, tourism contributes a fair amount of its revenue as well, with visitors attracted by the unspoiled country villages and gently rolling hills that spread to the shores of Loch Leven. The villages of Kinnesswood and Scotlandwell are especially beautiful, and there are several ancient standing stones to be seen at Orwell.

The historic county of Perth gradually extends from Strathmore in the east, the Drumochter in the north, and Rannoch Moor, and Ben Lui in the west. Upon the banks of the River Tay lies the city Perth, a name with origins reaching back to the Pictish word for "wood" or "copse." Perth has been associated with the moniker the "Fair City" in reference to Sir Walter Scott's novel *The Fair Maid of Perth*; it has also been called "St John's Toun" or "Saint Johnstoun" due to the principal

Top: Equestrians line up with their mounts on the grounds of Blair Castle, which hosts a yearly country fair with horse trials.

**Kinnoull Hill Tower, a castellated folly, stands at the extreme edge of Kinnoull Hill overlooking the River Tay.**

church's dedication to St John the Baptist. Perth has been occupied since Mesolithic hunter-gatherers first roamed its lands and on through the Neolithic age. At one time, Perth was regarded as the "capital" of Scotland due to the frequency with which members of the royal court visited the county. Over the years, Perth became one of the richest counties in Scotland and engaged with the trading of luxury goods with France, Spain, the Netherlands, and the Baltic countries.

## BLACK WATCH CASTLE AND MUSEUM

The Black Watch Castle and Museum is housed in Balhousie Castle in Perth, which dates back to 1631. The site has its origins in a stone castle built here in the 1100s that in 1631 George Hay, 1st Earl of Kinnoull developed into an L-plan tower house overlooking the North Inch. Having fallen into disarray in the early 19th century, the castle was "restored" and extensively remodeled on a larger scale in from 1862 to 1864 in the Scottish Baronial style. The building you see today largely dates back to that major redevelopment. The castle served several purposes over the years, until the army took over in 1940 and has remained ever since. The castle has been home to the Regimental Museum of the Black Watch since the 1960s. There was no notable change until the Regimental Trustees of the Black Watch bought Balhousie Castle in 2009 and oversaw the addition of a large annex that is home to the visitor reception, the shop, and an excellent cafe. During the refurbishment the museum was brought up to the very best modern standards of lighting, display, and design. Detailing the history of the Regiment from 1739 to the present, the museum's collections are divided between 13 galleries, most of which are organized chronologically from "The Early Years" to "The French Wars" and "Empire." The World War I displays are especially poignant, offering a sobering experience that remind us that between 1914 and 1918 some 50,000 officers

**At the Black Watch Castle and Museum, a cascade of thousands of ceramic poppies flowed from a second-floor turret window across the castle grounds in remembrance of those lost in World War I.**

169

# PERTH AND KINROSS

Above: Deer graze near the chapel on the grounds of Scone Palace. Below: Light snow dusts the Loch Leven Heritage Trail as it meanders between tall Scots pine trees.

and men served in the Black Watch Regiment and 8,000 of them were killed and a further 20,000 were wounded. You then move on to World War II and the post-war era, before arriving at the final galleries that examine the life of a modern member of the Black Watch. Each gallery features remarkable artifacts representing the era, such as medals, weapons, personal objects, maps, pictures, and sculptures.

## KINNOULL HILL PARK

Kinnoull Hill Woodland Park, located to the east of Perth, is actually home to five hills—Corsiehill, Deuchny Hill, Barn Hill, Binn Hill, and Kinnoull Hill, the tallest. This landmark shares a border with Perth's River Tay and has been named a Site of Special Scientific Interest. Opened in 1991, it was the first official woodland park of Scotland, and now attracts countless hikers, birdwatchers, tourists, and horticulturists who travel its windings trails and take note of the thriving local flora and fauna. Roe deer and red squirrels can be found throughout the park. The many paths that meander through the park are marked according to difficulty, making Kinnoull Hill Park a perfect destination for hikers of all levels of ability. The northernmost slopes of the park are relatively gentle. For those not wishing to hike, the car park attached to the grounds actually offers some lovely, scenic views of Perth and the River Tay, along with the whimsical Kinnoull Tower.

## SCONE PALACE

Few places of interest in Scotland are as historically potent as Scone Palace. Most famously, it was an important religious gathering place of the Picts, it was the site of an early Christian church, and it housed the Stone of Destiny. In the intervening centuries, it has been the seat of parliaments and the crowning place of the kings of Scots, including Macbeth and Robert the Bruce. The Stone of Destiny—also known as the Stone of Scone—was used in the coronations of the kings of Scots until it was captured by Edward I in 1296 as spoils of war and taken to Westminster Abbey. It was fitted into a wooden chair, known as King Edward's Chair, on which most subsequent English sovereigns, including Elizabeth II, have been crowned. That this ancient symbol of Scotland's monarchy remained in English possession never sat well with the Scots, and on Christmas Day 1950, four Scottish students removed the stone from Westminster Abbey; three months later it turned up 500 miles away at the high altar of Arbroath Abbey. In 1996, the stone was officially returned to Scotland.

Set in the village of Scone, the red sandstone palace features a castellated roof and is a typical example of the Gothic-Revival style of architecture. The present palace is said to stand on the site of an Augustinian priory built where the early Christian church stood; when its abbey was

**Opposite:** Scone Palace was once the home of the Stone of Destiny.

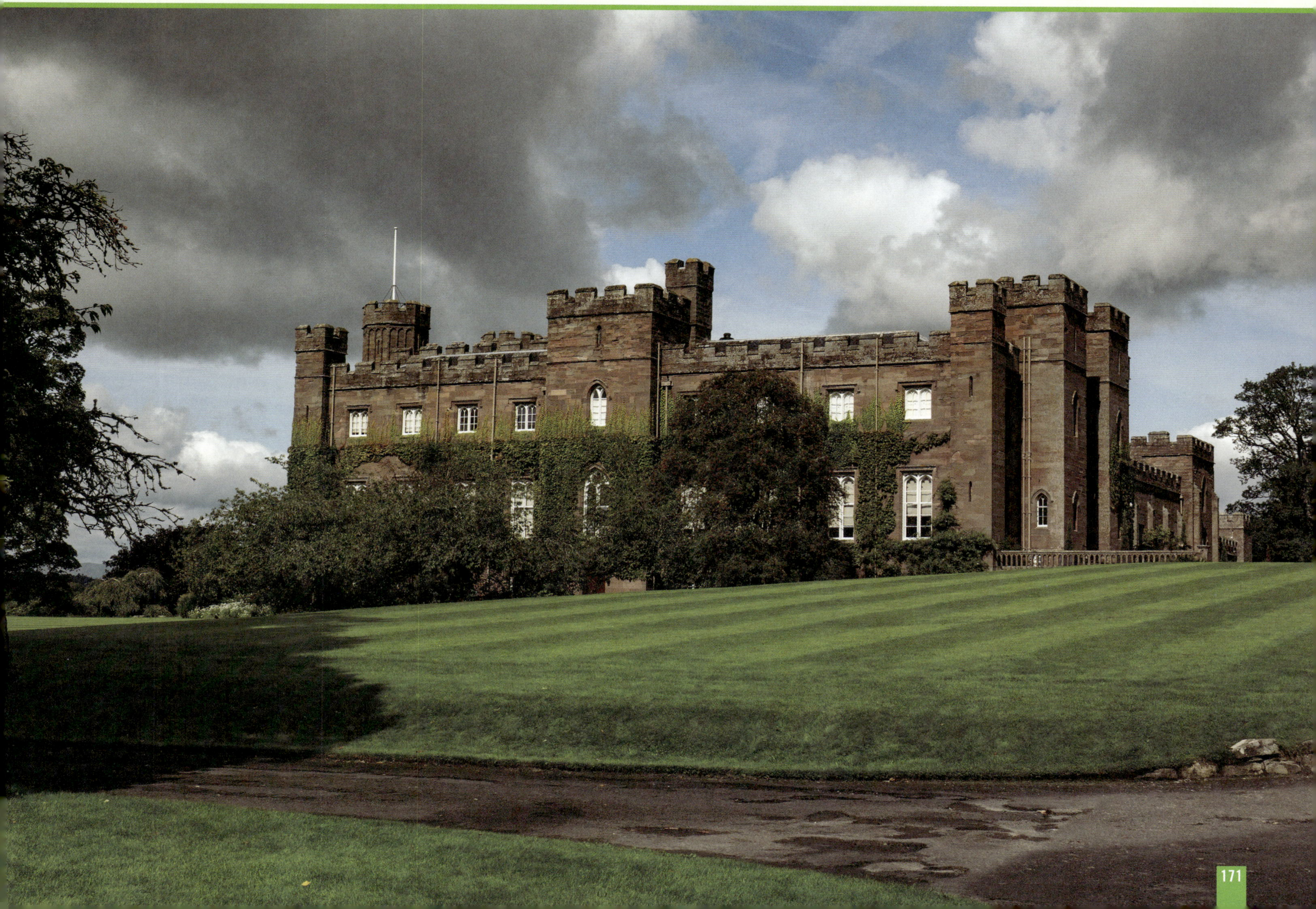

# PERTH AND KINROSS

seriously damaged in 1559 during the Scottish Reformation, the core structure survived and was restored. The palace now houses an outstanding collection of antiques, paintings, and rare artifacts, including elegant French furnishings, delicate pieces of china, and beautiful paintings. The royal residence's gardens and grounds are stunning, too, and feature fir trees, a butterfly garden, and a novel star-shaped maze.

## LOCHLEVEN CASTLE

Built around the early 14th century, Lochleven Castle is infamous for being the tower in which Mary, Queen of Scots, was imprisoned in 1567. She remained there for almost a year, until she was compelled to abdicate her throne to her young son, who was crowned James VI of Scotland that year, and then James I of England in 1603. She later made a daring escape with the help of a boatman. Today, the remains of this great castle are protected as a scheduled monument in the care of Historic Environment Scotland. The beautiful residential tower, although only open to the public during summer and accessible only by ferry, is worth visiting if only for the weight of the many historic events embedded in its stone walls. A minor excavation in 1995 found the footings and two steps of a stone stairway that gave access to the great hall, and 16th-century pottery and animal bones were found buried in debris near the forestair. Upon reaching the castle, you can see the tower rooms where Queen Mary was held, explore the calm lands of the island itself, and simply enjoy both the natural beauty and the long-running threads history present here.

**Mary, Queen of Scots, was held prisoner in Lochleven Castle; it was where she was forced to abdicate the throne in favor of her son, James.**

## RSPB LOCH LEVEN NATURE RESERVE

This nature reserve is considered the largest lowland freshwater reserve in Scotland, and it is an exceedingly popular spot for families looking to spend a day out experiencing nature. Formerly known as Vane Farm, it was bought in 1967 and transformed into a center for environmental education. The wildlife and natural terrain provide an excellent environment for kids to explore nature. You can climb the trail through the woodland to get a lovely view of the countryside or stroll down to the wetland trail to relax and enjoy the fresh air. This reserve is home to thousands of geese, ducks, and swans, as well as other, rarer birds. In summer, visitors can see ospreys over the loch, and during winter may even catch a glimpse of a visiting white-

**Opposite: The freshwater Loch Leven is home to a wonderful nature reserve.**

# PERTH AND KINROSS

A still centers a seating area outside the ivy-clad Blair Athol Distillery.

## HAVE A DRINK

Perth and Kinross is home to several outstanding distilleries and breweries. Among them are Dewar's Aberfeldy, which was built in 1898 and produces one of the most recognizable names of all Scotch whisky. Claiming to be the smallest distillery in Scotland, Edradour Distillery (above) is based in Pitlochry. The Glenturret Distillery, Scotland's oldest working distillery, is located 2 miles northwest of Crieff on the banks of the Turret River. For a switch from the hard stuff, you can take a tour of the Loch Leven Brewery, Located next to Loch Leven in Kinross. A visit here gives you the opportunity to sample their award-winning craft beers and tour the facilities to learn all about the delicate craft of beer brewing.

tailed eagle. Different kits are available for purchase at the visitor center with everything one might need depending on the season and the weather.

A great way to see the reserves is to follow the Loch Leven Heritage Trail. This largely traffic-free path lies in the east of Scotland's Central Lowlands and offers opportunities for trekking and cycling and is even suitable tracks for wheelchairs. This trail takes you past scenic loch shores, an ancient graveyard and historic church, and also provides some breathtaking views of the infamous Lochleven Castle. The deep woods, the vibrant marshland, the thriving bird life, and the café stops along the way will ensure that you remain both entertained and refreshed while making your way along the trail. This level circuit traces a circular path all the way around the Loch Leven National Nature Reserve. Although dogs are permitted on the trail, they must be kept on a leash at all times in order to prevent them from disturbing the birds and other wildlife.

## ELCHO CASTLE

Elcho Castle is an exhibit of the division of the Scottish nobility during the Middle Ages and early Renaissance. It is a characteristic construction of Scotland: a small castle belonging to a noble family with a power over a specific portion of the region. The perfectly preserved castle is located near the city of Perth beside the River Tay in the town of Rhynd, and open to visitors as a 17th-century museum. The castle contains a switchback staircase leading up the main tower, as well as fragments of a surrounding wall with attached corner towers. Interestingly, the castle was built on an older structure from about 1560 and is one of the best surviving examples of its era in Scotland. A large part of the castle is accessible to the public—although floors in some rooms have been destroyed, much of the building can be safely walked on. The castle is to date owned by the family of the original builders, the Wemyss family, though it has not been inhabited in 200 years.

## BLAIR ATHOL DISTILLERY

Established in 1798, Blair Athol Distillery is one of the oldest working distilleries in Scotland. Standing at the gateway to the Scottish Highlands in the picturesque town of Pitlochry, this distillery is set in open moorland south of the town. John Stewart and Robert Robertson, who founded the distillery, were drawn to the site because of its ancient source of water, the Allt Dour—which in Gaelic means the "burn of the otter." The Allt Dour flows through the grounds of the distillery from the slopes of Ben Vrackie in the foothills of the Grampian mountains, contributing to the mellow quality and smooth finish of the whiskies produced here. Tours allow you to see how the whisky is made, as well as to sample some of their products.

**Opposite: Trees partially obscure the ruins of Elcho Castle.**

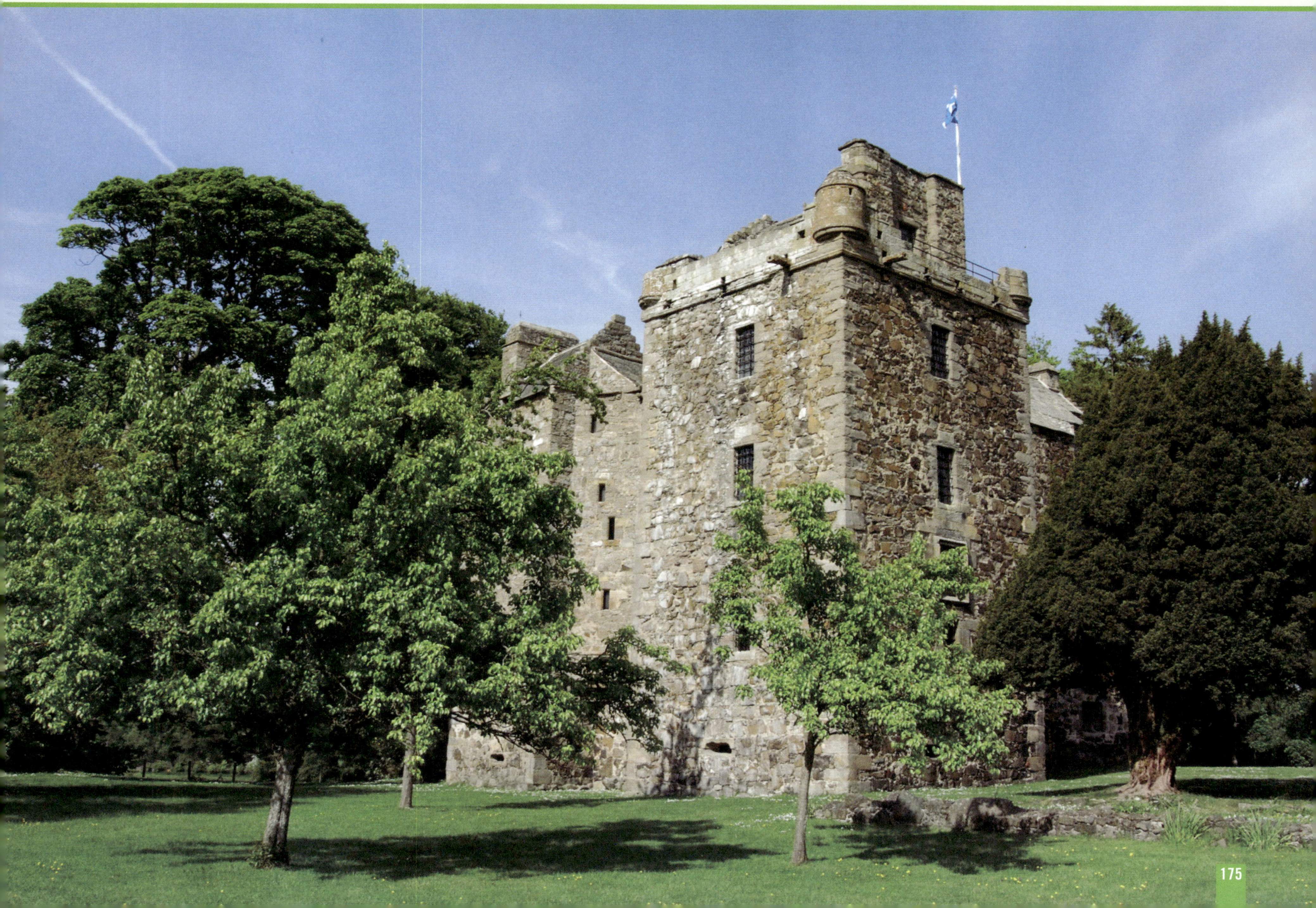

# PERTH AND KINROSS

## BIRKS OF ABERFELDY

With a name taken from the song "The Birks o' Aberfeldie" penned by Scotland's national bard, Robert Burns, in 1787, this circular walk takes you through mature mixed woodland on the western outskirts of Aberfeldy. Originally called the Dens of Moness, the Birks (Scots for "birch trees") overlook the Falls of Moness and line the slopes of the Moness gorge. The well-defined path is overhung by mature birch, oak, ash, and elm trees and offers excellent views to the roaring white water of the falls and during winter, when the trees are bare, across to Strathtay. Much of the gorge is designated as a Site of Special Scientific Interest for its botanical features. The gorge is a place of immense natural beauty in any season but perhaps most photogenic in the cooler days of late autumn.

## FALLS OF BRUAR

Another great way to immerse yourself in the spectacular natural beauty of Perth and Kinross is to follow the sometimes steep path to the Falls of Bruar. This one-to-two-hour walk will take you through some lovely countryside that offers splendid views. Long known as a spectacular local beauty spot, it is where in 1787 Robert Burns was inspired to write "The Humble Petition of Bruar Water" as a request to John Murray, the 4th Duke of Atholl. He writes as if he were the waters themselves, which then wove through a barren landscape of rock and stone, imploring the Duke to "shade my banks

**A contemplative statue of Robert Burns sits in the Birks of Aberfeldy.**

Georgian Picture Staircase; the grand State Dining Room and Drawing Room; and the magnificent Ballroom, bedecked in hundreds of antlers.

The castle is set in breathtaking landscape, and you can stroll the 250-year-old Hercules Garden. The now-gorgeous garden had become overgrown by the 20th century, but ongoing restoration has turned it into a must-see destination. Named after a statue of Hercules, which was originally set on the hill as a focus for the landscape to the east, the gardens and grounds feature a nine-acre walled garden, a peaceful wooded grove, a ruined kirk, a red deer park, and a whimsical Gothic folly.

*A stone bridge looks out over the tumbling waters of the Falls of Bruar.*

wi' tow'ring trees, and bonnie spreading bushes." Since then, the falls have been set in a landscape of verdant greenery.

## BLAIR CASTLE AND HERCULES GARDEN

Nestled in the landscape of Highland Perthshire, Blair Castle has been home to 19 generations of Stewarts and Murrays, the dukes and earls of Atholl. A visit here tells you the story of its 700 years of Scottish history, including a visit by Mary, Queen of Scots, to the Civil War and from the Jacobite cause to Queen Victoria's famous stay, which led to the creation of Europe's only surviving private army, the Atholl Highlanders. Highlights of the castle tour include the Baronial Entrance Hall, featuring weapons used at the Battle of Culloden; the classic

## OTHER TOP SITES

### • BRANKLYN GARDEN

Found near Kinnoull Hill, within a short walk's distance from Perth's city center, Brankyln Garden is a small but beautiful landmark, home to an impressive collection of rare and exotic plants. After exploring the vibrant garden, stop by the terrace for tea, coffee, and freshly made baked goods while looking out over the flowers. The garden also includes a gift shop, where you can pick up souvenirs and plants to take home and nurture.

### • ORWELL STANDING STONES

These two massive stone monoliths stand 15 yards away from each other, located opposite Orwell's farm. The stones are ancient and are so large that they can be seen from over half a mile away. They are also quite different in character; the western stone is angular and jagged with sharp edges, while the eastern stone is smooth and rounded. When one of the monoliths was being re-erected after it fell over in 1972, four cremation deposits were found buried in the ground underneath the stone. Upon testing the remains, it was determined that they had been buried beneath the stone somewhere around the year 2000 BCE.

# RENFREWSHIRE AND INVERCLYDE

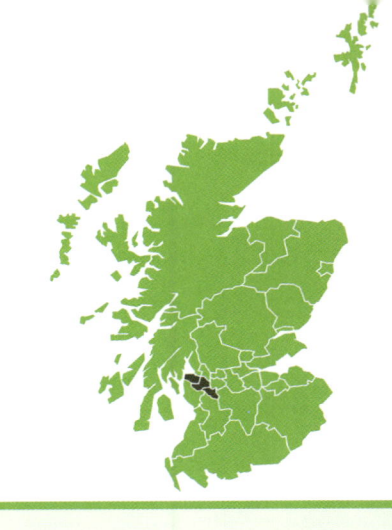

## TOP SITES IN RENFREWSHIRE AND INVERCLYDE

- Newark Castle
- Finlaystone House
- Paisley Abbey
- Cloch Lighthouse

Nestled in the central west Lowlands, Renfrewshire is home to many of Glasgow's commuter towns and villages. It is one of three council areas of Scotland contained within the historic county's boundaries and is also known as the county of Renfrew or Greater Renfrewshire. This county was originally established by King Robert III from lands centering on the ancient lordship of the Strathgryfe in 1402. It had formed part of the county of Lanarkshire and earlier had religious authority over the area. Renfrewshire today contains Glasgow International Airport, Scotland's second-busiest airport. It is also known for the stately River Clyde, the second-longest river in Scotland, which flows into the Firth of Clyde. Named from the Old British *rhyn frwd* for "point at the current," Renfrewshire was once home to the 12th-century Renfrew Castle, built for its strategic location that made it ideal for protecting western Scotland from Norse invaders. Renfrew Castle was destroyed and rebuilt twice over the years, and was later re-dubbed "Inch Castle" due to its proximity to the river islet known as the King's Inch. The castle was demolished by the 18th century, and today nothing remains above ground to indicate its presence.

The area's main settlement and center of local government is the town of Paisley. Historically, the town of Renfrew undertook shipbuilding and engineering as its primary economy, though today it relies mostly on service sector businesses for its principal source of revenue.

Now its own council area together with the East Renfrewshire and Renfrewshire council areas, Inverclyde, one of the smallest in terms of area, once formed part of the historic county of Renfrewshire.

**Top: The cream-colored walls of Finlaystone House stand out against the varied greens of acres of lush gardens and ancient woodland.**

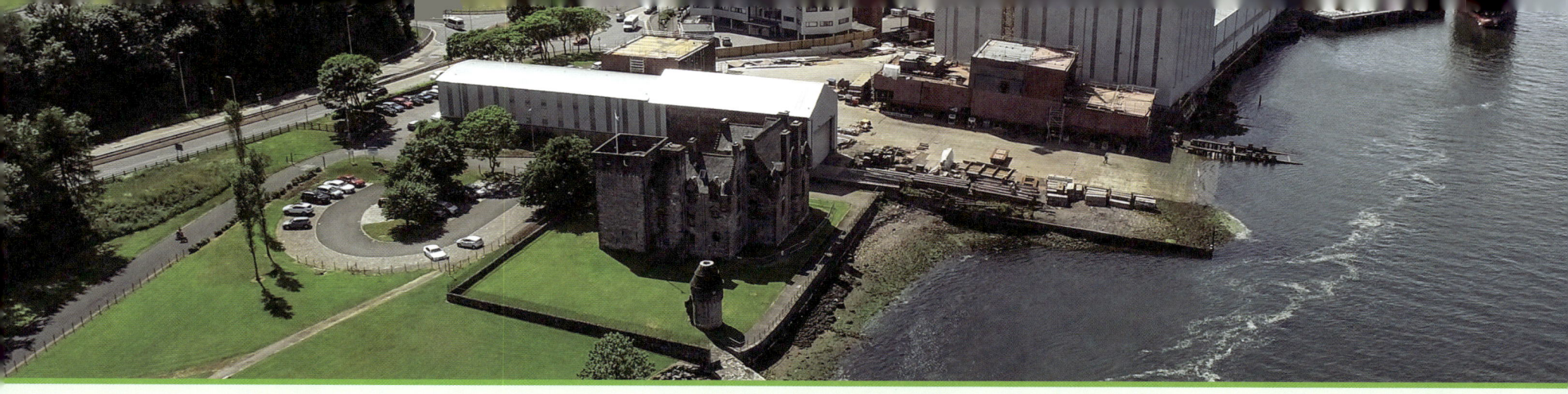

An aerial image of Newark Castle shows its tucked alongside the Ferguson Marine shipbuilding yard on the River Clyde.

## NEWARK CASTLE

With splendid views across the river, the elegant and still virtually intact Newark Castle sits on the south shore of the Firth of Clyde less than half a mile from the center of Port Glasgow. Built by George Maxwell in the 15th century after he inherited the Barony of Finlaystone, the oldest part of the castle is a tower with a gatehouse erected soon after 1478. The castle was then called the "New Werke of Finlastoun." In the 16th century, his descendant Patrick Maxwell added the elegant connecting range. Patrick might have had architectural taste, but he is best known—or rather infamous—for murdering two of his neighbors and beating his wife of 44 years who bore him 16 children. When the last Maxwell died in 1694, the castle passed through a series of nonresident owners and served a number of uses. An early tenant was rope-maker John Orr, who besides making rope made money from wild animals, such as big cats and bears, that he acquired from ships docking in the Clyde. His often housed the animals in the castle cellars. The last of the nonresident owners passed the castle into state care in 1909, and it is now looked after by Historic Environment Scotland. Newark Castle is a remarkably well-preserved building and still sits amid Port Glasgow's shipyards, which once completely blocked any inland view of it. There is now plenty to explore, and views provided by its River Clyde frontage add to its appeal. You can tour the inside, and the ground floor is wheelchair accessible, but only spiral or steep straight stairs lead upstairs.

## FINLAYSTONE HOUSE

Near the southern bank of the Firth of Clyde, beside the village of Langbank in Inverclyde, you will find the lovely Finlaystone House. On lands granted to him by Robert II in the late 14th century, Sir John de Danyelstoun built the original castle here, which was completed in the early 15th century. In 1764, a new house incorporated parts of the 15th-century castle. George Gordon MacMillan is the current chief and owner of Finlaystone, with his family

The round tower of Newark Castle is the site's oldest structure.

179

# RENFREWSHIRE AND INVERCLYDE

running the estate. Set in 500 acres of ancient woodland and renowned gardens, this handsome historic mansion is now open as a tourist attraction with marked walks, a visitor center, and play areas, as wells as monthly and annual events. The 10 acres of garden are perfect for a stroll, with intricate Celtic paving and serpentine herbaceous borders, as well as sweeping lawns and sculptured hedges. You can also enjoy a hot drink in the walled garden's tea room.

## PAISLEY ABBEY

Founded in 1163 by Walter Fitzalan, the High Steward of Scotland, as a Cluniac monastery, Paisley Abbey began life when 13 monks from Shropshire set up a priory on the site of an old 6th-centuty Celtic church founded by St Miren. By 1245, the priory had been raised to the status of an abbey, and under royal patronage, it became increasingly wealthy and influential; yet in 1307, Edward I had the abbey burned down. Rebuilt in the 14th century, it became a center of learning, and it is believed William Wallace, who played such a prominent part in the 13th-century Scottish Wars of Independence, was educated here. In 1499 a new, larger pilgrims' chapel had been built, and the magnificent stone frieze depicting scenes from the life of St Miren was added. Over the years, a succession of fires and the collapse of the tower significantly damaged the structure, leaving it in a partially ruined state. The western section, however, was still used for worship, but the eastern section was widely plundered for its stone. Restoration beginning in 1858 and lasting until 1928 saw the north porch and the eastern choir rebuilt on the remains of the ruined walls, and work on the choir was completed. The abbey also houses the mortal remains of all six High Stewards of Scotland, as well as Marjorie Bruce, mother of Robert II, and the wives of Robert II and King Robert III. The Celtic Barochan Cross, once sited near the village of Houston, is now also inside the abbey itself. The stunning Wallace Memorial Window was donated to the abbey in 1873 and is located in the nave. Events in the abbey are a breathtaking spectacle, and these days this architectural gem still performs religious ceremonies and also hosts concerts and cultural events throughout the year.

## CLOCH LIGHTHOUSE

Cloch Lighthouse stands at Cloch Point near Inverkip on the eastern shore of the Firth of Clyde, opposite Dunoon, where the river turns from flowing west to a southerly direction into the estuary and then the open sea. This lovely lighthouse became a landmark for many Scottish emigrants and a welcome sight for travelers returning home. Completed in 1797, the lighthouse was erected to warn boats away from the Gantocks, a dangerous reef of rocks directly west of the Point. The site includes two generations of keepers' houses, the older now used as stores and the more recent having crow-stepped gables.

**Cloch Lighthouse guards the waters of the Firth of Clyde.**

## OTHER TOP SITES

- **INTU BRAEHEAD**

Intu Braehead is Scotland's favorite shopping destination, featuring more than 100 well-known stores, as well as a long list of ways to keep the whole family entertained. Notable features are the Braehead Arena, where you can catch an ice hockey game or watch live entertainment, and Snow Factor, Scotland's first indoor ski slope. It also contains restaurants, food courts, movie theaters, bowling, laser tag, and mini golf, ensuring there will be something to keep visitors of all ages and preferences entertained for hours.

- **ARDGOWAN HOUSE**

You can book a private tour and tea at this stately home and 10,000-acre coastal estate that has remained in the possession of one family, the Shaw Stewarts, since 1406. Just 35 minutes from Glasgow Airport, it is also available for events and celebrations.

**Opposite: Cheerful daffodils brighten the lawns of Paisley Abbey.**

# SCOTTISH BORDERS

## TOP SITES IN THE SCOTTISH BORDERS

- Melrose Abbey
- Jedburgh Abbey
- Bowhill House and Grounds
- Dawyck Botanic Garden
- Smailholm Tower
- The Haining Estate
- Halliwell's House Museum
- Sir Walter Scott's Courtroom
- Abbotsford
- Dryburgh Abbey
- Paxton House
- Floors Castle and Gardens

Created in 1975 by merging the historic counties of Berwickshire, Peeblesshire, Roxburghshire, and Selkirkshire, along with a bit of Midlothian, the Scottish Borders council area sits in the eastern part of the Southern Uplands at Scotland's southern border with England. Because of its proximity with England, the area has seen a great deal of conflict throughout its history. Berwickshire and Roxburghshire, in particular, bore the brunt of the conflicts, whether in declared wars, such as the Wars of Scottish Independence, or undeclared battles, such as those of the Border reivers, the Scottish and English raiders who harassed the entire Anglo-Scottish border from the late 13th century to the beginning of the 17th century. There was even a strip of land at the western end of the border known as the "Debatable Land" that was constantly a point of contention between England and Scotland until its boundaries were adjusted in 1552. It is no surprise, therefore, that you will find the ruins of many castles in the area.

Berwickshire, initially the name for Berwick-upon-Tweed's region, was caught in the midst of many battles, and Berwick was lost to England in 1492. Today, the River Tweed forms the southern border of Scotland and the northern border of England. Between the Tweed and the Lammermuirs is the low-lying district known as "the Merse," from an old Scots word for a floodplain. The name is sometimes extended to the whole of the county, and the inhabitants referred to as "Merse-men." Like Berwickshire, Roxburghshire, nestled between Dumfriesshire and Berwickshire, was repeatedly captured and recaptured between the Scots and the English during

**Top:** The River Tweed runs through pastoral countryside near Peebles.

*The sprawling Floors Castle in Roxburghshire is the seat of the Duke of Roxburghe.*

the Scottish Wars of Independence. Primarily rural, Roxburghshire is dotted with a few lochs with rolling hills along the border with England. Located in some of Lowland Scotland's most fertile ground and close to the River Tweed, Roxburgh once had an illustrious agricultural industry and a large economy centralized around transporting goods along the river.

As one of the earliest royal burghs in Scotland, the name *Selkirkshire* comes from the old Scots language meaning the "church in the forest," named after Ettrick Forest. Although Selkirkshire is not directly adjacent to England but a little northwest, it still suffered the constant tug-of-war between the two rivals, changing hands between the two countries numerous times over the years. Like Roxburghshire, it is rural, with a handful of small settlements set within hill and forest countryside. Peeblesshire, also known as Tweeddale, is a landlocked section of the Scottish Borders, with the River Tweed and multiple reservoirs dotted throughout. The settlements in the county consist mostly of low hill country, including parts of the Pentland Hills and Moorfoot Hills.

## MELROSE ABBEY

A focal point of the Borders, Melrose Abbey is a magnificent ruin on a grand scale. Founded in 1136 on a fertile spot beside the River Tweed by David I, it was the first Cistercian monastery in Scotland, one of a number of abbeys that he set up in the Borders to show both his piety and his power over this highly contested territory. Monastic life continued at Melrose for the next 450 years, until the last monk died around 1590. In its heyday, the great abbey church of St Mary the Virgin at Melrose loomed large in the lives of many people on both sides of the border. It was a place so beloved by Robert the Bruce, he chose it as the final resting place for his heart, although his body was interred

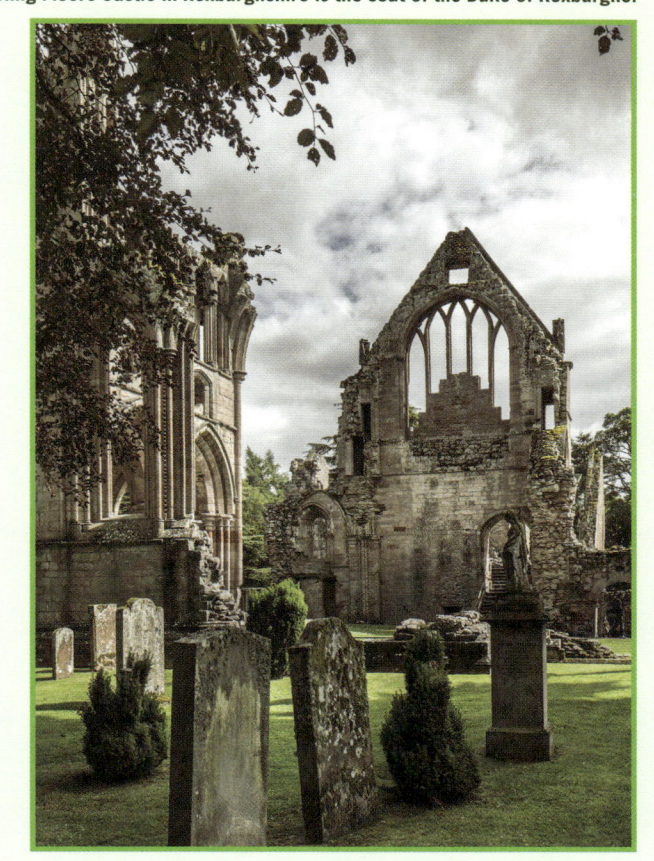

*Scotland's famed author Sir Walter Scott lived and died in the Scottish Borders and was laid to rest at Dryburgh Abbey.*

# SCOTTISH BORDERS

**Above:** A view from the top shows some of Melrose Abbey's carved hobgoblins. **Right:** Even in its ruined state, the abbey still retains its splendor.

at Dunfermline Abbey. Its site meant that it was on front line of conflict with England during the later Middle Ages, and it suffered major damage requiring repairs after attacks by Edward I in 1300 and 1307 and Edward II in 1322. Richard II's attack in 1385 led to a complete rebuilding of the abbey church and the War of the Rough Wooing in the 1540s caused further damage. Eventually the deteriorating abbey church was used as a parish church until a new kirk was built nearby in 1810. Only a very small part of the first abbey church survives, and the rose-colored stone building you see dates almost entirely to the post-1385 rebuilding. Still some highlights remain remarkably intact, including the presbytery at the east end where the high altar once stood, with its ornate

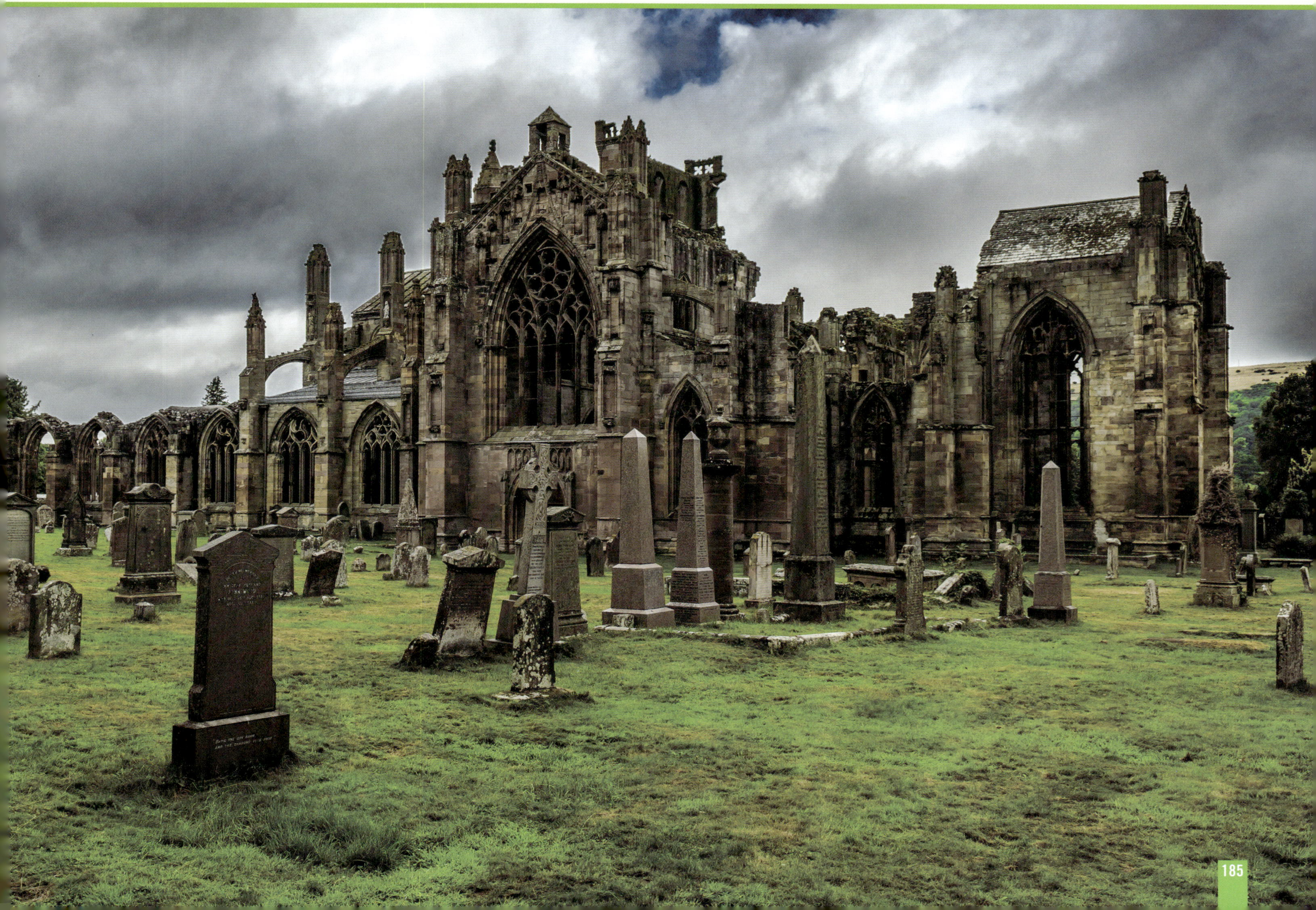

# SCOTTISH BORDERS

stone vaulting, the monks' choir and transepts, and part of the nave. Despite any damage it once suffered, Melrose is still considered one of the most magnificent examples of medieval church architecture anywhere in the British Isles. The exterior displays some amazing sculptures that depict a wide array of subject matter, including demons and hobgoblins, lute-playing angels, cooks with ladles, and a bagpipe-playing pig. Little remains standing of the two great cloisters that lay to the north and west of the abbey church, but their ground plans are largely complete. A visit to the restored Commendator's House, built in the late 1500s, will give you a glimpse of monastic life, with artifacts such as cooking pots.

## JEDBURGH ABBEY

One of the four border abbeys, Jedburgh was founded by David I around 1138 for Augustinian canons. The church combined Romanesque and early-Gothic styles to create a magnificent edifice that David was proud to display to his English neighbors to demonstrate he could match any grand building in England. It might have shown that, but its site on the border meant it was a focus of conflict, and it was badly damaged and rebuilt several times during the Wars of Independence. What you see today, however, still possess the magnificence that David I wanted to convey, and although in ruins, the remains of the building are sufficiently intact to still present an awe-inspiring profile. It has been said that rather than

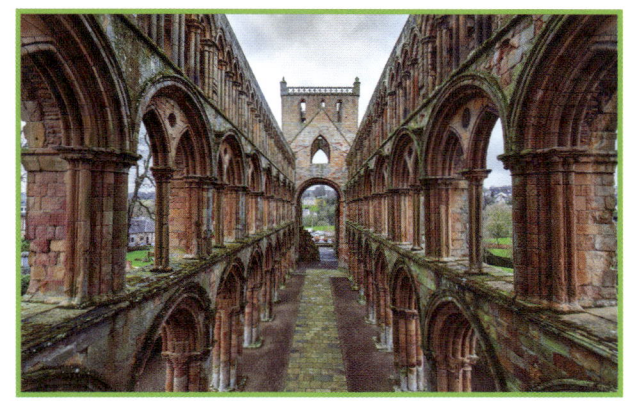

**Above: Inside Jedburgh Abbey the scale of the interior arches gives you a sense of the sheer size of the building. Left: The abbey lies on south-facing slopes close to the center of Jedburgh.**

looking like a building in decline, it almost looks as if the building were in the process of construction and is just awaiting a new roof and windows. At the west end of the abbey, a very narrow spiral staircase leads you to a balcony that overlooks the abbey interior, and throughout the abbey there are information boards in five languages that supply a great deal of info about its various points of interest. You can also check out the adjoining visitor center, where you can view artifacts found during excavations that uncovered remains of the cloister, including the priceless "Jedburgh comb," a delicately carved ivory relic of the 12th century and an 8th-century shrine.

## BOWHILL HOUSE AND GROUNDS

Bowhill is a lovely spot to visit with the entire family. It is the magnificent country home of the Duke and Duchess of Buccleuch and home to

# SCOTTISH BORDERS

*Above: Dawyck Gardens near Peebles is one of Scotland's Royal Botanic Garden sites. Below: This 65-foot Smailholm Tower was built in the first half of the 15th century*

the famous Buccleuch art collection. The estate features a theater, a jungle gym for the children, beautiful walking paths through the grounds, and a picturesque lunch nook. Visitors can also take a guided tour of the house and the grounds; other events are occasionally offered depending on the season. Bowhill House regularly hosts private events like parties, weddings, and corporate events, as well as an occasional craft fair where locals can sell their hand-made goods to visitors. The house was first constructed in 1708 by Lord John Bowhill, although the final layout was not completed until 1876.

Also on the grounds of Bowhill House is Newark Tower, a large, ruined tower house standing in the valley of the Yarrow Water 3 miles west of Selkirk. Along with the keep, you can see sections of the surviving gatehouse and wall.

## DAWYCK BOTANIC GARDEN

Located in the hills of the Scottish Borders, 65-acre Dawyck is one of the four Royal Botanic Garden locations in Scotland, along with Edinburgh, Logan, and Benmore, each with its own specialized collection. Dawyck's almost continental climate, with warm dry summers followed by cold, snowy winters, means that plants from the mountainous regions of Europe, China, Nepal, Japan, and North America thrive here. Features of this lovely site include one of Scotland's finest tree collections, including some of Britain's oldest and tallest trees, dating back to 1680. A visit here in May and June is the perfect time to catch the blaze of color of the Azalea Terrace and see the carpet of blue poppies that appear under the tree canopy in early June. The Heron Wood Reserve is the world's first reserve for mosses, liverworts, lichens, and fungi. The Garden is truly a sanctuary for endangered plants, a collection not only for conservation and study, but also a place of beauty to be enjoyed.

## SMAILHOLM TOWER

Smailholm Tower is approximately halfway between Melrose and Kelso as the crow flies. The Pringle family originally built the tower, known as a peel tower, in the 15th century. It was named after the landowning family of Smailholm, who were followers of the Lord of Douglas. The word *holm* is derived from the Old English term for the "little island," and the word *smail* is derived from the Old English term for "small, slender, or thin." Smailholm's beautiful Norman church is worth a visit. The nearby surroundings of Smailholm Tower are also breathtaking. Even though the tower is less than 2 miles north of the River Tweed, the surrounding jumble of rocky outcrops is strangely reminiscent of the much rockier northwest Sutherland.

## THE HAINING ESTATE

The Haining is a Scottish Borders country house sitting close to Selkirk and overlooking the beautiful Haining Loch. The main house was built

**Opposite: The ruins of Newark Castle lie within the grounds of Bowhill House.**

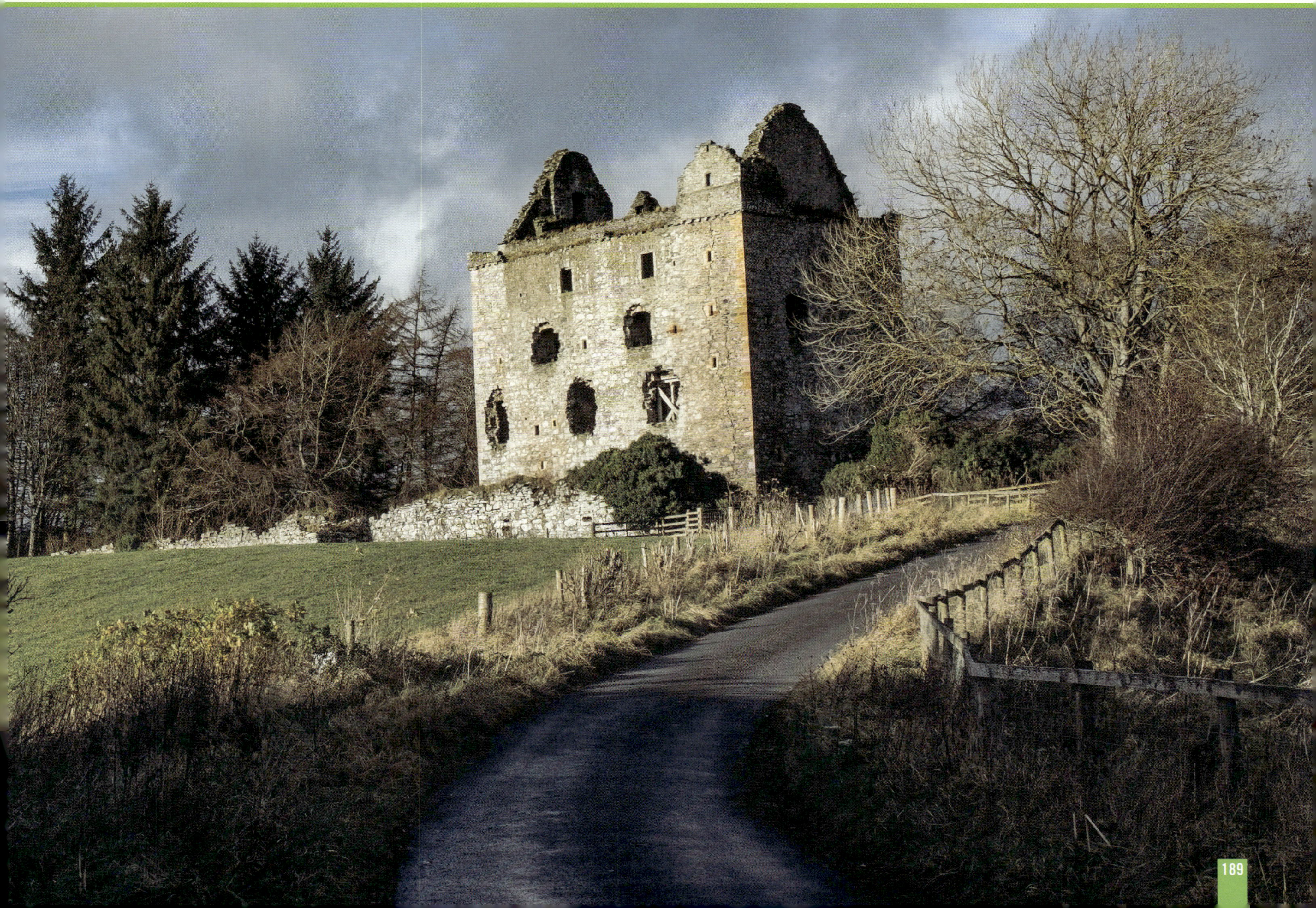

# SCOTTISH BORDERS

in the 1790s, predated by an older house nearby on the estate that was constructed in the 1500s. The home and gardens were left to the inhabitants of Selkirkshire and the public in 2009. The Haining Charitable Trust is by and by endeavoring to change the structure into a scene for craft, culture, and historical displays and events. The house's ground floor has been heavily renovated and is currently open to the public, as well as for a variety of private events. The Haining Loch nearby is a lovely place to walk or explore; many visitors stop here to relax by the water or try to spot some of the local wildlife. Numerous trails and paths—some marked, some not—cross through the forests near the loch and the Haining Estate. The officially marked paths are well maintained and help to make for a relaxing wander in this little bit of countryside. There is plenty of clear and visible signs asking that dogs and presumably humans do not enter the water, as there are rare birds nesting near the water's edge.

## HALLIWELL'S HOUSE MUSEUM

The Halliwell's House Museum offers a genuinely stand-out experience. This extraordinary 18th-century home can be found in Halliwell's Close, a small cobbled street named for hairpiece producer Walter Halliwell. Halliwell's Close is located just off of the bustling Selkirk Marketplace, where many shops featuring hand-made and historic goods can be found. Inside the museum, you are welcome to explore one of Selkirk's oldest standing homes; the museum features several exhibits detailing the rich history of the area, and a guided tour will take you through the house room-by-room. An old ironmonger's shop has been recreated on the ground floor of the building; this display is filled with the tools that would have been used in the workshop that originally stood in this very place centuries ago. The museum also delves into the many other trades and crafts that once made up the bulk of Selkirk's local economy, featuring displays covering every profession from shoe-making to barrel-making to butchery. One of the most notable historical exhibits is the "Flodden Flag," a captured English flag brought home by Selkirk's only soldier to survive the battle of Flodden Field in 1513.

## SIR WALTER SCOTT'S COURTROOM

The Courtroom of Sir Walter Scott is one of only a handful of direct connections to the prestigious Scottish creator. Sir Walter Scott served as Sheriff of Selkirkshire for more than 30 years. The famed Scottish writer lived his entire life in the Scottish Borders, and it is commonly believed that the area's beautiful scenery and rich, troubled history were great sources of inspiration for his works. He tirelessly balanced his writing and creative work with his duties as sheriff, dispensing justice until his death in 1832. His courtroom—first

**Opposite: The Haining, a country house near Selkirk, sits on the shores of Haining Loch, a perfect place for a peaceful stroll.**

**Above: Bowhill House, the stately country home of the Duke and Duchess of Buccleuch, is open to visitors. Below: Halliwell's House Museum is located in part of the oldest surviving row of dwellings in Selkirk and features a re-created ironmonger's shop.**

# SCOTTISH BORDERS

> Breathes there the man, with soul so dead, Who never to himself hath said, This is my own, my native land!
>
> —SIR WALTER SCOTT

built in 1804 and located in the heart of Selkirk Marketplace—was renovated and rebuilt so that visitors from all over the world can explore the rooms within and learn all about the history of Sir Walter Scott and the town he lived in. The historic courtroom features displays of artifacts and the personal effects of Sir Walter, as well as some detailed overviews of the many crimes and sentences addressed in this building. This historic structure stands next to the statue dedicated to Sir Walter himself, which helps this landmark stand out from far away.

## ABBOTSFORD

Home of the "Great Scott" himself, Abbotsford stands on the banks of the River Tweed in Melrose. This creation of Sir Walter Scott, while not literary, is still a grand achievement. Built between 1817 and 1825 on the proceeds of Scott's phenomenally successful literary career, Abbotsford is an enduring monument to its creator, one of Scotland's most important and beloved national figures. He intended it to be a family home, work space, and private museum for his numerous interests. The house was opened to the public in 1833, a year after Scott's death, it but continued to be occupied by Scott's descendants until 2004. Today this Scottish Baronial–style home, which Scott called a "flibbertigibbet of a house," attracts scores of visitors from all over the world. A visit here in the heart of the beautiful Borders countryside, lets you discover the life and times of Scott, who was an obsessive collector who jam-packed his home with curios, books, weaponry, and more; in the Abbotsford Collections, you can view some of these fascinating artifacts. Scott also gave a great deal of attention to the grounds and garden of the estate. The South Court is the first of his three "outdoor rooms," which

**Left: A statue of Scott, affectionately known as the "Shirra," stands in front of the courthouse. Right: The amazing Gothic architecture of Abbotsford makes it an icon of 19th-century European Romanticism.**

193

# SCOTTISH BORDERS

joins with the sunken Morris Garden. A stone archway from there leads to Scott's kitchen garden. A walk through the estate's ground will highlight Scott's obsession with tree planting. Abbotsford also includes a chapel and a visitor center.

## DRYBURGH ABBEY

Nestled in a secluded woodland site by the River Tweed you find the graceful ruins of Dryburgh Abbey. Established by Premonstratensian canons in 1150, Dryburgh became the premier house in Scotland of this French order. Although never as wealthy or influential as the abbeys at Kelso, Jedburgh, and Melrose, it was a perfect place to practice the contemplative monastic life. Its Scottish Borders location, however, meant it wouldn't be spared from the violence of the Scots-English wars. It suffered four savage attacks, the most famous in 1322 when Edward II's soldiers turned back to set fire to Dryburgh having heard its bells ringing out as the English army retreated. The Protestant Reformation of 1560 effectively ended monastic life at Dryburgh. Today you can wander this remarkably complete ruin, where you can admire the warm-pink sandstone transepts flanking the presbytery, which are said to be some of the best Gothic church architecture in Scotland, and still see plaster and paintwork inside the 13th-

**Opposite: The charming landscape of Dryburgh owes much to David Erskine, 11th Earl of Buchan, who bought the estate in the 1700s. He is buried here, along with his close friend Sir Walter Scott.**

# SCOTTISH BORDERS

century chapter house. Dryburgh is also the burial place of Sir Walter Scott and home of the Dryburgh yew, one of Scotland's oldest trees. Nature lovers will also be pleased to catch sight of one of three bat species that use the magnificent veteran trees and abbey ruins as roosts.

## PAXTON HOUSE

This fully renovated house, built in the 1760s by Patrick Home of Billie, is complete with a tea room and art gallery that is open to the public year round. Patrick Home commissioned architects John and James Adam, the sons of renowned Scottish architect William Adam, to design the building. Paxton House is a Neo-Palladian Georgian mansion constructed of pink sandstone overlooking the River Tweed and surrounded by 80 acres of woodland, gardens, and parklands. The estate sits right on the border of Scotland and England, about 4 miles from Berwick-upon-Tweed. Here, visitors can enjoy a variety of walks and trails, including the especially well-loved Fairy Trail and Woodland Trail. There are boat trips up the river Tweed to Horncliffe available according to season, and these serve as great ways to learn about local wildlife and history. This grand House has a croquet lawn and 9-hole putting green, picnic areas, two adventure play parks, a children's playground, nature trails, and many more special events and outdoor activities.

**Opposite: Lily pads float in a fountain at Paxton House.**

## FLOORS CASTLE AND GARDENS

Floors Castle is one of Scotland's most renowned castles, and it is its largest inhabited castle. This beautiful family home, which has housed 11 generations of the dukes of Roxburghe, is a treasure of Scottish architecture and political history. Visitors are invited to peruse the castle's expansive collection of fine art, china, and tapestries, while exploring the building's many lavishly decorated rooms. Spectacular scenic views over the River Tweed and the Cheviot Hills toward the south can be seen from the castle and gardens. It was built for the first Duke of Roxburghe somewhere between 1721 and 1726 by famous Scottish architect William Adam. The Castle has been featured in the 1984 movie *Greystoke* and was also featured on an episode of "An American's Aristocrats Guide to Great Estates" on the Smithsonian channel. The gardens outside the castle are a beautiful in their own right; they are home to a carefully cultivated array of flowers and trees that only add to the rich, vibrant atmosphere of the estate. The castle and grounds are open to the public year-round.

The ruins of Roxburgh Castle can be found on the grounds of Floors Castle. It is one of Scotland's most historically significant castles, although it often goes unnoticed by tourists. Only two parts of the wall can be seen from the street, which runs very close to the base of the castle. Built some time before 1128 by David I, it was destroyed by the Scots in 1460. There are also fragments of stone walls around the castle.

## OTHER TOP SITES

**• KELSO RACECOURSE**

The Scottish Borders is known as the homeland of equestrianism in Scotland, so it is no surprise to find this Thoroughbred racing course, which has been voted "best small course in Scotland" several times over the years, within the area. Kelso Racecourse is widely believed to be one of the foremost venues for horse racing in all of Scotland and northern England. Steeped in history and tradition, it was opened in 1822 as the Duke's Course, although the site was recorded as a location for horse racing as early as 1734. The original building is still a center of activity on a race day, with coal fires blazing during the cold winter months and maintaining a unique charm that has welcomed racegoers for over a century. Kelso stages 15 National Hunt Race days throughout its season, which runs from September through to late May.

**• LOCHCARRON VISITOR CENTRE**

The Lochcarron of Scotland Visitor Centre can be found in the Selkirk marketplace near a massive statue of Sir Walter. Lochcarron Visitor center is a combination of a plaid, tweed, cashmere, and knitwear retailer—one that has been going since 1947—a cafe, and a textile mill

**• 7STANES OF GLENTRESS**

The 7stanes are seven mountain biking centers that stretch from the Scottish Borders to Dumfries and Galloway. The 7stanes incorporate Fredrick Park for riders to try out tricks and a visitor center with a wildlife room. These venues are known as the 7stanes because each site features a special "stane," the Scots word for "stone", created by Gordon Young and placed somewhere along the forest trails. You can reach them by foot, horse, or bicycle. The 7stanes sites are Ae, Dalbeattie, Glentress and Innerleithen, Glentrool, Kirroughtree, Mabie, and Newcastleton.

**• JOHN BUCHAN STORY MUSEUM**

This specialty museum and gallery in Peebles explores the life and works of John Buchan, 1st Baron of Tweedsmuir.

**• KAILZIE GARDENS**

West Kelloch, which means "forested valley," was the first name for Kailzie. The garden dates back to 1812, and sits at the center of the Tweed Valley just a mile east of Peebles, occupying a beautiful position on the River Tweed.

# SHETLAND

## TOP SITES IN SHETLAND

- Broch of Mousa
- Clickimin Loch
- Hermaness National Nature Reserve
- Croft House Museum
- Jarlshof Prehistoric and Norse Settlement
- Haroldswick

The islands of Shetland are bordered by the North Sea to the east and the Atlantic Ocean to the west. They are the northernmost landmass of Scotland. Of Shetland's 16 inhabited islands, the largest is known as the Mainland, and it is known for its rolling hills, rich geology, and jagged coastline. The name *Shetland* originated from the Old Norse word *hjalt*, meaning "hilt."

The history of human habitation on the Shetland Islands goes back to the Mesolithic period. Early in Shetland's history, its primary influence came from Norway—the Scottish did not claim the islands until the 15th century.

Shetland's leading source of revenue comes from North Sea oil, but fishing, long a major part of its economy, remains important to the region. Perhaps Shetland's most famous legacies are found in the Shetland croft sheepdog (sometimes called a "Sheltie") and the Shetland pony.

The scenery of Shetland is wild and beautiful, with deeply indented coasts (the sea lochs, or fjords, are locally called voes) enclosed by steep hills. The winds are nearly continuous and robust, and trees are therefore sparse, but the climate is very mild for such a high latitude—only 400 miles south of the Arctic Circle—because of the warming influence of the North Atlantic Current, an extension of the Gulf Stream system. Shetland has long been world famous as a mecca for bird enthusiasts. The availability ranges from the ultra-rare to the quirky; birds of all breeds flock to the isles in their droves. From a crime perspective, Shetland is a highly safe place. If you are mugged, robbed, or treated with anything other than courtesy during your stay, you can consider yourself extremely unlucky.

Top: The wind tousles a distinctive Shetland pony in a Shetland moor.

*Mousa Broch stands on a low promontory overlooking Mousa Sound.*

## BROCH OF MOUSA

The mysterious round stone tower on the Scottish island of Mousa is one of Europe's best-saved old developments. It is the most noteworthy of all the current towers—knowns as brochs—in the country, tracing back to the Iron Age and remaining intact for 2,000 years. The genuine capacity of the Broch of Mousa, which is assessed to have been raised somewhere in the range of 300 and 100 BCE, is obscure; it is thought to have had two significant ages of utilization. The broch can be found on the western shore of the island of Mousa. The site is accessible by boat from Sandwick and stands on the flat rock surface of a low peninsula close to the shore overlooking Mousa Sound. The Broch of Mousa is the tallest broch still standing and among the best-preserved prehistoric buildings in Europe. It is famous among birders for its breeding European storm petrels, which are best seen after dark on wholly or partly cloudy summer nights. The island hosts around 6,800 breeding pairs, representing 8 percent of the British population and roughly 2.6 percent of the world population. Most of the birds nest in burrows within the broch itself.

## CLICKIMIN LOCH

The Loch of Clickimin is Lerwick's most ample open space on the town's southwest edge. The Clickimin Center, with its games offices, pool, and camp and caravan site, is a great place for travelers, tourists, and locals alike to start before making their way around the rest of the loch. The loch itself is a spectacle of natural beauty; there is an abundance of wildlife for bird-watchers and nature enthusiasts to observe, and the waters of the loch are something to behold. Potentially even more interesting, however, is Clickimin Broch: this ancient stone dwelling can be found on an island to the loch's southern side and was built some 3,000 years ago. The broch—a carefully constructed stone roundhouse that was occupied several times over a period of over 1,000 years—is relatively well-preserved, as it has been maintained by expert historians since its discovery and

*A recessed pathway leads to the entrance through the blockhouse of Clickimin Broch, an Iron Age defensive building.*

# SHETLAND

excavation in 1861. This unique site is managed by Historic Scotland. Several fascinating artifacts have been found on the grounds surrounding the broch, including stone lamps, fragments of Roman glass, and objects carved from whale bone. Clickimin Broch is one of the best-preserved broch sites in Shetland.

## HERMANESS NATIONAL NATURE RESERVE

The Hermaness National Nature Reserve is well-loved by tourists and locals alike for its stunning natural beauty, thriving wildlife, and rich history. The white crests of the waves mix in with the white stains on the bluffs where seagulls lay their eggs every year. Around an hour's stroll from the nearby parking lot, the sheer and dramatic cliff faces are home to various seabirds that build their nests on the rocks, including fulmars, gulls, shags, gannets, puffins, and kittiwakes. The history of this reserve can be traced to 1831, when conservation activities first began at Hermaness. The original owner of this plot of land, Dr. Lawrence Edmondston, began the first conservation efforts here in an attempt to protect bonxie nesting sites from egg poachers. The area of conservation widened in later years when the Royal Society for the Protection of Birds took the responsibility of monitoring and maintaining the birds' population. In 1955, the area was declared a National Nature Reserve, and surveys of local seabird populations have been taken regularly since the 1980s.

## CROFT HOUSE MUSEUM

This old croft house was built in the 1800s and was inhabited until the latter part of the 1960s, but today it serves as a preserved cross-section of rural Shetland life. It can be found on the shore of Boddam, a small but beautiful village in Dunrossness. The living quarters, byre, and outbuilding would have been sheltered under one rooftop, intended to help the residents withstand Shetland's unforgiving climate conditions and avoid going outside unnecessarily. The Croft House has been renovated and maintained expertly over the years. The property is presented in the style of how it would have looked in the 1870s, with very little changes made in terms of modernization; the fireplace still holds peat fuel, and much of the furniture and decorations present are preserved original pieces. The Croft House also has a lovely garden. The museum offers regular guided tours for visitors interested in learning about the culture and practices of the people who once lived here, as well as informational placards detailing specific aspects of the house. Around the grounds are piles of peat, crumbling stone walls, and even Shetland ponies for visitors to admire.

## JARLSHOF PREHISTORIC AND NORSE SETTLEMENT

This site is widely believed to be the most historically significant prehistoric archaeological site in all of Scotland. The ruins and remains

**Top:** Gannets congregate on the sea cliffs at Hermaness. **Bottom:** The Jarlshof complex has buildings dating from a wide range of eras, including the early-17th-century Old House of Sumburgh.

**Opposite:** Sheep calmly graze on the perilous cliffs of Hermaness

# SHETLAND

Opposite: The Jarlshof complex boasts an impressive Norse settlement that possibly originated in the 9th century.

excavated here date back as far as 4,000 years ago, although some remains buried in the grounds of Jarlshof are dated as recently as the 1600s. The site was inhabited several times over the millennia, featuring distinct ruins from the Pictish period, the Bronze Age, the Iron Age, and the Viking Age, the last of which makes up the bulk of the still-standing ruins. Visible on the grounds are several Bronze Age roundhouses, an Iron Age broch, and several Viking longhouses. One peculiar structure with a large hearth has also been preserved, which historians believe may have served as a sauna. Several painted and carved Pictish stones have been found on the grounds, as well as a bronze dagger, carved-bone tools, pottery, shears and scissors made from bog-iron, and molds once used in forging bronze weapons and tools. It is also believed that this site served as the inspiration for Sir Walter Scott's original work *The Pirate*. Jarlshof has the most considerable amount of visible remains of any historic Viking site in Britain.

## HAROLDSWICK

To find out more about Shetland's Viking past, a visit to Haroldswick in Unst should be on your must-see list. Thought to have been the first foot-fall of Vikings in the North Atlantic, the island of Unst is home to more than 50 settlements.

Originally built in Sweden, the *Skidbladner* is a full-size replica of a Viking longship.

Haroldswick is named after Harald Fairhair, the first king to claim sovereignty over all Norway, who had to bring the Shetland Vikings under control in 875 CE. A highlight here is the *Skidbladner*, a full-size replica of the 9th-century Gokstad ship found in a Viking burial mound in Norway in 1880, which you can board. There's also a replica Viking longhouse that was constructed according to a design based on excavation results.

### OTHER TOP SITES

- **SHETLAND MUSEUM AND ARCHIVES**

This fascinating historical center covers the story of Shetland's past and culture and is situated on the waterfront in Lerwick inside a modified 19th-century dock. The Shetland Museum and Archives' collection reveals the archipelago's development, from its topographical beginnings to the current day. Its exhibitions house everything from choice Shetland ribbons to fine examples of Pictish craft.

# STIRLING

## TOP SITES IN STIRLING

- Stirling Castle
- National Wallace Monument
- Cambuskenneth Abbey
- Stirling Old Town Jail
- Loch Lomond and the Trossachs National Park
- Church of Holy Rude
- The Battle of Bannockburn Visitor Centre
- Doune Castle
- Stirling Old Bridge

Stirlingshire is a historic county and registration area of Scotland and now a council area. The history of Stirling dates back to the prehistoric era, as stone age carvings can still be seen near King's Park to this day. In 1890, the county was granted a coat of arms by Lord Lyon, King of Arms. Nestled in the heart of Scotland near Glasgow and Edinburgh, Stirling contains a sizable historic fortress and a medieval town. Due to its strategic position near the River Forth, it has a history of attracting invaders over the centuries, primarily English and Viking forces. It is also the site of several historic battles, including the Battle of Bannockburn at Bannockburn, a significant Scottish victory in the Wars of Scottish Independence, and the Battle of Stirling Bridge in 1297.

Stirling occupies an essential position on the Forth-Clyde isthmus, commanding the main overland routes from Glasgow and Edinburgh to central and northern Scotland, and it is often referred to as the "Gateway to the Highlands." The western "arm" of the county is sparsely populated, as most of the region is taken up by Loch Lomond. The central part of the county is dominated by the Carron Valley Reservoir and the Campsie Fells, the Kilsyth Hills, and Gargunnock Hills. The larger towns, like Lennoxtown and Kilsyth, are spread out along the southern border and A891/A803 roads. In the southwestern region, near Milngavie, lies the Greater Glasgow conurbation, as well as several small reservoirs and lochs, including the Burncrooks Reservoir, Kilmannan Reservoir, Mugdock Loch, Carbeth Loch, Bardowie Loch, Craigallian Loch, Dumbrock Loch, and the Mugdock/Craigmaddie Reservoir.

**Top: A cobbled path leads to Stirling's medieval Old Town.**

*Stirling Castle perches on craggy volcanic rock at the heart of Stirling Old Town.*

> "Stirling, like a huge brooch, clasps Highlands and Lowlands together."
>
> —ALEXANDER SMITH

The much flatter eastern part contains the bulk of the county's population, especially near the Firth of Forth, which provides access to the North Sea.

The county town is Stirling, where according to legend, a wolf once howled to alert the townsfolk of an incoming Viking attack in time for them to prepare for battle. As such, Stirling is historically associated with the wolf. Stirling was once an agricultural market town, but today its most significant sources of revenue come from financial services and tourism.

## STIRLING CASTLE

Stirling Castle is one of the most historically and culturally significant castles in all of Scotland, and it is certainly one of the largest. This sprawling castle and its outer estate can be found atop Castle Hill in Stirling. Built in or before the 1100s, the castle was initially the favored seat of the Stewart lords and sovereigns, who were well known for hosting extravagant feasts and parties there. The site was also the location used for the inauguration of many Scottish kings and queens, notably including Mary, Queen of Scots, and many other Scottish royals were born and died in the castle. Stirling Castle holds an extensive collection of fascinating historical artifacts, works of art, and original interior decoration, but one of the highlights is the Great Hall, which has been fully restored to its 16th-century splendor. Visitors are welcome to take guided tours through the castle and the surrounding grounds, where expert historians can explain fascinating details pertaining to the deep history of Stirling Castle.

*The remains of the abbey that takes it name from the village stands in Cambuskenneth, which is enclosed within a loop in the River Forth.*

# STIRLING

## NATIONAL WALLACE MONUMENT

This monument to Sir William Wallace, the warrior who became known as Scotland's National Hero, is a fantastic landmark and one of Stirling's most well-known attractions. Inside this monument, visitors are transported back to the 13th century as they learn about the life and deeds of the soldier who led the Scottish army to victory at the Battle of Stirling Bridge during the First War of Scottish Independence. This battle, on September 11, 1297, saw the forces of Andrew Moray and William Wallace defeat the combined English forces of John de Warenne, 6th Earl of Surrey, and Hugh de Cressingham. Many will know the bare bones of this event through the 1995 film *Braveheart*, but here you will find the true—and just as riveting—tale.

The Wallace Monument is divided into three main parts: the exhibition floor is the first, and it tells the story of William Wallace, focusing in particular on the 1297 Battle of Stirling Bridge that led to Wallace's appointment as the Guardian of Scotland. The second floor features a display of 16 marble busts of important Scots whose notable achievements are explained with in-depth audio guides. The third floor tells the story of how the monument was built in 1870. The tower's staircase comes to an intimidating 246 steps in total, but the climb is well worth the effort; the top floor of the tower is an observation deck that offers unparalleled views from the Abbey Craig hilltop over the site of the famous Battle at Stirling Bridge.

## CAMBUSKENNETH ABBEY

David I founded Augustinian Cambuskenneth Abbey in about 1140 to serve the royal castle of Stirling, which stands a short distance to the west. Most of the abbey was built in the 1200s, and much of the surviving structure, although reduced to ruins, dates from that era. In its heyday, it was the scene of Robert the Bruce's parliaments in 1314 and 1326. In 1488 the Battle of Sauchieburn between the armies of James III and his son, the future James IV, took place just south of the abbey. James III was killed sometime during the rout, and he was buried in front of the abbey's high altar next to his queen, Margaret of Denmark, who had died two years earlier. The altar no longer exists, with only the abbey's doorway remaining, although evidence shows that it had been laid out in a cross shape with an eight-bay nave with a north aisle, a choir and a square-ended

**Opposite:** The National Wallace Monument stands high overlooking the site of the 1297 Battle of Stirling Bridge. **Left:** A statue of William Wallace, who led his troops to victory over the English at this famous battle

The Wallace Monument, completed in 1869, is a 220-foot sandstone tower, built in the Victorian Gothic style.

# STIRLING

*Above: The menacing exterior of the Stirling Old Town Jail fits its grim purpose. Below: The Falls of Falloch are tucked away in the Loch Lomond and the Trossachs National Park.*

presbytery flanked by two transepts, each with two chapels, and a cloister to the south of the church. Also surviving is a free-standing bell tower with lancet windows and ornamental arcades that mark it as an excellent example of 1200s architecture. On a visit to Cambuskenneth, you can also explore the small, peaceful cemetery.

## STIRLING OLD TOWN JAIL

In the heart of Stirling's Old Town, just a short walk from Stirling Castle, stands the foreboding Stirling Old Town Jail. Costumed interpreters, who remain in meticulous character throughout your visit, introduce you to the rules of your new "life" as a prisoner her before leaving you to explore the old cells and passageways. A self-guided audio tour and Scene of the Crime Exhibition allow you to safely explore the dark history of local crime and punishment and give a remarkable insight into prison life and prison reform. A visit here teaches you much about methods of corporal punishment, the ground-breaking prison reform movement, prison life, the antics of a few famous felons, and more.

## LOCH LOMOND AND THE TROSSACHS NATIONAL PARK

Combining two of Scotland's favorite tourist destinations, Loch Lomond and the Trossachs National Park straddles the Highland Boundary Fault, which divides it into two distinct regions—lowland and highland—that differ in underlying geology and topography. With its amazingly lovely landscape of hills and glens, the Trossachs was one of the first regions of Scotland to become a recognized tourist destination. Familiar to many from the song "The Bonnie Banks o' Loch Lomond," this loch is a picturesque freshwater lake. It is often considered the boundary between the lowlands of Central Scotland and the Highlands. At 22.6 miles long and with a surface area of 27.5 square miles, it is the largest lake in Great Britain by surface area, although Lough Neagh and Lough Erne in Northern Ireland take the title for the entire United Kingdom. Within the loch are numerous islands, including Inchmurrin, the largest freshwater island in the British Isles. The surrounding hills make this a stunning place to visit, with views of Ben Lomond on the eastern shore, as well the most southerly of the Scottish Munro peaks. These impressive views have made this one of Stirling's top attractions, and it has been called "the sixth greatest natural wonder in Britain." A highlight not to miss are the Falls of Falloch, which tumble down a straight 30-foot fall and are reached via a well-marked, easy path.

Considered one of Scotland's premier boating and water sport venues, Loch Lomond offers canoing, kayaking, paddleboarding, water skiing, and many other activities. Anglers are welcome, too, and for those who want to stay on land, the Loch Lomond Golf Club is situated on the southwestern shore. The hills adjacent to the loch are crisscrossed

*The deep blue waters of Loch Lomond's Milarrochy Bay reflect the surrounding mountains.*

209

# STIRLING

with numerous trails and cycling paths; the Luss Heritage Path is a local favorite. The path meanders through beautiful, lush farmland and the quaint Luss village, complete with old cobblestone houses. The park offers a wide range of routes for walkers, from very easy strolling paths to strenuous hillwalking on the park's highest summits, including Ben Lomond in Dunbartonshire and the Cobbler in the Arrochar Alps. Several of Scotland's Great Trails—officially designated long-distance footpaths—can be found in the park, including the West Highland Way, which follows the eastern shore of Loch Lomond, as well as the Loch Lomond and Cowal Way, the Three Lochs Way, and the Great Trossachs Path.

## CHURCH OF THE HOLY RUDE

Sitting on the shoulder of the city's highest hill, the Church of the Holy Rude (Holy Cross) has the notable honor of being one of only three still-standing churches in Britain to have facilitated a coronation: in 1567 the infant James VI was crowned King of Scotland here following the forced abdication of his mother, Mary, Queen of Scots. The church dates back to the reign of David I and the original church on the site was built in 1129 as Stirling's ward church. A catastrophic fire tore through it in 1405, leaving nothing of the original structure intact. The church was reconstructed in 1414, although renovations and additions to the church were still being made as recently as 1530.

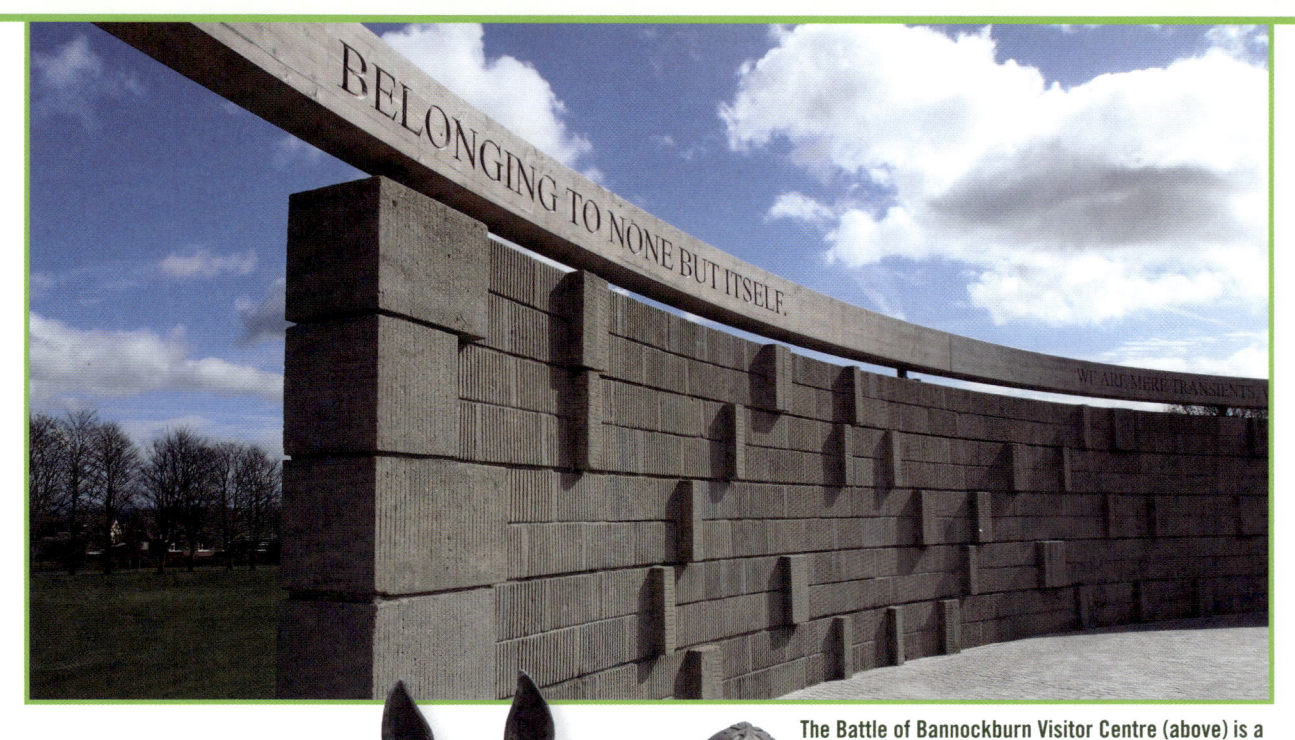

The nave's exposed oak ceiling, restored in 1940, is one of Scotland's few remaining old wooden rooftops built in this style. This ancient church is the second-oldest building in Stirling (after Stirling Castle) and is the parish church of Stirling. The church has historically had the close support and patronage of the Stuart kings, especially in the 15th, 16th, and 17th centuries.

The Battle of Bannockburn Visitor Centre (above) is a short walk away from a towering statue of Robert the Bruce that was constructed in 1964 (left).

## THE BATTLE OF BANNOCKBURN VISITOR CENTRE

This site memorializes the Battle of Bannockburn, where King of Scots Robert II led his soldiers to victory against the armies of King Edward II in the first War of Scottish Independence in 1314. The monuments and

**Opposite:** Ancient headstones crowd the cemetery behind the Church of the Holy Rude.

# STIRLING

*The atmospheric Doune has stood in for many historical film castles.*

## OTHER TOP SITES

- **DEANSTON DISTILLERY**

Deanston Distillery is situated on the River Teith at the entrance to the beautiful Loch Lomond and Trossachs National Park, roughly 8 miles from Stirling and a short way from Edinburgh and Glasgow. The original building was built in 1785 and served as a cotton mill for almost two centuries. When the mill closed, it was repurposed into a distillery in 1966 that gave the local population a new craft, and with hard work and some innovation they produced the very first bottle of Deanston Highland Single Malt Scotch Whisky.

- **STIRLING DISTILLERY**

Scotland doesn't just make whisky, and you can find an alternative at the Stirling Distillery. Founded in 2015, this maker produces gin, and you can tour the facilities, as well as get a taste.

exhibits on display at this landmark are dedicated both to the battle itself—which was a vitally important moment in Scottish history—and to Robert the Bruce, one of Scotland's most beloved heroes. The visitor center offers fascinating insights into the events and political circumstances surrounding the battle, as well as a gift shop and some light refreshments. One highlight of the center is the "Battle of Bannockburn Experience," which uses 3D animation to simulate exactly how the battle went. The Experience also includes several informative films, exhibits, and carefully preserved weapons and armor on display.

## DOUNE CASTLE

Strategically located at the confluence of the Ardoch Burn and the River Teith, the striking Doune Castle was originally built for Robert Stewart, the son of Robert II in about 1381. Named after the Gaelic word for "fort," Doune has played many different roles in its long history, including serving as a medieval fortress and later a retreat and hunting lodge for the Scottish monarchy, as well as a prison and military garrison. Many notable Scots walked its halls, including Mary, Queen of Scots, her son, James, and Charles Edward Stuart (aka Bonnie Prince Charlie). The castle was damaged and rebuilt several times over the centuries, especially during the War of Scottish Independence, but it contains one of the best-preserved great halls of all the castles in Scotland. The layout of the castle has gone mostly unchanged—it includes a fortified central lord's tower, a great hall, a kitchen tower, and a courtyard and surrounding curtain wall. Doune Castle has also been used as the backdrop for many historical productions, most notably as Castle Anthrax in *Monty Python and the Holy Grail;* it was also used as the setting for Winterfell in *Game of Thrones,* as well as Castle Leoch in *Outlander.*

## STIRLING OLD BRIDGE

The Stirling Old Bridge—most famously known for the Battle of Stirling Bridge when Sir William Wallace and Sir Andrew Moray defeated the English in 1297—is a medieval stone arched bridge that crosses the River Forth. The 262-foot-long bridge was rebuilt between 1400 and 1500 to replace the much older original timber bridge that had begun to collapse from wear and decay over the centuries. It has four semicircular arches, supported by three piers, and at each end arched gates once controlled access to the bridge. The gates were probably removed under order from Stirling Castle's governor General Blackeney in an attempt to forestall Bonnie Prince Charlie's forces as they marched south at the beginning of the 1745 Jacobite Rising. The bridge has been closed to traffic since 1833 and is currently designated a Category A structure, but you are free to walk its length. Out of all the ancient stone arched bridges left in Scotland, Stirling Old Bridge is one of the most historically significant.

**Opposite:** Stirling Old Bridge was the site of William Wallace's victory against English forces in 1297.

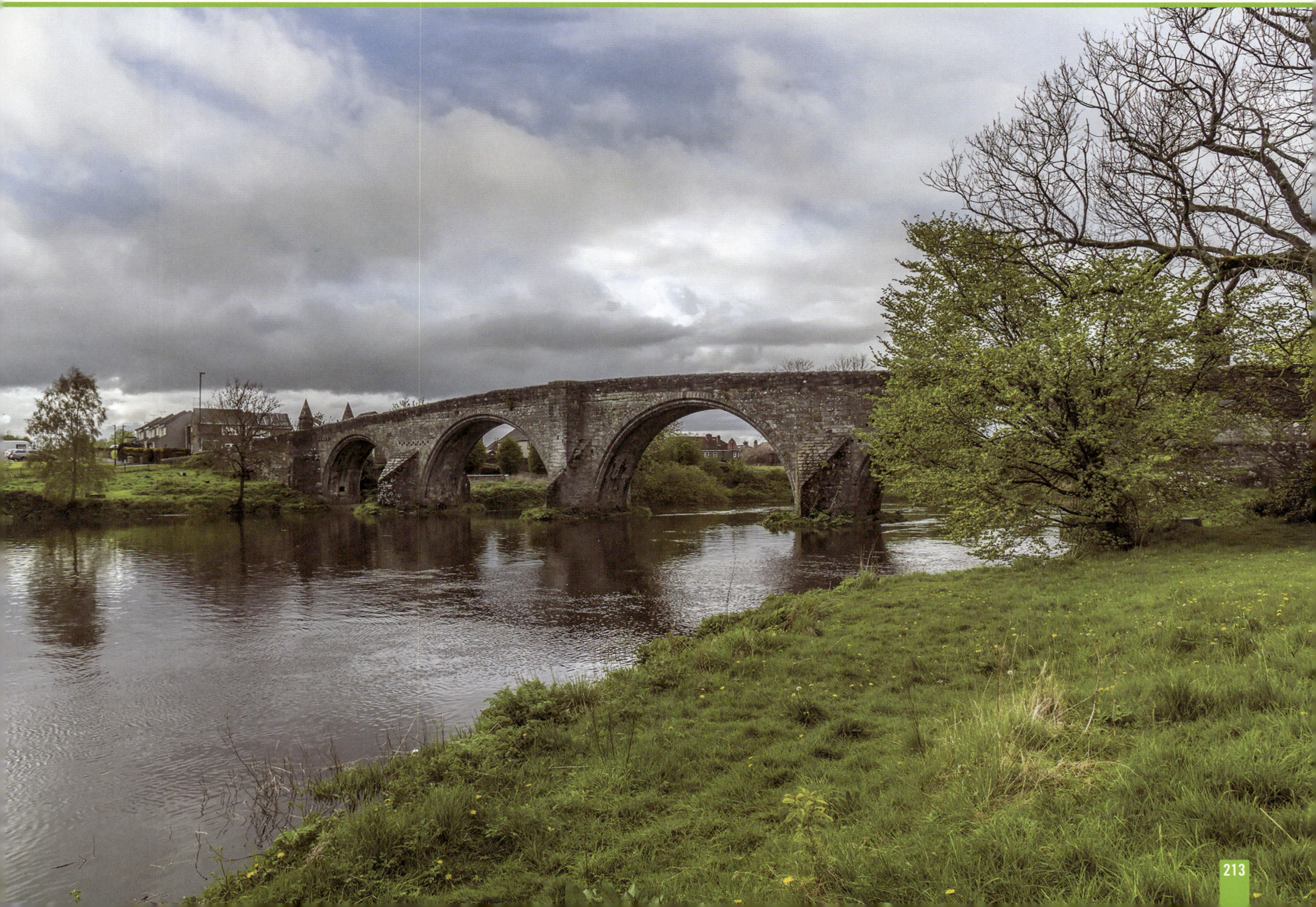

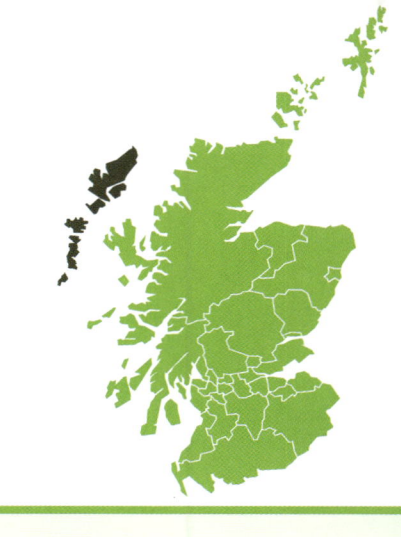

# WESTERN ISLES

## TOP SITES IN WESTERN ISLANDS

- Lews Castle
- Garenin Blackhouse Village
- Calanais Standing Stones
- St Clement's Church
- Luskentyre
- Kisimul Castle

Most familiarly known as the Outer Hebrides, the Western Isles, or Comhairle nan Eilean Siar, this chain of islands form part of the Hebrides archipelago, sitting off the western coast of Scotland and separated from the mainland and from the Inner Hebrides by the waters of the Minch, the Little Minch, and the Sea of the Hebrides. There are more than 50 uninhabited islands greater in size than 40 hectares in the Outer Hebrides, including the Barra Isles, Flannan Isles, Monach Islands, the Shiant Islands, and the islands of Loch Ròg. Much of the archipelago is a protected habitat, including both the islands and the surrounding waters. There are 15 inhabited islands; the major ones are Lewis and Harris, South Uist, North Uist, Benbecula, and Barra. Most of the inhabitants speak Scottish Gaelic, although in a few areas English speakers form a majority. The cool temperate climate is remarkably mild for islands in such a northerly latitude, due to the influence of the North Atlantic Current.

Tourism is one of the islands' main commercial activities, so sea transport is crucial, and several ferry services operate between the islands and the mainland. In the past the stormy seas claimed many a ship, but modern navigation systems have now minimized the dangers. Other commercial activities are crofting, fishing, and weaving, which includes the making of the famous Harris tweed.

### LEWS CASTLE

Lews Castle, near Stornoway on the Isle of Lewis, was built in the mid-19th-century by architect Charles Wilson. The three-story castle originally belonged to Sir James Matheson, who owned the entire island, but was purchased by William Lever in

*Top: The northern lights illuminate the Calanais Standing Stones, an extraordinary setting of stones that predate Stonehenge.*

Blackhouse Village in Garenin is a remarkable collection of thatched-roof cottages.

1918 and later donated to Stornoway parish. Lever thoroughly renovated the castle, adding necessities such as electricity, heating, and a phone system to allow communication between the many rooms of the castle. The castle served as a hospital for the Navy during WWII, and was converted into a college after it was sold to the Ross and Cromarty County Council in 1953. The castle was used as a school until 1988. Today, the castle is in the care of the Western Isles Council; it currently houses the museum, archive, and cultural center Museum Nan Eilean, which is open to the public year-round. Visitors can tour a restored grand ballroom, visit the resident cafe, and even rent rooms in the castle itself.

## GARENIN BLACKHOUSE VILLAGE

Garenin is a small crofting town that can be found on the west coast of Lewis. The town—with a population of only 80 people—is best known for "Blackhouse Village," a historic preservation project that took over a decade to complete. The village features nine stone-walled "blackhouses," which are a type of traditional thatched-roof cottage that were commonly built in rural Ireland, the Hebrides, and the Scottish Highlands as recently as 150 years ago. Garenin Village is home to the last inhabited blackhouses—they were only fully vacated in 1974—and the site has become a popular tourist destination since the cottages were finally restored by the Garenin Trust. Today, the Blackhouse Village cottages can be rented out by tourists and travelers; the village also offers a museum, visitor center, and a seasonal cafe and gift shop. This restored village feels as though it has been preserved in time and is a great way for visitors to learn what rural life in the Hebrides was like decades ago.

## CALANAIS STANDING STONES

The Calanais Standing Stones, also known as Callanish, are one of Scotland's many enigmatic megalithic monuments. This landmark consists of 13 large stones arranged in a cruciform pattern with a central stone circle, under which a chambered burial site is buried. The stones around the center

A view from the harbor shows the green grounds of Lews Castle.

# WESTERN ISLES

## LIGHTHOUSES OF THE WESTERN ISLES

Lovers of lighthouses will find much to appreciate in the Western Isles, which has close to 20. The four light stations reasonably accessible without a boat are all on or close to the Isle of Lewis. On Lewis, not far from the town of Stornoway, you will find the diminutive Arnish Point Lighthouse, which dates to 1853. At the very northern end of Lewis is the more famous Butt of Lewis Lighthouse, built in 1862, where you can stroll the imposing sea cliffs while waves crash against the rocks far below. Built in 1900, Tiumpan Head, also on Lewis, is a great place for whale-watching. On Scalpay is Eilean Glas (above), which lies along one of the Western Isles most popular walking routes that gives amazing views of the Isle of Skye. This red-and-white tower dates back to 1824. If you want to take a boat trip to Mingulay or around the Barra Islands, you can catch sight of Barra Head Lighthouse, built in 1833, which sits atop vast sea cliffs. For wildlife watching, the red-brick lighthouse at Shillay in the Monach Islands is the spot. The Gaelic name, *Siolaigh,* is thought to derive from the Old Norse word for "seal," and at least 10,000 grey seals call the islands home. From the west coast of Lewis, a boat trip will take you to the Flannan Islands and its mysterious lighthouse. Built in 1899, it is known for the three lightkeepers who disappeared, leaving no trace, shortly after it was constructed. A memorial to the vanished keepers stands at the shore near the village quay in Breasclete.

are joined to five rows of smaller stones, all of which appear to form makeshift roads leading outwards in every direction. Archaeologists believe that the site was constructed around 2900 to 2600 BCE. Some assume that the circle was used to mark the location of the burial chamber beneath the center stone, but an excavation revealed that the tomb was added after the original construction of the circle. The Calanais Standing Stones have been a part of local Scottish culture for centuries—the first known written recording of them comes from the 1680 journal of John Morisone, who believed they had once been men before magic turned them to stone, and local folklore states that the stones were giants who were turned to stone for refusing to convert to Christianity. In more recent years, it has been suggested that the stones may have been used as a type of calendar or lunar observatory or that they served a religious purpose.

## ST CLEMENT'S CHURCH

St Clement's Church is located in Rodel, Harris. The church was built in the late 15th century for the chiefs of Harris's MacLeods clan; it is believed that an older church previously stood on the land where St Clement's was built, although there is no remaining physical evidence of an older structure. Although the Reformation caused this Catholic church to crumble into disrepair in the 16th century, it remained in use as a burial ground for the MacLeod family for several

**The Butt of Lewis Lighthouse stands guard over wild coast of Lewis.**

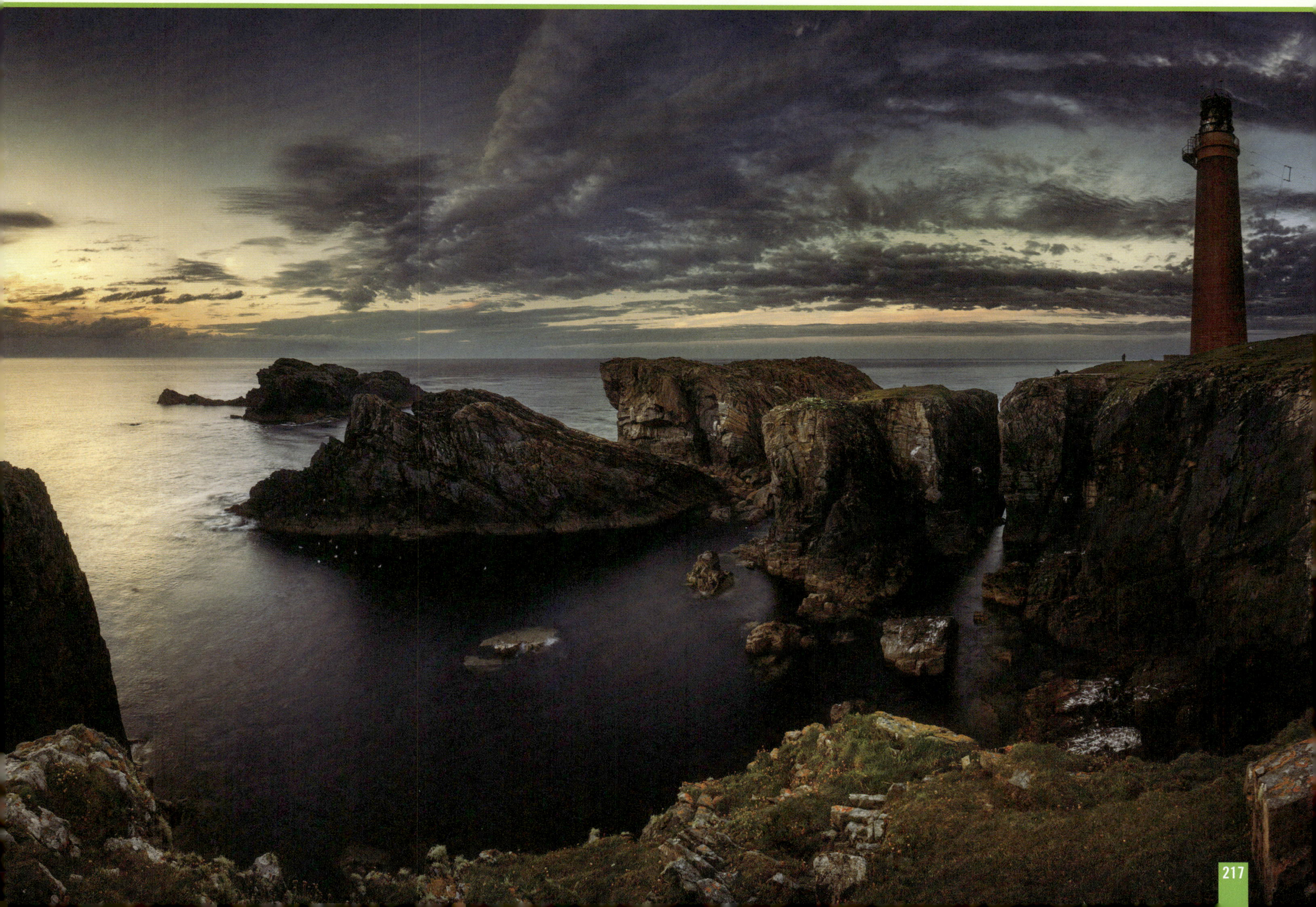

# WESTERN ISLES

*Above: The medieval Kisimul Castle sits in the center of Castlebay on Barra. Below: With miles of white sand and clear, sparkling waters, Luskentyre beach is a breathtaking hidden gem.*

centuries, potentially including 17th-century poet Mary MacLeod. The church has been restored a number of times over the centuries, and today it is maintained and protected by Historic Environment Scotland. The church, which Historic Environment Scotland refers to as "the grandest medieval building in the Western Isles," is also home to the tomb of the 8th chief of the MacLeod clan, Alasdair Crotach MacLeod, whose tomb is one of the most ornately carved in all of Scotland.

## LUSKENTYRE

Luskentyre is located on the western coast of Harris, a mountainous region to the south of Lewis and Harris. Luskentyre is best known for its beach, which—although lesser-known than some of Scotland's more famous shores—has a reputation as one of the most beautiful scenic beaches in all of the Outer Hebrides. The beach, kept in pristine condition and rarely crowded, is also a great location for walking, cycling, fishing, and swimming. Luskentyre is also a popular destination for birdwatching, as several species of ducks and other waterbirds can commonly be spotted here.

## KISIMUL CASTLE

Kisimul Castle is a 15th-century castle that can be found on an island near Castlebay, Barra. The island itself is small enough that the castle takes up almost the entire island; its name comes from the Gaelic word *ciosamul,* which literally means "castle

*Opposite: The ancient St Clement's Church is located on Harris.*

island." It was owned by Clan MacNeil for centuries until it was sold by the current clan chief to Historic Environment Scotland—or, more accurately, it was leased for a period of 1,000 years, in return for an annual payment of £1 and a bottle of whisky. The castle has been the subject of several excavations and archaeological surveys, but experts have had difficulty determining when exactly the structure was first built. It is believed that much of the original castle was supported with wooden beams and roofing, which have since decayed, leaving only the stone walls still standing. Excavations have uncovered pieces of gold, animal bones, flint tools, and shards of pottery, as well as a buried prison beneath the floor of the great hall. The island is open to the public, but it can only be reached by boat.

## OTHER TOP SITES

- **HERCULES THE BEAR**

This wooden sculpture commemorates a grizzly who appeared in a number of movies and TV shows during the 1970s and '80s. It stands in North Uist, where Hercules once evaded capture for more than three weeks, launching a massive land, air, and sea search.

- **MUSEUM NAN EILEAN**

This museum, cultural center, and historic archive service can be found in Lews Castle on the Isle of Lewis.

- **VUIG SANDS**

This beautiful beach on the Isle of Lewis is beloved for its miles of pristine shoreline and stunning natural beauty. It is especially popular for camping and hiking.

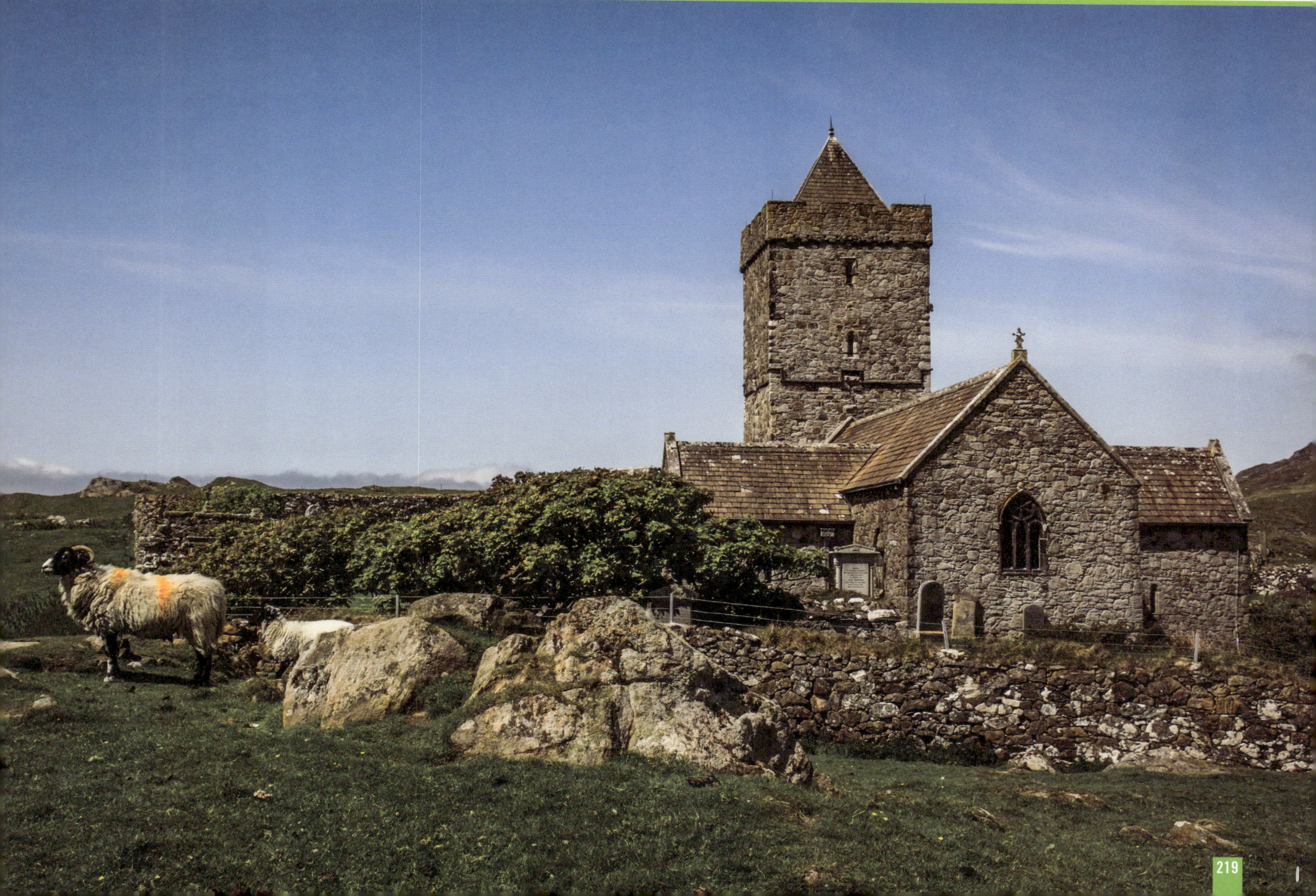

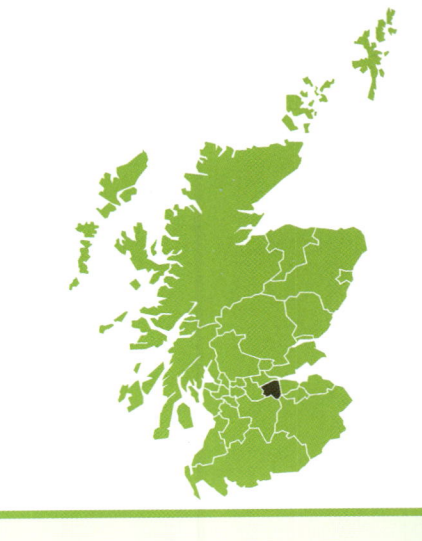

# WEST LOTHIAN

## TOP SITES IN WEST LOTHIAN

- Linlithgow Palace
- Beecraigs Country Park
- Blackness Castle
- Cairnpapple Hill

West Lothian is located on the southern shore of the Firth of Forth. This mainly rural county was once home to booming coal, shale oil, and iron mining industries. In fact, West Lothian was the site of the world's first oil boom. Today, two-thirds of West Lothian is agricultural, with silica sand and coal industries still in place. There are also several large-scale wind farms used to produce electricity for the region. This county also features a good range of leisure pursuits offered to anyone in search of relaxation or adventure. There are a dozen golf courses in the area, and the Low Port Centre is a great place to sail. There are also quite a few beautiful trails for walking, hiking, and cycling, especially in the Bathgate Hills and the Pentland Hills, which offer more than 60 miles of trails to explore. West Lothian is also home to an abundance of historical attractions, prehistoric burial sites, ruins, castles, and stately homes that date back hundreds, sometimes thousands of years.

With a history reaching back to prehistoric times, West Lothian was once inhabited by a tribe of Britons known as Votadini and Gododdin. Southern Scotland had been claimed by Romans by 83 CE, but the Romans eventually withdrew; about two centuries later, the Anglo-Saxons arrived in the 5th and 6th centuries. The region didn't become part of the Kingdom of Scotland until the 11th century.

**Top:** The tranquil Beecraigs Loch lies within Beecraigs Country Park.

### LINLITHGOW PALACE

Linlithgow Palace in West Lothian was originally built as a resting destination for royals on the path between Stirling Castle and Edinburgh Castle, this "pleasure palace" was the birthing place of several monarchs, including Mary, Queen of Scots. Linlithgow Palace sits on a low hill above a tiny

The great Royal Palace of Linlithgow is set in its own park on a small hill above Linlithgow Loch.

inland loch. The name *Linlithgow* means the "loch in the damp hollow." The site was first occupied during Roman times about 2,000 years ago, and James I had the present palace built on an older royal structure here. The palace is centered in a large square yard with a flawless stone spring. The entire structure is open to the public, and visitors are often drawn here to pick their way through the many rooms—although some areas of the castle are in a state of ruin. Many of the main rooms of the castle now feature informative displays explaining the various purposes of each area. Linlithgow also hosts the annual Spectacular Jousting event each summer.

## BEECRAIGS COUNTRY PARK

Beecraigs Country Park covers 370 gorgeous hectares close to the notable town of Linlithgow, high in the Bathgate Hills. Beecraigs is the biggest of West Lothian's three country parks, with miles of woodland streets and trails to investigate by foot, bicycle, or even on horseback. The Ranger Service offers any information visitors might need about the park's trails, as well as the local wildlife and plants. Many nature enthusiasts visit Beecraigs park to see red deer, highland and belted Galloway cattle, and several kinds of sheep. The park is open to the public, and a free map can be downloaded online so that ambitious hikers and cyclists can plan their route ahead of time. Refreshments, souvenirs, and self-guiding-leaflets are also available at the visitor center, and nearby areas are specially reserved for picnics and barbecues.

Left: A statue of Mary, Queen of Scots, stands in the grounds of Linlithgow Palace, where she was born. Right: Every year Linlithgow Palace hosts a medieval jousting tournament.

221

# WEST LOTHIAN

*The imposing Blackness Castle, built in the 15th century, has been used variously as a prison, fortress, arsenal and powder magazine, and most recently as a shooting location for historic films.*

## BLACKNESS CASTLE

Built in the 15th century by the Crichton family, Blackness Castle, one of Scotland's most fabulous castles, is a fortress near the village of Blackness, on the south shore of the Firth of Forth. Cobbled pathways encircle the yard, and the grounds have some dazzling greenery. There are information displays posted at intervals around the yard that provide detailed insights into the site's history. The castle was briefly used as a garrison during World War I and is now a scheduled monument in the care of Historic Environment Scotland. The striking appearance of this castle, with its high defensive walls and enclosed courtyard, have made it very attractive to filmmakers over the years; Blackness castle has appeared in several movies and shows, including the feature film version of *Hamlet* and the BBC adaptations of *Ivanhoe* and *Outlander*.

Cairnpapple Hill is home to an ancient ceremonial complex.

## CAIRNPAPPLE HILL

One of the most important prehistoric monuments on the mainland of Scotland, Cairnpapple Hill is a rare ceremonial complex in the Bathgate Hills. For at least 4,000 years its broad summit was a significant site for ceremonies and burials. The henge here dates from about 3800 BCE, and the surrounding land was also a chosen site for a number of Bronze Age burials before Christians began burying their dead here even later. It is just a short, gentle walk to the summit of Cairnpapple Hill, but as well as learning about this great example of a Neolithic henge monument, you can take in the stunning vistas across the Forth Valley and beyond—on clear days it is even possible to get a glimpse of Goat Fell, Arran's highest peak.

### OTHER TOP SITES

- **LIVINGSTON DESIGNER OUTLET**

Livingston Designer Outlet is the largest outlet mall in Scotland, and is one of the most popular shopping locations in West Lothian. Featuring over 100 stores, restaurants, and activities for children and adults alike—including a 3D movie theater and stores featuring all of the most well-established name brands—it would be difficult to think of something one couldn't find here.

- **FIVE SISTERS ZOO**

This zoo in West Calder offers a great value family day out. It is home to more than 120 different species from all around the world, from bats to bears and lemurs to lynx. The zoo offers daily handling sessions, keeper talks, and feed-the-lemur sessions.

# PHOTO CREDITS

**Cover photo:** Old Man of Storr by Lukasz Pajor/Shutterstock.com

**Back cover:** Calton Hill by SAKhan Photography/Shutterstock.com; Mull of Oa by Kevin Standage/Shutterstock.com; Falkirk Kelpies by Derek Skinner/Shutterstock.com

**Locator maps:** Ingo Menhard/Dreamstime.com

**Key**

DT = Dreamstime.com  SS = Shutterstock.com  CC = Creative Commons

l = left  r = right  t = top
m = middle  b = bottom

4 Rusel1981/DT; 6 pql89/SS; 7t Harald Lueder/SS; 7m Fabio Giaiotto/DT; 7l cornfield/SS; 8t Serge Bertasius/DT; 8b Gyvafoto/SS; 9 Swen Stroop/SS; 10–11 David Ionut/SS; 12t chrisdorney/SS; 12b Mylmages - Micha/SS; 13 Ingo Menhard/DT; 14 Adam Wrobel/SS; 15t anastas_styles/SS; 15b JASPERIMAGE/SS; 16t Jonas Muscat/SS; 16b Thomas Lukassek /DT; 17 Miroslav Liska/DT; 18 J.thephotograph/SS; 19t Jaroslav Moravcik/SS; 19b anastas_styles/SS; 20 Mino Surkala/DT; 21 Yulia_Bogomolova/SS; 22l Iain Gray/DT; 22r Mark Eaton/DT; 23 Iwom22/DT; 24t S Buwert/SS; 24b Denisbin/CC–Attribution-NoDerivs 2.0 Generic; 25 Checco2/SS; 26t roy henderson/SS; 26b Moomusician/SS; 27 Adam Wrobel/SS; 29 Helen Hotson/SS; 30 Paul Butchard/DT; 31t Jacqueline Satchell/SS; 31b Jan Holm/SS; 32 James McDowall/SS; 33t Iain Coull/SS; 33b D MacDonald/SS;

34–35 Reimar/SS; 36 angus reid/SS; 37t R K Hill/SS; 37m TreasureGalore/SS; 37l Kevin George/DT; 38t Office50633/DT; 38b Grian12/DT; 39 Ruth Peterkin/SS; 40 Shafiq Khan/SS; 41 Ianthraves/DT; 42t Mark Williams/DT; 42m Richardjohnsonuk/DT; 42b DeFacto/CC–Attribution-ShareAlike 4.0 International; 43 Sgar80/DT; 44 David Woods/DT; 45t Grian12/DT; 45b David Woods/DT; 46t Kevin Standage/SS; 46b Andreas Demel/DT; 47 Martin Molcan/DT; 48 Jerryzuo/DT; 49 Swen Stroop/SS; 51 Apostolos Giontzis /DT; 52 Georgesixth/DT; 53t Jim Mcdowall/DT; 53b Jim Scott/SS; 54t Carole MacDonald/SS; 54b George Robertson/DT; 55 Chris148/DT; 56 Sasalan999/DT; 57t Mason Taylor–Simon Taylor/CC-Attribution-NonCommercial-NoDerivs 2.0 Generic; 57b Sasalan999/DT; 58 Serge Bertasius/DT; 59 Richard Semik /DT; 60 Daniel Ietford/SS; 61 Jameselkington6/DT; 62 Geoffrey Allerton/DT; 63t Jaahnlieb /DT; 63b Mark Paterson/SS; 64 Paul Bradburn/DT; 65 Steve6326/DT; 66DonaldJudge/CC-Attribution 2.0 Generic; 67Terence A R Watts/DT; 68 Jaahnlieb/DT; 69t Richard Goodrich /DT; 69m Ollyhitchen01/DT; 69b TheUntravelledWorld/DT; 70 Claudine Van Massenhove/SS; 71t Juliane Jacobs/DT; 71b Hatheyphotos/DT; 72t SnapTPhotography/DT; 72b Stocksolutions/DT; 73 Heartland Arts/SS; 74 Helen Hotson/SS; 76 Mick Atkins/SS; 77t TreasureGalore/SS; 77b dave_sousa/CC–Attribution-ShareAlike 4.0 International; 78–70 Wayleebird/SS; 79 Paolo Amiotti/DT; 80 Anthony Renton/DT; 81t Attila Jandi/DT;

81b Garyellisphotography/DT; 82 Creativehearts/DT; 83t Studio Karel/SS; 83b Geoffrey Allerton/DT; 84 David McElroy/SS; 85 George Robertson /DT; 86 Photofires/DT; 87t SAKhanPhotography/SS; 87b T.w. Van Urk/DT; 88t Maurie Hill/DT; 88m Serge Cornu/SS; 88b cliveWa/SS; 89 Dan Breckwoldt/DT; 90 Richie Chan/SS; 91t Fotokon /DT; 91b Cliff Hands/SS; 92l stefan dzalev/SS; 92r Songquan Deng/SS; 93 By Scott Heaney/SS; 94 Jaroslav Moravcik/SS; 95l Kamira/SS; 95r f11photo/SS; 96 Vicki_Smith/SS; 97 Jaroslav Moravcik/DT; 98t Claudiodivizia/SS; 98b David Ridley/DT; 99 Photofires/DT; 100 Giuseppe Di Paolo/DT; 101 John Selway/SS; 102–103 Have a nice day Photo/SS; 103 Muzzyco/SS; 104 Rosser1954/CC–Attribution-ShareAlike 4.0 International; 105t Miroslav Liska /DT; 105b Scottturner/DT; 106 Derek Skinner/SS; 107 By Martin Donald Smith/SS; 108 Catalina Panait/DT; 109t Karminc/DT; 109b Dennis Dolkens/DT; 110Hikersmurf /DT; 111 Andrea La Corte/DT; 112 Catalina Panait/DT; 113 Sasalan999/DT; 114 Anthony Renton/DT; 115t ALBAimagery/SS; 115b Chris148/DT; 116 Klodien/SS; 117tr Martin Gaal/DT; 117m Claudio Divizia/SS; 117br Emma manners/SS; 118 Tosca Weijers/DT; 119 Joulian/SS; 120 Jeff Whyte/DT; 121 Meunierd/DT; 122 Leonid Andronov/DT; 123 Jeff Whyte/DT; 124 Ken Taylor/DT; 125 Leonid Andronov/SS; 126 Maaster/SS; 127t Henner Damke/DT; 127b Shaiith/DT; 128t App555/DT; 128b Lukas Bischoff Photograph/SS; 129 Wiesel/DT; 130 Tomas Marek/DT; 131l Bennymarty/DT; 131r Andre

Goncalves/SS; 132 John Holmes/DT; 133 Catuncia/SS; 134 John & Anna Marie Carter & Mearns/DT; 135t Catuncia/SS; 135b Rob Atherton/SS; 136t Ineke Mighorst/DT; 136b Francesco Bonino/SS; 137 A. Karnholz/SS; 138 Toni Lucena Viudez/SS; 139 Helen Hotson/SS; 140t Megs Pier/SS; 140m K.F.Photo/SS; 140b Sslater2/DT; 141 Dejonckheere/SS; 142 Jan Holm/SS; 143 Jiri Vondrous/DT; 144l Mino Surkala/SS; 144r Fencewood Studio/SS; 145 David W Bird/SS; 146 Licancabur/DT; 147 Jacqi/DT; 148 Sasalan999/DT; 149t Ctollan/DT; 149b Ollie Taylor/DT; 150t TreasureGalore/SS; 150b Grian12/DT; 151 TreasureGalore/SS; 152 Beth/CC-Attribution-NonCommercial 2.0; 153b Tom Parnell/CC-Attribution-ShareAlike-2.0; 153t Jamie Wills/SS; 154 Calculici83/DT; 155t Powerofflowers /DT; 155b Photofires/DT; 156 JASPERIMAGE/SS; 157t David Head/DT; 157b Ayome Watmough/DT; 158l Christoph Lischetzki /DT; 158r Robert Porter/DT; 159l Osnuya/DT; 159r Micuzzzu/SS; 160 Geoff Eccles/DT; 161t Giuseppemasci/DT; 161b H368k742/DT; 162 Harold Stiver /DT; 163 Juan Vilata/DT; 164t Paolo Giovanni Trovo/DT; 164b Jeremy Brown/DT; 165 Rallef /DT; 166 Harold Stiver /DT; 167 David Woods/SS; 168 Crystalpoteat/DT; 169t Joannepanton photography/DT; 169b Iain Coull/SS; 170t Christoph Lischetzki /DT; 170b Deborah Macdonald/DT; 171 Mino21/DT; 172 Stefano Valeri /DT; 173 Elenarostunova/DT; 174t Paolo Amiotti/DT; 174b Lowsun/DT; 175 Sasalan999/DT; 176 George Robertson/DT; 177 Sergejus Lamanosovas/DT; 178 Allan

Ogg/CC-Attribution-NonCommercial-ShareAlike-4.0; 179t TreasureGalore/SS; 179b Julian Gazzard/SS; 180 Ales Micola /SS; 181 Ilonawillemsen/DT; 182 Angelacottingham /DT; 183t Binson Calfort/SS; 183b John Holmes/DT; 184 Susanne Pommer/SS; 184–185 Grafxart/DT; 186–187 Ulmus Media/SS; 187 Serge Bertasius/DT; 188t MichaelY/SS; 188b John Holmes/DT; 189 JPOfford/SS; 190 Jan Holm/SS; 191t Tom Parnell/CC-Attribution Share Alike-2.0; 191b Scottfocus/CC-Attribution-ShareAlike-4.0; 192 Morag Fleming/SS; 192–193 WApted/SS; 194 Serge Bertasius /DT; 196 Kevin Eaves /DT; 198 Ollyhitchen01/DT; 199t Grian12/DT; 199b Grian12/DT; 200 Orion9nl/DT; 201t Alan5766 /DT; 201b Marcin Kadziolka /DT; 202 Attila Jandi /DT; 203 Alan5766 /DT; 204 Stefano Valeri/DT; 205t Martin Valigursky/DT; 205b Emily Goodwin/SS; 206 Catalina Panait /DT; 207l Nui7711/DT; 207r Jaroslav Moravcik/DT; 208t Nicola Pulham/DT; 208b Whiskybottle/DT; 209 Mcwarrior/DT; 210 Jaroslav Moravcik/DT; 211t Silviaanestikova /DT; 211b Jacek Buller/DT; 212 JMDuranPhoto/DT; 213 Nicola Pulham/DT; 214 Luca Quadrio/SS; 215t Fintastique /DT; 215b Photosvit /DT; 216 MyTravelCurator/SS; 216–217 Wojciech Kruczynski /DT; 218t Luca Quadrio/DT; 218b Photowitch/DT; 219 Jaroslav Sekeres/SS; 220 Dougie Milne Photography/SS; 221t Esaumi1911/DT; 221m Attila JANDI/SS; 221b Serge Bertasius/DT; 222 TreasureGalore/SS; 223 Nicola Pulham/DT